# Derek McGovern

## ON SPORTS BETTING
## ... AND HOW TO MAKE IT PAY

**RP**
ROWTON PRESS

# Dedication

In memory of my Mam and Dad

**Jacket design by Pure Design & Advertising Ltd, Shrewsbury.**

© Rowton Press Ltd 1999
First Published 1999
by Rowton Press Ltd,
P.O.Box 10, Oswestry,
Shropshire SY11 1RB.

Typeset by Rowton Press using MICROSOFT WORD FOR WINDOWS
Output on a Hewlett Packard HP Laserjet 4000.

Printed and bound in Great Britain by Biddles, Guildford

1-871093-43-0

# foreword

**by Brough Scott,** Channel 4 Racing presenter and Racing Post editorial director

It was in August 1990 that Derek got the challenge. Could he take over at least two pages a day of the *Racing Post* and devote it to sports betting? He never hesitated. History, and the odd histrionic, was on the march.

Looking back, it's hard to imagine that this seemed any sort of a risk at the time. Betting on sport is now a totally established fact of life. But people had been slow to move. What they needed was a quick-witted, sharp-fingered Scouser to liven them up and make himself some luck. In 1991 he got it.

When, and some say it cannot happen soon enough, they finally lay Derek McGovern to rest we all know the two names that will be written on his heart if not his liver. The doubters had a bad time when his team tipped Michael Stich to win Wimbledon at 40-1, but when the Open golf preview came up with Ian Baker-Finch at 50-1, Sports Betting was truly off and running.

Of course there have not been too many wins as big as Stich and Baker-Finch but the trail was laid. You could enhance your enjoyment of sport by matching your judgement against the bookmakers. More and more people got involved, more and more pages were wanted. In 1995 Racing Post editor Alan Byrne led it on the back cover. By 1999 we were running up to 20 pages on Saturdays.

It was possible to believe you would know as much about the form as the bookies did. But the number of their advertisements amongst the sports pages suggested that there were plenty of traps for the unwary. It is past those traps that the intrepid McGovern tries to steer you with his own opinionated mix of fact and fantasy.

To judge by his clothing it is debatable just how much he has made his own betting pay. But he always was a case of being better at giving advice than taking it. Whatever you make of this book you are unlikely to find it dull. You won't want to put it down – except perhaps to smack it over his incorrigible little Liverpool head.

# contents

# chapter 1

## the birth of sports betting

Ten years ago I was mocked, ridiculed, even despised for daring to suggest that racing's days as the No.1 betting medium in Britain were numbered. What an idiot, the experts said. The man's lost his marbles. How they all laughed. But as each year has passed with racing's share of the punters' pound dwindling, the laughter has taken on an altogether more hollow ring.

Racing's share of the betting market ten years ago was something like 85 per cent. Now it's 70 per cent and in free-fall. Betting shop innovations like Lucky Numbers and one-armed bandits are partly responsible for luring punters from the pull of the turf, but the chief culprit is sports betting. More and more punters, every day, are learning that not only does betting on sport offer far more excitement than a fiver each-way at Fakenham, it also gives us the chance to take on the bookies on something like level terms.

Bookies have almost unimaginable power in the racing game – moles in all the top stables, trainers and jockeys on the payroll, and the ability to manipulate starting prices. It is practically impossible for them to lose. In sport, though, they are by comparison impotent, as this book will make stunningly clear.

They say that where America leads, Britain follows. Well, given that of the $2.5billion bet legally on racing and sport every year in the gambling state of Nevada, the split is 75-25 in sport's favour, we should have little doubt what the future holds.

Bookmakers like to play down the incredible rise of sports betting because if true figures were ever revealed they would face searching questions about the rate of deductions ('tax' in layman's terms) they charge. This is a very controversial subject, which will be tackled at length later in the book. It's enough to say here that for every £10 wagered on sport, bookies are immediately 15p better off no matter if the bet is a winner or loser. The more bet on sport, the higher their automatic, risk-free profit, and the louder the inevitable calls for an inquiry; so it is clearly in their interests to mask the true figures.

Ten years ago, when sports betting was in its infancy, it was reckoned to account for no more than five per cent of bookmaker turnover. That figure has now more than doubled and I would estimate that sports betting accounts for at least 12 per cent of bookmaker turnover. One leading bookmaker representative told me in 1995 that, on a typical winter Saturday, 15 per cent of turnover is generated by the day's football fixtures.

Yet although it's easy to regard such growth as a phenomenon, we could perhaps more accurately describe it as inevitable. The only reason racing could puff out its chest as the undisputed king of betting for so long was that there was precious little else, greyhounds apart, to bet on. If you're starving and only pizza is on the menu, you'll eat it. You may think it tastes like cardboard but you'll eat it all the same. You've got no choice. It was the same with racing – that is until sports betting was born.

For decades, men and women with a natural instinct to gamble had only one outlet – racing. They might have known absolutely nothing about it, maybe even have loathed it, but it was the only thing that could satisfy their craving. So, out of necessity, they would bet on races at Ascot and Aintree, Carlisle and Kempton, and in time this forced interest, almost a chore to begin with, became a daily habit. Racing, to the natural-born gambler, offered a quick, regular and fairly exciting fix.

But over the last ten years we have witnessed the emergence of a new generation of gamblers. Punters who have grown up with the same instinct to gamble, but with a far wider choice of targets. The 18-year-old cricket-mad gambler will no longer gravitate towards racing to satisfy his hunger; why should he when there is so much cricket to bet on? Soccer fans have no need to pore over Plumpton when there's wall-to-wall football, much of it live on TV. No longer are punters forced by lack of choice to bet on something they know little about. Now they can bet on what they want, and what they know. Be sure racing will be at the bottom of the list.

I would suggest that the three figures most responsible for the astonishing growth in the popularity of sports betting in Britain are, in no particular order: Ron Pollard, former Ladbrokes' PR guru; Graham Sharpe, his William Hill counterpart; and, erm, erm, me. That comment may raise a few eyebrows but will be explained later in this chapter.

It's likely, though, that both Pollard and Sharpe, like me, will bow the knee to the real godfather of sports betting: the man whose knowledge of odds-making, coupled with the personality of a true extrovert and a genius for public relations, persuaded America to cold-shoulder horseracing and establish betting on sport as a thriving multi-billion pound industry.

Jimmy Snyder, better known to millions of American gamblers as Jimmy The Greek, made betting on sport almost a way of life in the USA, even though gambling is legal in few states. When you next have a 72-hole match bet in a big golf tournament – say Lee Westwood to beat Justin Leonard over four rounds of the Open Championship – Snyder, up there in that great casino in the sky, will permit himself the faintest glow of satisfaction. For it was Snyder, despite a deep ignorance of golf, who invented such a form of betting.

Not long after his arrival in Las Vegas in the 1950s, the popular Desert Inn Hotel staged the Tournament Of Champions, now known as the Mercedes Championship, which kicks off the annual US PGA Tour each season, and the hot topic of conversation in Vegas was golf. It was all anybody would talk about. Snyder, who'd majored in American Football, basketball and horseracing, was clueless about golf – he'd never even held a club in his hand – but he knew he somehow had to cash in on this massive interest in the sport. He spent a couple of days looking at the forthcoming tournament from every angle, searching for a new way to bet on it. Then, Eureka, he found one. By coupling certain players together according to their Vardon Trophy record – average strokes per round throughout the season – he reckoned it was a take-your-pick affair who won, therefore allowing the house to lay 5-6 each player and virtually guaranteeing a profit.

Punters who reckoned Gary Player at 8-1 was too risky a bet to win the tournament outright would have no hesitation in plumping for Player at 5-6 to beat, say, Billy Casper. Golf match betting quickly became as popular as a Vegas hooker giving freebies.

Snyder, of Greek parents but born in a town called Steubenville in Ohio, found his spiritual home in Vegas. He loved it there, his legend grew; that was until the city of sin sold out to the faceless public companies. Snyder, in his autobiography, *Wizard of Odds*, described the early flavour of Vegas and how the gambling oasis in the heart of the Nevada Desert became almost unrecognisable in the space of just ten years.

"The late fifties were the heyday for Vegas. From Monday to Thursday the town belonged to the professionals. The public, riding free junkets, came in on the weekends. Almost any big bettor who flew in from anywhere in the country was known by name by the floor men and pit bosses. Until about 1961 it was a world of its own. Then the computers and business people began taking over and it got bigger and bigger. The casino hotels became attuned to the masses, instead of the elite, and the place lost some of its romance, intimacy and excitement. The high-roller stopped coming, and the slot machines were lined up row after row.

"In times gone by, the bigger casino hotels would not deign to have slots because they felt they detracted from the atmosphere. Today most of the hotels are owned by public companies. You can buy their stock in the market. But those gamblers who built Las Vegas are gone. Some died, some got rich and semi-respectable, others grew old and complacent and sold out.

"Hookers are part of the mystique of Las Vegas, but it is not the industry some people seem to think. The sexiest girls in the world go there, and in many cases they do enjoy a kind of temporary visa. Any schoolteacher, secretary, airline hostess or model who wants to supplement her income can go to Las Vegas for a weekend and score. They come from all over the United States –

straight girls and housewives, who turn professional from Friday to Sunday. These girls from Utah, Texas, Nebraska and thereabouts cannot miss. They may earn £500, $1,000, or $1,500 depending on how pretty or cute they are, who they run into, and how well his luck runs at the tables. A few have scored big, from $10,000 to $15,000, because the guy they were escorting got hot at the craps table and shared his winnings with her. Any pit boss in town can give you a story like it. In Las Vegas even the hookers tend to look like ingenues. They are in demand because gambling is a sensual sport, and a fellow can grow attached to his lady of the evening."

Early in his gambling career, Snyder was paid the ultimate compliment by bookmakers – they adjusted their line to whichever way he bet. For instance, if the Greek backed, say, Miami Dolphins with a six-point start, the bookies would happily lay him his bet and then quickly shave the line to five. They were prepared to lose to him so long as they could benefit from his research and contacts.

That's a tactic the big bookmaking firms in Britain have perfected. They will allow a well-known racehorse trainer to get on at big stakes because such a bet helps mark their card on a race – knowledge almost certainly worth far more than the lucky trainer will win. David Lowrey, group racing director for British bookmaking giants William Hill, admitted: "A client who wins consistently has knowledge we would like to share. We have clients we use for information. We'd be stupid not to."

What gave Snyder an edge in betting was his contacts. He made sure he cultivated the friendship of high school football players tipped to make the grade at pro-level by offering them summer jobs – at a strip mine he had an interest in, or through friends who owned companies. He figured, correctly in most cases, that he could call in those markers once the kids had graduated to the NFL. Snyder's home neighbourhood, the Ohio River Valley, was a hotbed of young football talent, so much so that national coaches were forever on scouting missions at southern Pennsylvania or West Virginia. Snyder, with a naturally amiable nature, quickly befriended them.

He adopted a similar strategy for basketball and baseball. All this spadework paid rich dividends – Snyder was in the know whenever a key player was injured. He tells the story in his autobiography about how one week during the basketball season he called Tennessee coach Mike Paidousis for a chat. It was the night before Tennessee were to take on Dayton, and Snyder believed Dayton were a severely under-rated team. Tennessee, the hot favourites, had no injury worries, the coach told him, but the team's top scorer and captain was under a cloud because earlier that week he'd been dumped by his girlfriend of three years. Snyder upped his intended bet on Dayton and won big.

Snyder had on his payroll the coach of a college basketball team – in America college sport is big business – who helped him win a small fortune over the course of one season. The Greek knew that the coach's star player, who had made the team among the highest-scoring in the college ranks, had a dodgy knee, an injury that needed urgent repair work before he could even take to the court. An hour before the start of each game, the coach would ring Snyder to give him the lowdown on the kid's knee. If it was stiff, Snyder backed the opponents; if in full working order, he'd stick with his coach's team. This Battle Of Wounded Knee saw Snyder emerge victorious – he won 18 out of 19 bets on matches involving the coach's team that season.

Snyder's reputation as a gambler and an odds-maker grew steadily. Press agencies would ring him to ask his thoughts on major sporting events. If news of a big Snyder bet broke, fellow punters would rush headlong to join him. Texas oil millionaire H L Hunt challenged Snyder to a season-long series of bets on the Super Bowl campaign – and was to regret it. To give you an idea of Hunt's wealth, he once said he quit smoking when he realised that just taking the wrappers off cigars had cost him $380,000 over the years – that's how valuable his time was. The same practice almost cost Bill Clinton a hell of a lot more, but that's another story.

Hunt would bet $50,000 per game, at evens each time, none of this 10-11 nonsense which has become the norm in betting. Once again the Greek capitalised after finding an edge. He learned the name of Hunt's secretary and got her on his payroll after being told that Hunt had a habit of jotting down his favourite teams on a notepad, with a star alongside his top choice. Hunt and Snyder had agreed to follow the points spread (the handicap) set by a local bookie called Shaeffer for their private bets, and every time Snyder got advance warning of the team Hunt was due to back he would place $20,000 on them with Shaeffer. Consequently, by the time Hunt placed his bet, the line would have changed in Snyder's favour by at least one point. On the occasions the Greek was convinced Hunt had chosen correctly, he would find ways of laying off the whole $50,000 at evens. After two seasons Hunt was down $600,000 and decided to call off the challenge.

So high profile was Snyder in Vegas, and so much money was passing through his hands, that the Justice Department began to suspect he had Mafia connections. Attorney-General Bobby Kennedy instructed his staff to examine Snyder's operation, convinced he was knee deep in Mob money. Snyder didn't help himself at the time with a widely-publicised comment that was to haunt him.

In an interview with the well-respected and widely-read *Sports Illustrated*, the Greek said about the Kennedy administration: "They lost in Laos; they lost in Cuba; they lost in East Berlin; but they sure are giving the gamblers a beating." This just after a law had been passed forbidding interstate transmission of gambling information, and wrecking a lucrative sideline Snyder had established in selling his odds nationally at $25 a week.

Had Snyder uttered such words for the pages of the *New York Times*, they would possibly have passed without comment, but he made the grave mistake of bad-mouthing the Kennedys in the most damaging of all vehicles – a sports magazine. His comment was even referred to by President John F Kennedy in September 1962. "One Las Vegas gambler is supposed to have said he hoped we'd be as tough on Berlin as we've been on Las Vegas. Well, we intend to be," Kennedy is quoted as saying.

Though Snyder was well known among the gambling community at this time, his was not yet a household name in America generally. More Alastair Down than John McCririck, if you like. But the fall-out from the Kennedy investigations and the nationwide clampdown on gambling convinced him that he needed to ditch his big-time gambler image, especially as, by now, he had a wife and

children and such a lifestyle was not conducive to domestic bliss. The Greek's next career move, later to spark a nationwide controversy, earned him a life of luxury and woke up ordinary Americans to the enjoyment, the enchantment, the sheer unequalled excitement of betting on sport.

First Snyder penned, for the *Las Vegas Sun*, a sports betting column that proved so popular it was syndicated in countless other newspapers. His name suddenly became respectable and he quickly launched a new career in public relations, confident that the network of contacts on national newspapers he'd built during his days as a big-time gambler would stand him in good stead.

He was handed the PR account in September 1965 for Caesar's Palace, the luxury Las Vegas hotel-casino. Caesar's had been open only a month and was struggling. Half the rooms were empty and the place, despite monumental outlay, had just not caught on. That was until the Greek took a hand. He flew in relays of entertainment writers from all over the States and spoiled them rotten. He instructed telephonists to inform would-be guests that all the rooms were occupied but that they would be notified if there were any cancellations. More memorably, he staged a photo-shoot for a big-selling magazine with his PR colleague Jay Sarno, dressed in a white toga, sprawled across a couch being fed grapes by two buxom slave girls. All of sudden Caesar's was the place to be.

Given that Snyder had made a success of his gambling career by always finding an edge, it was no surprise when he was asked to do a TV commercial for Edge shaving cream. The ad agency sent him a script which called for him to say, "For a smoother shave it's Edge, three-to-one," a boast based on results of a poll. But when Snyder checked the poll figures he found the odds were closer to 5-2 and demanded a script change.

"What the hell difference does it make?" the agency screamed.

"The difference is that it's not three-to-one, it's five-to-two," said Snyder, and that's how the advert was filmed.

Snyder's greatest PR coup was the night of the famous tennis showdown between 'male chauvinist pig' Bobby Riggs and Billie Jean King at the Houston Astrodome in August 1973. Snyder made Riggs the 2-5 favourite in this battle of the sexes, but knew hours before the contest that the only possible winner was King.

American writer Ginger Wadsworth, who collaborated with Snyder on his autobiography, pictures the scene beautifully.

"When the publicity for the show began to take off and it became apparent that this was not going to be a sports event but a 'happening', Charley Diker, president of a Nabisco subsidiary, wanted Jimmy to get involved.

"Nabisco's candy division sold an all-day sucker called the Sugar Daddy, which seemed to fit right in with the male chauvinist angle Riggs had pushed for months. All Jimmy wanted was for Bobby to present Billie Jean with a giant Sugar Daddy, which they would bill as 'the world's largest' at mid-court before the match, on national television. The company was prepared to pay them $15,000 each.

"Jimmy made the proposal first to Riggs and Jerry Perenchio, the promoter of that cosmic event. Jimmy Welch, the president of Nabisco candies, was with Jimmy. They almost laughed them out of the room. 'Think it over,' Jimmy said, looking at Perenchio but talking to Riggs. 'After this match this may be all he has. He ought to get it while he can.'

"The idea began to grow on Bobby, as did the $15,000 Jimmy offered him, and a contract as the tennis host at the Tropicana in Vegas for $100,000 a year. In a few days Perenchio called and said it was set. Billie Jean had agreed to go along. Jimmy's only concern now was that Riggs would carry it too far and get them all thrown out of the arena. But the night of the match turned out to be a press agent's dream. The ABC cameras covered the whole ceremony. (Billie Jean, who had refused during the weeks of the build-up to lower herself to Riggs' level, maintained her dignity by entering the Astrodome on a litter borne by male galley slaves. Under one arm she carried a piglet, which she gave to Riggs after accepting the Sugar Daddy.)

"Fifty million viewers looked on, with commentary by Howard

Cosell. It was one of the last great moments of pure comedy the country ever knew. Bobby gave his all, even wearing a yellow warm-up jacket with 'Sugar Daddy' emblazoned in blue across the back. He did not discard it until after the fourth set, trailing early and headed for an inglorious, upset defeat.

"What all this had to do with tennis was never made clear, but it turned on the whole country. For months afterwards people asked Jimmy if Riggs had thrown the match.

"The answer was no. He lost because he wore himself out promoting it. He wore himself out in another way too. It may have been billed as 'the battle of the sexes' but Jimmy could tell you Bobby collaborated like hell with the enemy. He needed those 400-odd vitamins he was washing down daily. Over the ten-day period preceding the match, Bobby entertained a total of 26 ladies in his room, around the clock. The number was an educated guess. Jimmy may have missed one or two, but Bobby did not.

"The night before he was to meet Billie Jean, Jimmy told Riggs he was going to lose. 'You've done a great job,' he said, 'but you forgot one thing – the tennis match.' It was just a tired old man who lost to Ms King the next evening before an international crowd of 30,000 who dressed like they were at the opera.

"Sugar Daddy was one of the night's biggest winners. They got a million dollars' worth of television time for $30,000. Sales for the first quarter after the match went up nearly 30 per cent (although Jimmy Welch said sugar costs did too).

"For Jimmy's money, Bobby Riggs established himself as one of the great public relations men of all time, better than some of the acknowledged giants of the field; Joe Namath, Evel Knievel, even Muhammad Ali. Jimmy based this on what he had to work with – a 55-year-old body and a face like Bugs Bunny."

All this time, although his public relations business was flourishing, Snyder would continue to set odds and distribute them to the national media. It cost him up to $50,000 per year on research and contacts, but he reckoned it was money well spent – it kept his name out there among the public.

In 1976, he was asked to join CBS's *NFL Today* show as a

resident panellist, predicting the outcome of games and examining the odds. Snyder was a revelation. The public, even those viewers who'd never had a bet in their life, lapped up everything he said, revealing an untapped wealth of potential gamblers.

To have someone like Snyder on such a massively popular show was like, say, John McCririck being chief guest on BBC's *Match Of The Day* – every single week. Suddenly betting and odds was an everyday topic of conversation in millions of homes throughout America, as common as mom's apple pie. Snyder had sanitised it, dignified it, stripped away its faintly sordid air. Suddenly all America woke up to the excitement of sports betting – Snyder had sown the seeds of a multi-billion pound industry.

Yet just as quickly as his star had risen, it plummeted. At the height of his celebrity, Snyder was interviewed by a WRC-TV reporter, Ed Hotaling, on 15 January 1988. He was in Washington, taping a feature for *NFL Today* on the NFL Championship between Washington Redskins and Minnesota Vikings. But it was also the date of Martin Luther King's 59th birthday and for some reason Hotaling believed Snyder was fair game for questions on the progress of black people in society.

Everything went well until Hotaling asked Snyder about the success of black athletes in sport.

"The black is the better athlete to begin with," Snyder said. "Because he's been bred to be that way, because of his high thighs and big thighs that goes up into his back, and they can jump higher and run faster because of their bigger thighs, you see. The white man has to overcome that. But they don't try hard enough to overcome it.

"... In football and baseball and any other game that you have to run a lot, I mean your thighs come into prominence, very much so, because that's what gauges your speed and your jump, in situations such as that, in basketball, your thigh's the thing that makes you jump high. I'm telling you that the black is the better athlete because this goes back all the way to the Civil War, when the slave owner would breed his big black to his big woman so that he could have a big black kid, you see. That's where it all started."

Though Snyder's comments were a rehash of an article he'd read in which black Olympic gold medallist Lee Evans aired the same views, and although of 4,000 letters he received on the subject not one was from an offended African-American, Snyder was given the bullet by CBS, who branded his remarks "reprehensible".

The public supported him but the TV companies thought he was poison and Snyder lived out the later years of his life – he died in April 1996 aged 76 – in relative obscurity.

Of his many obituaries, one paragraph stands out. The *Las Vegas Sun* wrote: "The colourful tout with the gift of the gab was responsible for making sports betting one of the most popular forms of mainstream entertainment." And this in a country where, Vegas and a few other states apart, gambling is illegal.

Snyder's counterpart in Britain was Ron Pollard, for many years the public face of Britain's biggest bookmakers, Ladbrokes. Unlike Snyder, Pollard didn't have to fight against anti-gambling laws – at least after betting shops had opened in the early sixties – but, like the Greek, he revolutionised the betting habits of a nation by a genius for odds and for public relations.

Pollard changed the face of betting in the UK when he set odds for the Conservative leadership race in the wake of the Profumo affair in 1963. Although he doesn't admit it, it's likely Pollard was influenced by a famous Snyder story, 15 years earlier, when the Greek flew in the face of the mood of the nation and nailed his colours to underdog Harry S Truman's mast in the 1948 US Presidential Election. In landing a monster coup, Snyder underlined how painstaking research must be the platform of any successful punting strategy.

Tom Dewey was something like a 1-25 chance to turf the unpopular Truman out of office. Quite simply it wasn't a betting contest – Dewey was a shoe-in. But it was while adjusting his tie in a mirror one morning that Snyder was given the first hint that a major upset was on the cards. "I think I'll grow a moustache," said the Greek, to no-one in particular. "Don't do it, Jim," his sister Mary said. "Girls don't like moustaches."

That day Snyder spotted in the newspaper a picture of Governor

Dewey - complete with pencil moustache. Remembering from newspaper stories that 52 per cent of the electorate were women, Snyder began to wonder whether his sister's words were true. He hired three women, at $15 per day each, to stand in front of a department store and ask every woman who came out one simple question: do they like moustaches? Altogether 500 shoppers were questioned – 347 said they did not like a moustache, 122 said they did, and 31 said they did not care as long as it was on a man.

Snyder's pulse began to quicken. He could be on to the best long-shot in betting history – Truman at 20-1 in a two-horse race. Next, Snyder got his three hired ladies to take another poll – at various stops like a grocery store, an expensive boutique, an African-American district – with again just one simple question: will you vote for Truman or Dewey? The result put the two politicians neck and neck. Snyder quickly made it known he had $10,000 to put on Truman. He was offered portions of the bet at varying odds up to a maximum 22-1 but opted to put the whole ten grand on with one layer at 17-1, taking the shorter odds to guarantee pay-out from what was a respectable bookmaker. Truman won to give Snyder the biggest pay-out of his gambling career up to then.

Pollard never had the gambling background of Snyder, but his eye was just as alert to the main chance, and it was his flair for introducing a betting angle into the big stories of the day that first taught the British public that horses and greyhounds were not the only games in town.

Pollard was the man who, every November, would eye up a procession of beautiful young women as part of his job – come on, someone had to do it. He wasn't a professional pervert – he was merely assessing the form for the annual Miss World contest for which, each year, he set the odds. It was part of growing up to be confronted with a double-page spread in the national tabloid newspapers of pictures of the Miss World contestants, their age, their nationality, their vital statistics, and the real vital statistics – the odds.

In 1965, Britain was transfixed by the plight of Goldie the eagle when he escaped twice from London Zoo. Goldie enjoyed his 12 days of freedom so much in February that, ten months later, in the run-up to Christmas, he broke out again, with the newspapers once again lapping up the story. Pollard released a story that Ladbrokes were offering 12-1 against Goldie being recaptured before midnight on Christmas Eve.

Goldie was recaptured hours before the deadline, to cost Ladbrokes £14,000, but the publicity value was worth far more. All these stunts had a drip-drip effect on the public. Slowly they began to realise that betting wasn't all about the privileged world of the turf, where only the true insiders knew which races were bent; betting was available on everything. Above all, betting was fun.

But it was really the great Conservative Party Stakes of 1963 that put Pollard, and Ladbrokes, on the map. The background to the race should by now be well known: Defence Minister Jack Profumo resigning after a dalliance with a young lady, Christine Keeler, also involved with a Russian diplomat. Prime Minister Harold McMillan was also forced to resign to spark a fierce leadership battle. Pollard, by nature a political animal but still at this time a greenhorn at Ladbrokes, wondered aloud whether to get involved. He did – and it was the greatest move he ever made.

In his autobiography, *Odds And Sods*, Pollard wrote: "I had no idea of what was to come; I cannot claim any vision of the immense PR and financial success it was to be. Somehow it just seemed the ideal time to discover whether the public would bet on politics. So I spoke with Cyril Stein, my employer and the managing director of Ladbrokes, suggesting that 'here was the chance for us to get on the front pages rather than the back'. He did not hesitate. 'Well don't just stand there, Ron,' he said. 'Get on with it.'

"Thus, in 1963, I inaugurated the Tory Leadership Stakes, quite the most momentous move of my life. Nothing would be quite the same ever again. It was like a fever; for two weeks I did not know whether I was a bookmaker or a film star."

Pollard made Rab Butler the 5-4 favourite, Lord Hailsham 7-4 and Reginald Maudling 6-1, with the rest of the candidates 10-1 or more.

'10-1 bar three for No 10,' screamed the newspaper headlines, and political betting in Britain was born. For the record, Sir Alec Douglas-Home, a 16-1 chance, won.

Pollard wrote: "From all this we discovered something that would be vital to our future. Until this time we had thought of betting in terms of dogs and horses and very little else. Now we knew different and were on to a big, big winner. For it was abundantly clear that the public would gamble on absolutely anything. If it moved, if it was on TV, if it caused an argument in the pub, they wanted to bet on it. Miss World, elections, the Eurovision Song Contest, man on the moon, the next Pope, aliens from outer space, the Loch Ness Monster - we obliged them all."

Pollard does not claim to be a sports betting guru but it was his work in pioneering alternative forms of gambling that was to kick-start the sports betting revolution in Britain. Previously it was perhaps too big a step for punters to graduate from horseracing to other sports like snooker, tennis or golf. But once they'd dabbled on Miss World, the next logical step was the big wide world of sport. After all at least in football, cricket and rugby they could perhaps boast of knowing as much as the bookies. In racing that was, and always will be, impossible.

Towards the end of his career with Ladbrokes – he is now retired – Pollard's mantle was taken up by his William Hill counterpart Graham Sharpe, now perhaps recognised as the voice of the whole bookmaking industry. Sharpe, too, has shown a genius for PR, taking betting time and again on to the front pages of the national newspapers.

Sharpe was responsible for perhaps two of the greatest PR coups of the last 20 years – the Maradona 'Hand Of God' goal and the 'Who Shot JR' riddle.

Argentina beat England 2-1 in the quarter-final of the 1986 World Cup but their opening goal was famously knocked in by Maradona's fist. The English were outraged - Maradona would have been shot had he set foot on these shores - but it was not until Sharpe heard Sports Minister Richard Tracey arguing that the moral result was 1-1 that he hatched his fiendishly clever plan.

Sharpe pushed for his company to refund stakes to all punters who backed a draw in that quarter-final, while still paying out on a 2-1 win for Argentina.

"My boss, John Brown, asked me to calculate how much it would cost the firm and when I told him a few hours later '£50,000', he told me to get cracking," recalls Sharpe. "The rival bookies went bananas. One of them called it 'the most irresponsible act ever committed by a bookmaker', so we knew we were in the right. And the punters were delighted."

Yet that stunt couldn't match the shockwaves he sent through the betting industry six years earlier – quoting odds on a cliffhanging storyline in popular TV soap opera *Dallas*. Surely he'd lost his marbles – scripts are written weeks in advance.

Sharpe recalled: "My wife Sheila was an ardent *Dallas* fan and while she was watching it one night she mumbled out of the blue: 'it could be anyone.' I didn't have a clue what she was talking about. The next day a reporter from the *Sunday Mirror* rang me and asked if Hills would offer prices on the identity of the villain who shot JR Ewing. I thought there was no way on earth my bosses would give me the okay to bet on something which in all likelihood had already been decided and I was right. They looked at me as though I had a screw loose.

"The next day the *Sunday Mirror* rang again and said the series would finish with the shooting, the new series would not be screened for six months, and the producers were keeping the identity of the killer a closely-guarded secret to fend off any giant pay demands by the actors. This was definitely more promising, but when I rang around the Fleet Street TV critics they all reckoned I was a mug. They all knew already who shot JR. It was Sue Ellen. No, it was Pam. Another insisted it was Dusty Farlow. In fact no-one knew for certain. So my boss told me to go ahead as long as I accepted the consequences."

The consequences were astonishing, Sharpe remembers. "The world went mad. Every paper wanted the story. And the BBC *Nine O'Clock News*, which immediately followed the *Dallas* shooting episode, interviewed me about the bets we'd taken."

Once again Sharpe, like Pollard and Snyder before him, had woken up the public to the thrills of non-racing betting.

Yet while recognising the huge importance of those three very talented figures to the growth of sports betting, would I be immodest to claim some credit myself?

Many bookmaking insiders point to the 1990 World Cup in Italy as the event that really kick-started the sports betting revolution, the tournament that transformed it from the puny infant brother of horserace betting to a muscular, though not fully developed, rival. The reasons they give are valid – the startling progress of England and the Republic Of Ireland in Italia 90, the betting-friendly kick-off times, and the aggressive marketing strategy of the big bookmakers. But perhaps the introduction, at my prompting, a year earlier of a daily sports betting section in the pages of the *Racing Post* also played its part. Suddenly Britain's biggest gamblers were aware of real betting opportunities away from the turf. As their money piled on, say, Stefan Edberg, Cliff Thorburn, Ian Woosnam or Dallas Cowboys, so the odds shortened. As the odds shortened, so bookmaker PR departments sprung into action.

National newspaper sports editors and TV commentators were now being told of wholesale gambles on the tennis at Wimbledon, or the World Snooker Championship, instead of the Ayr Gold Cup. This was so much sexier, so much more refreshing. By the time Italia 90 came around, punters had been bitten big time by the sports betting bug.

The growing momentum was helped a year later by an astonishing tipping *tour de force* in the pages of the *Post*. Ian Baker-Finch was tipped – I didn't say he *might* win, I said he *would* win – at 50-1 for the 1991 Open Championship at Royal Birkdale, just a fortnight after Michael Stich's 40-1 triumph – again strongly recommended in the *Racing Post* – at Wimbledon. Winners at those kind of odds come along once in a blue moon for racing tipsters; we had two in a fortnight. Punters were quick to jump aboard a bandwagon gathering pace daily. Sports betting was here to stay.

Looking back, it seems incredible that in 1988 you would not find a word of copy on sports betting in either the *Racing Post* or *Sporting Life*, Britain's two betting dailies at the time. Now it's common to find 15 pages per day in the *Post* under the Sports Betting banner. Forgive me a certain feeling of pride. That was my baby.

# chapter 2

## how to con the bookies

We're told so often that bookmakers have an intelligence network that would put MI5 to shame that to try to pull a fast one over them is as futile, we must believe, as an escape bid at Alcatraz.

Yet nothing could be further from the truth. Bookies are vulnerable in many areas, none more so than sports betting, as this chapter will make abundantly clear.

To take advantage of the loopholes I am about to describe, it is necessary to loosen your morals a little. If you're the prim and proper, butter-wouldn't-melt type, this is not for you. If, however, you see nothing wrong in using deceit to hit back at bookmakers, then you may find this chapter ultimately very rewarding.

A few years ago, while writing for the *Racing Post*, I made clear that I believed there was nothing wrong with punters 'after-timing' – that is, placing a bet after the result is known – if they can get away with it. Bookies employ similar tactics all the time, using their considerable muscle to ensure profitability. For instance, they will continue to quote ante-post odds for a horse for a big race in the full knowledge (because they've been tipped off) that the horse has no chance of running. And although there's no proof, no-one can convince me that shadowy bookie-type figures aren't behind the inexplicably large number of scheduled eight-runner races which somehow manage to see only seven runners go to post, wrecking at a stroke the best-laid plans of each-way punters (bookies pay out to third place in eight-runner contests; only to second spot in seven-runner affairs).

Bigwigs of the leading firms hit the roof when my words appeared in the *Post*, accusing me of dishonesty and wanting to know how the *Post* could continue to employ someone who was urging punters to steal (their words).

They protested so loudly only because they know, no matter how much they hide behind this intelligence network myth, that they are vulnerable to the shrewd punter who can identify where they are weakest and who, perhaps more importantly, can sensibly limit his ambitions to a lumpy rather than life-changing win.

So often attempted coups are scuppered by sheer greed. In the summer of 1998, a small band of punters attempted a sting that may well have come off had the perpetrators not tried to be too ambitious.

An employee of Mirror Group Newspapers, publishers of the *Racing Post*, the only reliable (until then) source of results from minor greyhound meetings, arranged for false results to be published for four races, two at Reading and two at Yarmouth, on a Saturday night in mid-summer. The 9.08 at Reading was won by Trap 4, Brothers Beech, at 6-1, but in the following Monday's *Racing Post* the winner was listed as Trap 2, Kilacquinn, at 7-1. Lisnakill Roy, Trap 1, won the 9.54, just as the *Post* reported, but the true SP was 11-10 fav - not 3-1.

At Yarmouth, the results of the 9.12 and 9.29 were also incorrect. Trap 2, Sand Buster, was listed as the 4-1 winner of the earlier race when, in fact, first prize had gone to Trap 4, Granard Class, the 11-10 favourite. The later race was also won by a 4-1 chance, according to the *Racing Post* – Trap 1, Security Gaz. The real winner, though, was 9-2 shot Decoy Elm, running from Trap 3.

Now, because results from these very minor meetings are hardly compulsive reading, there's a chance, albeit slight, that the skulduggery would never have been noticed. Betting shop managers checking the results section on that Monday morning would have had no clue that three of the winners and four of the SPs were false.

True, there was always the possibility that connections of the real winners would ring to complain that their beloved greyhounds had not been given the credit they deserved, but we're not talking about the 2,000 Guineas here. Just as likely they'd have shrugged their shoulders and put it down to a *Post* cock-up. In fact such is the perceived nature of greyhound racing that the winning connections, once noticing the incorrect results, may just have suspected a hint of a betting sting and kept mum, silently wishing the perpetrators well.

But the sting was grounded by greed. Quite simply the organisers tried to win too much. Bets were reported - doubles, trebles, yankees, and other accumulators – in betting shops in East London, Littlehampton in Sussex, and Hull. The odd yankee here and there would probably never have raised eyebrows, but some shops faced pay-outs of up to £18,000 and that was always going to set alarm bells ringing given the insignificant nature of the races involved.

The other problem about this attempted coup was that it was very clearly a case of fraud. Once rumbled, the instigators had little chance of pleading ignorance, like the after-time punters always can, and police action was inevitable.

The *Post* employee involved, a 22-year-old called Neil Taylor, was sentenced to 180 hours' community service, but I wonder if it was mere coincidence that Taylor attempted his scam just a year after an article I wrote in the *Racing Post*, highlighting the dangers of the existing greyhound results service. This is what I wrote:

"Spare a thought for the small bookie who found himself well out of pocket as a result of an incorrect greyhound SP published in both *The Sporting Life* and *Racing Post* recently. A regular punter staked 10 x £4 doubles and a £2 accumulator on five dogs at evening meetings. The Liverpool-based bookie, playing safety-first, laid off a £4 accumulator on the same five dogs with another independent layer.

"When all five won, the first bookie cheerfully paid out £593 to the punter, expecting a cheque for £513 from the bookmaker with whom he had hedged. But then his problems began.

"The fifth leg of the accumulator had been listed as a 4-1 winner (at Milton Keynes) in both trade papers (*The Sporting Life* was still flourishing at the time) and it was at those odds that Bookie A had settled. But the dog was in fact 4-7, as both papers made clear in corrections the following day. Understandably, Bookie B settled at 4-7, sending a cheque for £150, rather than £513, to his bewildered counterpart.

"'What can I do about it?' a bitter Bookie A asked. 'I am almost £400 down through no fault of my own.'

"Evening greyhound results are provided for both papers by the Press Association. Errors are rare, but when they do arise they appear in both organs. What should worry the betting industry is the massive scope for an organised coup current greyhound SP practices offer.

The Press Association results desk is as honest as the day is long, but what is to stop any future employee deliberately filing an incorrect SP for newspaper use, having first tipped off a group of conspirators? It's a problem that has no easy solution and it's one we're sure to hear more about."

That was very much a sting that went sour, but bookies shiver whenever they remember the famous Hole-In-One Gang, who netted an estimated £400,000 on an ingenious golf betting coup in 1991. I described it at the time as gambling's greatest coup, and I believe it still merits that tag now.

Paul Simons and John Carter met in a betting shop in the late eighties. Simons tried to place £700 on a bowls match that was already over, but betting shop manager Carter was too sharp for him. The two shared a deep interest in betting on sport and their friendship developed.

In the spring of '91 they trawled Britain's smaller bookmakers asking for odds about a hole-in-one being scored in five of the year's leading golf tournaments, the Open and US Open among them. The brilliance of this idea has never fully been recognised.

Simons and Carter suspected that many bookies, while aware of the rarity of holes in one by amateur golfers, would be blissfully unaware that most professional tournaments throw up at least one ace and would therefore offer inflated odds. In fact the odds they were offered staggered even them. The intrepid duo were given anything up to 100-1 – when the true odds are closer to evens.

If you doubt that holes in one are so commonplace in

professional events, consider this. There are generally four par-3 holes per round, with up to 150 of the world's best golfers taking part in the first two rounds, and around 70 in rounds three and four following the halfway cut. That makes around 1,760 attempts at a hole-in-one per tournament – by the most accurate golfers on the planet. In fact it's a wonder there aren't more aces.

If you're still not convinced, chew on this: the lowest number of holes in one on the US Tour in the 1990s is 25 in 1993. And that from just 42 tournaments. In 1994 there were 44 holes in one.

Of course those statistics can be misleading because one tournament may throw up, say, six holes in one. So chew on this, too: leading in to the Benson & Hedges International Open in May 1999, ten European tournaments had yeilded a hole in one from only 15 staged since the beginning of the season. In 1998 16 of the 32 European Tour events witnessed a hole in one.

Yet although such mouthwatering odds were readily available, Simons and Carter still had work to do. First, they had to place their bets cleverly, careful not to raise the slightest suspicion. Second, they had to wait for those holes in one. Okay, they'd got 100-1 about an even-money shot, but even-money shots get turned over every day. I know - I back most of them.

To place their big-money doubles and trebles without setting off alarm bells, the duo had to adopt the personality of the kind of punters bookies love – the loud-mouthed Cockney with more money than sense, and the betting shop rookie. Simons played the first role to perfection, as he described in the duo's book *Hole-In-One-Gan*g.

"'Hello, guv'nor. There's no sweat in betting 18 thousand to two Faldo is there?' I asked, marching towards the counter already counting a fistful of readies. 'There's a few things I want to bet on,' I bulldozed on, completing count two of my readies and adding that I had done three large at the dogs the previous evening. 'I want to bet Mike Harwood to beat Brand Jnr, and while I'm here I'll lay out a few quid on the cricket. And where's the 2,000 Guineas betting? I want a price for Desert Sun.'

'The latest price is ten-to-one, sir.'

'Missed the effing train again,' came my disgruntled reply. 'There's no hole-in-one odds up on the screen – can you quote me a price, guv?'"

Sure that he's got a complete mug on his premises, the bookie relaxes his guard, asks Simons what price he's been given in the past, and then agrees to 66-1.

For Carter the task was to act ignorant, the innocent abroad. Something like: "Hello mate. I'm going to the golf in a few days and I just wanted an interest in it. Would you have any prices for a hole-in-one to be scored?"

Carter wrote: "The old bottle always took a bit of a hammering at this point because in the next few seconds the bookie's body language would reveal all. Permutations are endless, but the two most common to pick up on are a rush of blood to the face telling you they have definitely been stung before, so get out of the shop as quickly as possible, or a lethargic scratching of the head while mumbling 'well, that's the first time I've heard that one', encouraging you to go for the throat."

All five tournaments picked out by Simons and Carter delivered the goods and the pair were due to pick up £500,000. But some layers cried foul, claiming they'd been duped by con-men and refused to pay-out. One even called in police to arrest them when they called to collect their winnings, only to be given a verbal cuff around the ear by the long arm of the law which sided with Simons and Carter.

Even when the two were backed by the (now-defunct) Green Seal arbitration service and by the National Association of Bookmakers, which publicly criticised its non-paying members, the welchers still wouldn't cough. In total Simons and Carter failed to collect £100,000 of the £500,000 they were due.

The behaviour of those bookmakers who refused to pay up was disgraceful. All the two punters had done was take advantage of information, freely available information by the way, bookies were not aware of. There was nothing underhand about their operation. Indeed they risked their combined life savings of £30,000 on the devilish scheme. It was no more morally wrong than, say, bookies shortening the odds of an unraced three-year-old for the 2,000

Guineas after being tipped off by a stable insider about a sparkling gallop.

And the sad footnote to it all was that Simons died a few years later, aged just 40.

Many of the areas of bookmaker vulnerability I'm about to outline here are perhaps more morally questionable, but stuff 'em. They've taken our money without a token of mercy for years so it's about time we got our own back.

A few years back Josh Gifford trained a useful chaser called Vodkatini, who was capable of winning valuable prizes but who very often dug in his heels at the start and refused to race. It was incredible how many punters were willing to take a chance on these mulish tendencies. All they had to do instead was write out their bet, amble to the counter, and wait for the off before handing over their cash. Betting shop cashiers will normally take bets for steeplechases for up to half a minute after the off.

At the beginning of the 1998-99 Premiership season, Aston Villa were at home to Middlesbrough in a live Sky clash on a Sunday afternoon. Villa had recently sold star striker Dwight Yorke to Manchester United and, with Stan Collymore injured, fans wondered who would play up front for the Midlands side. Half an hour before kick-off, news filtered through that Villa centre-half Riccardo Scimeca was poised to partner Julian Joachim up front.

A friend of mine immediately rang the credit operation of Tote Bookmakers and asked for a price on Scimeca to score the first goal in the match. Told that he was a 50-1 chance, my friend had a £50 bet. Scimeca did indeed play as Joachim's strike-partner but didn't manage to get on the scoresheet, so the bet was a loser. That, however, didn't stop Tote writing to my pal to close his account, telling him his was not the sort of business they wanted. Yet what did Tote expect?

When a punter is armed with hot information like that, it's his duty to take advantage. Not all bookies will react as pettily as Tote. They realise, or at least should do, that what my pal did – act on useful information – is no different to them slashing the odds for Saturday's big race of a horse they've just been told by a stable lad has worked like a dream on the gallops.

Though I warned earlier of the dangers of greed, I'm still kicking myself for winning a paltry £80 on what in hindsight will go down as one of the great sports betting coups of all time. The Lance Todd Trophy, awarded to the man of the match in rugby league's Challenge Cup Final at Wembley, is voted on by a panel of rugby league journalists. It just so happened that, in 1989. a pal of mine, a regular punter, was on the panel for the Wigan v St Helens Challenge Cup Final. After a few pints in a London pub the night before the game, he let slip that he'd arranged with more than half the panel that the Lance Todd vote would go to Wigan's Ellery Hanley, the superstar of rugby league at the time and guaranteed to shine even if playing at only 50 per cent capacity, unless Hanley suffered an obvious nightmare.

This was dynamite. Better still, Hanley was 8-1 with Hills to win the Lance Todd. But as each lager was downed my mate became more and more worried about the implications of what he was about to do the following day. What if he got found out? He'd lose his job for sure. When we parted around midnight, he was adamant that the coup was still on, but I could see doubt in his, by now glazed, eyes. I stuck a measly ten quid on Hanley and I swear I was gutted when he went on to play a blinder and win the award in a canter. Not having at least a ton on Hanley is my second biggest regret in life. My first is not trying harder to nail a German beauty queen called Christine Hartmann who almost succumbed to my charms (honest) in Ibiza in the early eighties. What a corker. She could have had my Lance Todd award any day.

Whenever a contest is decided upon by a vote you can be sure that manipulation is always a threat. In March 1994, Michaela Pike was backed down in the space of two hours from 8-1 to 4-5 with Hills to win the Miss British Isles beauty contest. Miss Pike was, probably still is, an undeniably pretty girl but the pattern of betting suggested her rivals were Nora Batty and the Ugly Sisters instead of 19 other corkers.

Miss Pike was duly crowned Miss British Isles that night and Hills owned up to a pay-out of £25,000, but the story was to have a twist. It was later reported that Hills had been persuaded into betting on the contest by the organisers, who promised to take a full-page advert in a national newspaper of a swimsuit line-up of the 20 finalists. The advert never materialised and, two days after Hills had paid out, a Brighton bookie revealed he'd been told of the result two days before the contest was held.

Six weeks later a report suggested that Scotland Yard had been called in to investigate an alleged coup on the Miss British Isles contest. A newspaper alleged that the judges insisted after the contest that none of them had voted for Miss Pike. It was further alleged that hotels, restaurants and a limousine hire firm were owed £100,000 by organisers, who had disappeared. Clearly embarrassed, Hills backtracked on their earlier comments and said they'd lost "nowhere near" £25,000 on the beauty parade.

In the early days of live Monday night football on Sky, spread firm Sporting Index took the brave step of framing a market on the man of the match, voted for by viewers. They would issue a spread based on the shirt number of the game's star man. But this was asking for trouble. Sky won't reveal how many viewers take the trouble to ring up and vote – I have been told by a Sky Sports employee that sometimes it's as little as 30 – but it's not hard to imagine an organised gang of punters cashing in. All they had to do for a market framed at, say, 6-7, was buy at seven and then vote in their dozens for a player wearing something like No.23. Needless to say, this market did not last long, although Sporting refuse to say whether they were ever skinned in such a way.

A similar strategy once almost made a nonsense of the BBC's prestigious Sports Personality Of The Year award a few years ago. I remember at the *Racing Post* we read, without comment, the cramped odds in Surrey Racing's betting lists for all the usual suspects like Nigel Mansell, Steve Davis and Nick Faldo, but almost choked on our coffee when we spotted on the 25-1 mark a man called Bob Nudd. Bob who?

It turned out that a Surrey employee had read about a campaign in an angling magazine asking readers to ply the BBC with votes for top fisherman Nudd in an attempt to get recognition for angling which, perhaps not surprisingly, is generally overlooked in that annual Beeb backslapping-fest in London. Surrey Racing, fearing that it would not take too many votes for Nudd to become a realistic contender for the BBC award – the Beeb also jealously guard voting figures – decided to take no chances on Nudd, hence the 25-1 quote.

Surrey need not have worried. Eagle-eyed backroom staff at BBC HQ also got wind of the angling campaign and disregarded all votes, however genuine, for the Nuddmeister. Poor old Bob was the one that got away. To rub salt in the anglers' wounds, there was not a single mention of fishing once again on the show.

In 1991, Lennox Lewis fought Gary Mason at Wembley Arena for the British heavyweight title. This was a massive fight in Britain and, daft as it may seem now, Lewis was the marginal underdog at a top-priced evens. The day before the fight I, as sports editor of the *Racing Post*, contacted boxing writers from all the national daily newspapers to canvass their opinions. Although the *Post* was solidly behind Lewis, it was not too surprising that the majority of ring hacks were going for Mason. An hour before deadline, the phone trilled on my desk. It was Frank Maloney, Lewis' promoter and a man well clued up on betting.

"I hear you've been conducting a poll on tomorrow's fight," he began. "What's the verdict?"

I told him that although we believed Lewis was a good thing, most other experts favoured Mason.

"That's incredible," he said. "Lennox is evens, isn't he? Listen, do yourself a favour and lump on large."

Though it was nice to hear our opinion reinforced, we expected Maloney, well versed in boxing-speak, to say little different. After all which fight promoter is ever going to recommend a bet on an opponent? But Maloney wasn't finished.

"Do you have any round betting through?" he asked.

"Yeah," I said, "what are you interested in?"

"What price is Lennox in round seven?" he wanted to know.

I told him the best price was 33-1 with Ladbrokes.

"Well listen, son," he said. "If I were you, I'd have a nice few quid on that." And then he was gone.

Scepticism, cynicism, or maybe just plain stupidism stopped me following Maloney's advice. The next night I got home from work in good time to watch the fight – it was live on a Wednesday night on BBC's *Sportsnight* – and I mentioned Maloney's words to my wife just before the first bell.

"Oooh, can I have a bet on that?" she asked.

Instead of ringing a credit office, instead of saying no, instead of telling her to pipe down and get on with the washing up, I laid the bet - £5 at 33-1.

Lewis won in round seven.

I should make clear here that there is no hint that Maloney, nor Lewis or Mason for that matter, conspired dishonestly for the fight to end in the seventh. It's my view that Maloney knew Lewis was so superior – as history has since proven – that he could finish the fight at will. A sort of 'take him out in seven, Lennox, I've a few bob riding on it'.

What the incident did prove was that for sports insiders, for those truly in the know, there are small fortunes to be made from sports betting. I'll give you another example.

Newspapers in the run-up to the 1998 Open Championship at Royal Birkdale left no-one in any doubt that the course would play far tougher than it did in 1991 when Ian Baker-Finch took out its teeth on his way to victory. Weather forecasts also suggested that the Open contenders would find the going tough. Yet that did not stop spread firm City Index spreading the number of players to finish under par after four rounds at 11-14. Logically this was a sell, but I still needed reliable inside information before I could confidently place a bet. Then it arrived. And how.

Peter Coleman is the loyal caddie to twice US Masters champion Bernhard Langer. He's also a hardened punter who's won and lost fortunes during his years in the game. I've known Peter a few years and he'd offered the week before the Open to mark my Birkdale card, to fill me in on who was playing well in practice, who was short of confidence, who'd had a row with his girlfriend, that kind of thing. On the Tuesday of Open week, Peter rang me at home from Birkdale.

"Don't listen to what anyone else says," he told me. "The winning score this week will be over par."

"Are you sure, Peter?" I asked. "The spread firms don't seem to think so."

"Bugger them," he said. "The rough here is terrible, the winds are howling, there's no way anyone is going to break par for the four rounds."

When you get information like that from a man on the inside, a man who really does know what he's talking about after a lifetime in top-level golf, then you've really got to cash in.

But no sooner was the money down than the winds abated. The first round of the 1998 Open was played in beautifully calm conditions. The only thing raging was my pulse-rate. After day one, 27 players were under par, with a further 14 on level par. Coleman, your name was mud. But he was proved right in the end. Strong winds on day two and three saw scores sky-rocket and the return to calmer conditions on the final Sunday came too late to save the spread firms. Not a single player beat par.

But of course we don't all have access to such dynamite inside information. Many of us have to rely purely on our wits in that daily battle with the old enemy and the rest of this chapter will explain how we can take bookies to the cleaners, even if some of the methods are, to say the least, unethical.

The first thing to remember is that bookmakers cannot keep on top of everything. There is simply too much sport going on every single day of the year for them to keep tabs. Yes, there's sport on TV almost all day long, useful web-sites spring up almost daily on the Internet, but bookmakers, with a thousand other things to look after, do not always have the manpower to take advantage. Punters, on the other hand, can.

Oxfordshire-based bookmakers Stan James, with an impressive debit-card betting operation, bet regularly on tennis. It could be the most insignificant tournament around, the Croatian Open for example, but their odds will appear on Sky Sports teletext (page 364).

Although Stan James will frequently take the trouble to contact the tournament organisers directly, more often than not they will rely on the Internet, in particular the atptour.com web-site, for the order of play. But as any regular tennis punter will tell you, the order of play is never an exact science. It can tell us when the first match is scheduled to start, but it's pure guesswork when later matches will kick-off.

As a rule of thumb, Stan James, and also Hills, who tend to bet in latter stages of tournaments, estimate that a men's best-of-three-sets match will last no longer than an hour and a half. So if, say, Pat Rafter is first on at 11 o'clock in the morning against Jonas Bjorkman, the second match on that same court – let's say Pete Sampras v Goran Ivanisevic for argument's sake - will begin no earlier than 12.30pm. All well and good. But if Rafter withdraws with an injury after just two games of the first set, the second match is very likely to start at around the 11.30am mark. By noon, Ivanisevic could be one set up against Sampras, but bookies won't know. They'll still be offering, say, 7-4 Ivanisevic even though he's a set up and well on his way to victory.

Bookies will insist that by constantly monitoring the Internet (the atptour.com site gives live scoring from tennis tournaments) they will find out just as quickly as anyone about injuries or changes to the order of play, but this is baloney. Quite often the 'live scoring' is anything but and news and results won't leak through until much later in the day.

But how, you are entitled to ask, can we get this information before bookmakers? With diligence is the simple answer. A phone call to the tournament office is all you need. English is the language of tennis so you'll have no problems making yourself understood and results are freely given out to anyone who requests them.

The full schedule of ATP tour events, together with all the relevant telephone numbers, can be found in the annual Player Guide books published at the start of each season by the ATP Tour. This is essential reading material for any serious punter, since it offers a comprehensive result service plus biographies of all the players on the pro-circuit. These Player Guides should be available in most good bookshops, but if all else fails contact

Sportspages (see page 318 for details).

It may sound a touch extravagant to ring the four corners of the globe just on the off-chance of finding a snippet of injury news, but you'll be surprised how often a scheduled order of play is altered and information like that is gold-dust. Bear in mind, too, that even if the Atptour live scoring is functioning properly on the Internet, bookies quite often will not have the time to monitor it.

Golf also offers the hard-working punter chances to steal a march on the more unsuspecting bookies, although in both the instances I'm about to outline, it is probably necessary to have a colleague working at the course to have any chance of cashing in. Okay, this may be difficult in the more far-flung tournaments, but should pose few problems in those staged closer to home.

Stan James bet in-running on the final day of many European Tour events. That is a brave move, for they are at the mercy of the live TV coverage on Sky Sports, which breaks with maddening frequency for adverts. Over the closing holes of a tournament there could be several players in with a chance of victory. Every single drive matters, every missed putt affecting the odds massively. But it is very often impossible for Sky, with so many commercial breaks, to keep viewers sufficiently up to date. While Papa and Nicole are carrying out their illicit liaisons, Colin Montgomerie may be missing a simple putt which will put him out of the reckoning. Viewers, and bookies, won't learn of it until the adverts are over. But the punter with a mate and a mobile phone at the course hears of it immediately.

Bookmakers traditionally update their outright odds for a golf tournament after the second round has been completed, and in doing so leave themselves vulnerable.

To encourage turnover on day three – almost always a Saturday, the busiest day of the week for hard-pressed odds-compilers – bookies will not suspend betting until maybe half an hour before the leaders are due to tee-off in the final pairing of the day. They will have no way of knowing if one of the earlier starters has taken advantage of benign morning weather conditions to fire birdie after birdie and muscle onto the first page of the leaderboard. Very likely, with so many other duties to fulfil on a Saturday morning, the first inkling they will get of such a charge is the sight of the leaderboard when the third round coverage begins on Sky at around 1pm.

Argentinian Angel Cabrera narrowly made the halfway cut at the BMW International in Germany in late August 1998. His two-round total of 141, two inside the cut line, put him ten shots behind halfway leader Thomas Bjorn, the evens favourite by that stage.

Anybody foolish enough to want to back Cabrera could have got 200-1. With only 13 players with a worse total going into the third round on the Saturday, Cabrera was among the very early starters. Indeed by the time Bjorn teed off alongside Sven Struver at around 12 noon BST, Cabrera was coming to the end of his round and was just three shots off the lead after a superb 65. And you could still have got on at 200-1. The Argentinian went on to finish in a tie for fourth slot. Bjorn, incidentally, was unplaced.

A couple of friends of mine claim to have cleaned up over the years on top-batsman bets in one-day cricket matches. Under normal circumstances I wouldn't look twice at this form of betting but they insist that some games throw up unmissable opportunities.

Their passport to wealth, they say, is to step in and back both opening batsmen, generally at around the 4-1 mark, of the team batting second in a match which has yielded a low first-innings total. The theory behind this, of course, is that with such a small total to chase, only about two or three batsmen will be needed for the team batting second to clinch victory.

Bookies predictably shave the odds for the openers under such circumstances, but quite often only narrowly, and this is the time to step in. In the NatWest Trophy Final in September 1998, Derbyshire, batting first, scored a pitiful 108. Lancashire reached 109 for the loss of just one wicket, with opener John Crawley top-scoring with an unbeaten 53. Before the innings began, Hills had cut Crawley from 100-30 to 9-4 to be top Lancashire batsman, which in my book was more than enough. But my friends insist this was only because the 1998 NatWest Final was ruined by wet weather on the scheduled Saturday, with Lancashire not starting their innings until the following day. Given the luxury of time to assess the odds, Hills got it spot on. But on a busy Saturday, with a thousand other sports going on, they will not always be so accurate.

Although many punters believe there are a dozen or more experts on all different sports sitting vigilantly at the headquarters of the leading bookmakers and changing odds the moment team news or injury news leaks through, the reality is quite different. On many occasions there will be just two or three under-pressure employees trying to keep tabs on results, liabilities, dodgy bets, angry phone-calls, media inquiries, and maybe even making coffee. They are under the cosh, quite possibly under the weather, very likely there for the taking.

On 11 May 1999, England played Hampshire in a warm-up match for the World Cup. Hampshire batting first in a game shown live on Sky Sports, collapsed to 35-5, by which time news of the England line-up had already been revealed, with Alec Stewart and Nick Knight opening the batting. I rang Ladbrokes as the Hampshire tail-enders plugged on and was astonished to be told that they were still taking bets on England batsman, and that Stewart and Knight were still each available at 5-1. I got on, patted myself on the back, and near ejaculated when Hampshire were all out for 91.

Now all I needed was Knight or Stewart to score something like 35 runs to collect, surely simple against a weak Hampshire attack? The fact that Knight was out for a duck off the second ball and that No.3 batsman Graeme Hick came in to score 65 off 66 balls to wreck my attempted coup does not alter the fact that this was a fantastic bet, capitalising on lethargy, or perhaps intolerable workload, of the Ladbrokes sports odds-compilers.

But if there is a real golden opportunity for the after-timers, then it has to be on European football, for which kick-off times are very much a moveable feast. Believe me, bookmakers quake with fear whenever the three European cup competitions come around, particularly in the early stages, when there are so many countries represented.

A few years ago it was virtually impossible to find accurate kick-off times for European ties. The only source was UEFA but they were notoriously uncooperative with bookmakers, fearing the stigma of betting. UEFA's attitude has since softened – Ladbrokes were the official bookmakers for Euro 96 – but that doesn't mean the problems are solved. UEFA supply kick-off details to British bookies but all are local times. That means it's up to the bookies to translate local times to BST or GMT, depending upon the time of year, and that's where the fun and games really start.

Russia, for instance, has three separate time zones, And God only knows when their clocks go backwards and forwards. And if that isn't a difficult enough problem to grapple with, clubs in Eastern Europe often switch their kick-off times with just a day's notice, not informing UEFA until after the match has been played.

The chief soccer odds-compiler of a leading firm admitted: "The trouble is that everybody treats the kick-off times supplied by UEFA as gospel, but we know they are anything but."

Leading bookies at the start of the 1998-99 season began to print kick-off times on their coupons for big European programmes. The unsuspecting punter may have been highly impressed to see four separate firms in perfect synchrony but there's a simple explanation. All the coupons are published by the same printers, whose job it is to check whenever there is a disagreement in kick-off times. In other words, all the coupons may say that Dynamo Moscow kick off at 4.30pm against Galatasaray, but it ain't necessarily so.

On 29 September 1998, the midweek coupons of all the leading firms stated that the UEFA Cup first-round second-leg match between Slavia Prague and Schalke kicked off at 5pm. By 3.30pm, Slavia were 1-0 up, with just 15 minutes of the first-half remaining.

I have a mate in Czechoslovakia who rang me at half-time and begged me to get a bet on Slavia at 11-8. A mini-coup was very much on the cards but bookmakers were saved by an outrageous piece of good fortune. An employee of bookmakers Stan James was idly flicking through the satellite channels when, on German channel ZDF, he spotted a live match in progress. It was Slavia v Schalke and the home side were already 1-0 up.

Knowing that the industry had the game listed as a 5pm kick-off, he alerted Satellite Information Services (SIS), which beams live horseracing into betting shops, and they in turn tipped off bookies nationwide. But for that fluke, as several leading odds-compilers have admitted to me, there's little chance bookmakers would have spotted the early kick-off.

The secret for punters with access to that kind of information is to limit ambition. A sudden rush of £200 bets on the telephone mid-afternoon for Slavia would trigger even the most insensitive bookie antennae. Far better surely to trawl around the betting shops with a £25 bet here, there, and everywhere.

Of course there's still the problem of getting hold of this information in the first place. If bookies don't know, how can punters expect to find out? In the instance outlined above I was lucky enough to have a pal based in the country in question, but there are other avenues to explore.

Ignore the teletext services in Britain, which are by and large hopeless for European results. But there are one or two teletext pages on obscure foreign satellite channels that so far have enabled punters of my acquaintance to steal a march. There's no point in me revealing them here because that would play right into the bookies' hands but believe me, they do exist.

And for the more diligent there are other means of mounting a coup. Worldwide news agency Reuters have operatives in most Eastern European countries and although they'll probably very quickly get fed up with queries about football kick-off times and results, they may be worth a try before goodwill disappears entirely. But the best method is to phone the clubs themselves. All the relevant numbers are listed in the *European Football Yearbook*. The only snag is that English is not necessarily the language of football - not even in England – so be prepared for an uncomfortable call.

The leading odds-compiler mentioned earlier admitted to me in an unguarded moment: "We've been stung many times before on European matches and will no doubt suffer many more times in the future. On a vulnerability scale of 1 to 10, I'd say we're about five for European ties. But there's no point in us bleating about after-time punters. It's up to us to make sure we're as vigilant as we can possibly be."

I should perhaps add here that although I see little wrong in after-timing, I would never try to fleece the small independent bookmaker who will very often have money troubles worse than our own and who is scraping to earn a decent living. Leave those guys alone. Your targets should be the big bookies – Hills, Ladbrokes, Coral, Stanley and Tote.

As I said earlier in the chapter it may be necessary to ditch your scruples to take advantage of these opportunities, and there's always the possibility, despite the refreshingly adult outlook of the odds-man mentioned earlier, that bookmakers, if they rumble you, will close your account or bar you from their betting shops. To me it's worth the risk but I cannot close this chapter without recounting the horror story told to me by a punter whose attempt at an after-time coup backfired spectacularly.

He put £200 on Turkish club Galatasaray at 9-4, ten minutes after their UEFA Cup clash had finished. The Ladbrokes shop accepted his bet but when he returned to collect his winnings the next day all that was waiting for him were two police officers who accused him of all sorts of things, fraud being top of the list. Not only did Ladbrokes refuse to pay him his winnings, they also confiscated his stake money as police carted him off to the local nick, where he spent a night in the cell. It was only after the intervention of a Ladbrokes bigwig that the luckless punter was freed and his stake refunded.

But, please, don't let that put you off. I prefer to remember the comments of the Ontario Lottery Corporation – a state-run football betting organisation in Canada – after British ex-pats stung them for £350,000 over Christmas 1994. Dozens of Bank Holiday matches in Britain that festive period kicked off at noon rather than the normal 3pm, but the OLC were the last to know. They were still taking bets more than an hour after the games had finished. World spread through dozens of British pubs and a large bunch of shrewdies cashed in. But there was no carping from OLC. No whingeing, no calling the cops. They pledged to honour all bets "because those who placed them had done nothing illegal". All a spokeswoman said was: "We must have a better way of getting more accurate information to ensure that this doesn't happen again."

Are you listening, British bookies?

# chapter 3

## football betting

The incredible rise of sports betting during the 1990s has spawned one bewildering puzzle: how can football, far and away the hardest sport on which to make a profit, have become the most popular betting medium outside racing?

This book will show how bookies can easily be beaten in sports like tennis, golf and snooker; but football, if you excuse the pun, is an entirely different ball game. Make a profit from betting on football and you truly are among the chosen few.

There are a number of reasons for this, chief of which are the almost criminal restrictions imposed by British bookmakers. Saturdays see football betting go through the roof, but they also considerably boost the bank balance of the nation's layers.

You may fancy, say, Bournemouth at 8-11 at home to Blackpool but in most betting shops you will then, because of the minimum five-timer rule, have to find another FOUR teams to go with it. This is a practically impossible task.

Just imagine if you popped in for a bet on the favourite in the first race at Ascot and were told that if you wanted to back that horse, you could do so only if you put another four selections in your bet. It's utterly absurd but every weekend of every season the bookies are allowed to get away with this form of daylight robbery.

For those not familiar with bookmaker football restrictions on the weekend fixed-odds coupons, here's a shorthand guide: If your bet includes a home selection, you must come up with another four teams for a five-timer. But you are allowed trebles if you restrict your bet to teams in the top two English divisions and the Scottish Premier. If your bet contains an away team, you must find another two to go with it to satisfy the 'minimum trebles' requirement. And believe me, finding three away winners on a Saturday fixture list is mind-bogglingly tough.

In July 1994, bookies gave us a crumb of comfort by announcing grandly that from the start of the following season they would allow doubles, so long as one of the selections was in a match covered live on TV. This was a huge step in the right direction for punters force-fed a diet of five-timers, but still gives us an uphill battle because so many live TV games are ultra-competitive clashes, with rarely a good thing on offer.

It should be pointed out here that singles are allowed on cup matches, international fixtures, and live televised games. The thinking here, a throwback to the infamous match-fixing scandal of the 1960s, is that players are highly unlikely to be tempted into throwing matches of such importance like cup games and internationals or high-profile matches in front of millions of television viewers.

It seems incredible that bookmakers were ever allowed to implement such Draconian rules as minimum five-timers. It's widely believed that they did so at a time – in the early 1970s – when banker homes were commonplace. Punters blindly backing Liverpool, Leeds and either Celtic or Rangers when they were playing at home, more often than not found themselves on a winner, the theory went. Yet that is not true.

In the early days of football betting, bookies would highlight the minimum pay-out for five homes, any five homes, on the top of the coupon; and punters, in those days perhaps not so educated as today, would take the bait, judging the pay-out for a mere three winners too paltry to bother with. Recognising quickly that they were on to a good thing, bookies established the five-timer as a minimum requirement.

While at the *Racing Post*, I campaigned long and hard to persuade bookmakers to drop their weekend five-timer ruling. After all, unrestricted trebles are allowed for midweek soccer programmes which nowadays can be as lengthy as weekend fixture lists. Merseyside-based Stanley Racing, a rapidly growing force in the bookmaking world, responded and say their football profits are undamaged, so it's surely time for other firms to follow suit. But they won't because they know there are millions of gullible punters out there who will meekly abide by these rules forever.

Indeed representatives of the leading firms have told me off the record that there's no point in relaxing their rules because so many punters will continue to place their eight-, nine-, and ten-timers in search of that life-changing jackpot win. That's great, isn't it? The more discerning punters must suffer because of the idiocy of the great unwashed.

Stanley Racing say one of the reasons they relaxed their football betting rules to allow unrestricted trebles was to avoid confusion. With so many do's and don'ts on the weekend football coupons, so many restrictions, there was a danger bewildered punters would just drift away and find something more straightforward to bet on. Stanley certainly have a point.

I asked all the leading bookies whether they would accept the following football bet on the weekend coupons: a four-timer of three away teams and one Third Division side playing at home. Surely a punter staking such a bet had complied with the minimum-trebles ruling? If we can have three aways in our bet, surely we can have three aways and one home?

"No," said Hills. "You must have a five-timer if a home is included."

"Yes," said Ladbrokes. "We would allow that."

"No," said Coral. "The home selection would be void."

If the bookies themselves don't know, what chance has the poor punter got?

For a further example of how cynical bookies are taking advantage of naïve punters whose only contact with betting is a weekly football flutter, take a look at the Sections List on the weekend fixed-odds coupons. I've thought of many words to describe the Sections List and the most fitting is 'evil'.

Typically there will be seven sections of around nine matches and the punter is asked to pick one or two teams from each for a bumper pay-out. Obviously the more teams selected per section, the bigger the pay-out. Guaranteed minimum odds for one per section will be something like 78-1, for two 6,985-1. So far so good. But these matches and the order in which they appear on the coupon are fiendishly plotted by bookmakers.

The first section will feature nine long odds-on shots, for example Manchester United at home to Charlton, to tempt the suckers. The second section will also feature a handful of apparent good things. By then you're well and truly hooked. By the time you get to the third section where the matches are far more difficult to call, there's no turning back. You plough on regardless even though by now you're selecting teams you don't even fancy. Section Four is tougher still, while the final sections contain exclusively matches you normally wouldn't touch with a barge-pole.

It's like appearing on a TV game-show and being told that you can keep your £1,000 first prize or risk it to win a brand new car by surviving seven ordeals. You're told the first is a ten-second snogging session with the leggy blonde hostess, and the second a five-minute time limit to gulp down two pints of Guinness. You're hooked already. It's only when two white tigers are wheeled on and, for the third ordeal, you're instructed to wrestle with them that you realise you've been had.

Yet what's most baffling about the popularity of these unholy bets is that they offer no bonuses whatsoever. All the matches featured on the Sections List also appear on the Long List on the same coupon. What's the point in grappling with the sections featuring the most difficult matches on the coupon when there's absolutely no reward for doing so?

If bookies paid an extra ten per cent bonus for seven winning selections, or a compensation payment for six winners out of seven, we could perhaps understand punters having a crack on the Sections. As it is, their popularity is the eighth wonder of the world.

Regular soccer punters will know that in football betting the odds are very much in the bookmaker's favour. In a match in which theoretically all three potential outcomes – home win, away win, and draw – are equally likely, the true odds should be 2-1, 2-1, and 2-1. But such odds give bookmakers no profit margin, so instead they will offer, say, 6-4 the home team, 6-4 the away team, and 11-5 the draw (the draw being longest price because bookies know that few punters ever back it, something that will be explained later). This produces a book of 111 per cent, giving bookies a theoretical profit of 11 per cent whatever the result. And that's just for one match.

Punters who are asked to string five selections together face an in-built bookie profit margin of more than 55 per cent. No wonder bookmaker PR departments go to great lengths to ensure publicity for the football punter who manages to come up with a winning 12-team accumulator. News of such pay-outs tempts more and more punters into these near-suicidal bets.

Here's an example of what five-timer punters are up against. When you back a single, there are three possible outcomes – home win, away win, and draw. In a double it goes up to nine possibilities (H-H, H-D, H-A, D-H, D-D, D-A, A-H, A-D, A-A). By the time you get to five-timers you're up to 243 possible outcomes. So by demanding five-timers, bookies are telling you to bet in 243-runner races. Punters trying their hand at how to beat the bookies' profit margins increase with each extra selection.

Let's say you're going to have a five-timer and in each of the five matches the layers go 7-4 each of three. The five-fold comes to around 156-1, which equates to a betting percentage of 0.637. Multiply that by 243 (all 243 possible outcomes are 156-1) and you get a book of 156 per cent. And we are being charitable to layers here because three 7-4 shots yields a book of only 109 per cent when the more normal bookmaker margin for a football match is 112.

I asked leading bookmakers to justify the minimum five-timer requirement. Here's what they told me.

**Coral:** "We are far from convinced that there is any significant new additional turnover to be gained by offering trebles on all weekend matches. Our market research shows the vast majority of weekend football bets placed with us contain an average of seven selections. This pattern remains largely unchanged on FA Cup weekends, even though singles and upwards are accepted on vast numbers of games."

**Hills:** "We produce prices for the midweek and weekend coupons at the same time on a Saturday night to make available to our clients first thing Monday morning. Therefore any formalities and injuries after Saturday night cannot be taken into account for the weekend matches. While this is not such a problem for the the top divisions, in the lower leagues it is, as teams there operate on much smaller squads. So we feel justified in setting a minimum five-fold rule."

**Ladbrokes:** "On the weekend matches, trebles are available on the Premiership, Division One and Scottish Premier. We have not extended this to all divisions as too many matches in the other divisions become uncompetitive when the season is under way and formlines have become established."

**Stanley Racing:** "We tried out unrestricted trebles for four seasons in Ireland and found it to be highly popular with punters. If there's a 60-match midweek coupon with unrestricted trebles, why should punters not be offered the same scope at weekends?"

Faced with such anti-winning devices as minimum five-timers and fat bookie margins, the punter surely deserves the very nature of football to be in his favour, but here again he's at a massive disadvantage. Quite simply, form in football can never entirely be trusted. In straight head-to-heads like tennis or snooker matches, it is the form of only two players that matters and is therefore quite likely to be fairly consistent. In football, however, we must rely on the form of 22 players, plus subs. That's why we see so many shock results.

If I have given the impression here that it's impossible to make a profit from betting on football, then good. Far better to warn novice punters of the massive hurdles facing them than to kid them that just because they watch Gillingham every week they have bookies on the back foot. One informed source has told me that, on an average weekend, bookies can show an 80 per cent profit on their coupons. But I honestly do believe that punters can come out on top; that unforgiving odds can be defied, but only by the disciplined, diligent gambler, as I will explain later in the chapter.

## the spectre of match-fixing

There is only one sure-fire way of fixing a football match. Forget about bribing players: most of them earn too much nowadays to be tempted by brown envelopes, and even getting a few of the more poorly-paid onto your pay-roll is no guarantee of securing the outcome you want. A far more logical way of ensuring a particular result is to force the abandonment of a game during the second half. I'm not suggesting engineering a pitch invasion by fans – that would take an awful lot of organising. Far easier, surely, to pull (somehow) the plug on the floodlights.

Such a strategy will never help you take money from bookmakers in Britain - all the leading firms have changed their rules in recent years and bets on abandoned matches are now automatically void. But in the Far East, where betting on football, and in particular the FA Premiership, is a multi-billion pound (illegal) industry, the score at the time of the abandonment counts, so long as the second-half has started.

Given that background, is it more than coincidence that in the space of five months at the start of the 1997-98 Premiership season, THREE matches were abandoned through floodlight failure – all early in the second-half?

● On 13 August 1997, Derby's first match at their new Pride Park stadium was blacked out in the 56th minute with the home side 2-1 up against Wimbledon.

● On 3 November 1997, the West Ham v Crystal Palace match, televised live on Sky, was abandoned in the 65th minute when the floodlights at Upton Park failed. West Ham had moments earlier made it 2-2 after trailing 2-0.

● On 22 December 1997, the lights went out at Selhurst Park just a minute into the second-half, with Crystal Palace and Arsenal drawing 0-0 in another match televised live on Sky.

Two days later, a national newspaper hinted at the involvement of shadowy Far Eastern betting syndicates – perhaps the same figures allegedly at the heart of the match-fixing trial earlier in 1997, involving footballers Bruce Grobbelaar, John Fashanu, Hans

Segers and a Malaysian businessman – and police announced they were to investigate.

But the whole affair went quiet until February 1999, when three men were charged with conspiracy and criminal damage in connection with an alleged attempt to fix the result of the Charlton v Liverpool match on 13 February 1999. It was a night I remember vividly, the news wrecking the shock value of the extensive background work I'd carried out on the three earlier floodlight failures.

I am convinced that at least two of the three incidents listed above were deliberate. Sure, there have been cases of floodlight failure before, but normally always at lower-division grounds where facilities were perhaps in need of an overhaul. Sure, there was just a chance that the brand new equipment at Pride Park would suffer teething trouble, but where was the explanation for similar problems at well-established Upton Park and Selhurst Park?

Even if we accept that the electricity supply at those two grounds was perhaps faulty, isn't it an enormous coincidence that it happened to blow on both occasions during a live televised match – when betting turnover sky-rockets – and on both occasions after half-time?

I have been told by a well-respected source in the betting industry that an Arsenal victory at Selhurst Park that night would have cost illegal bookmakers in Europe and the Far East a fortune. He had been told a day before the match that if Arsenal were not in front when the second-half started, the game would not last 90 minutes. How suspicious, therefore, that the lights went out as soon as the second-half began.

As for the West Ham v Palace game, it's important to understand the way punters in the Far East bet. Not for them the normal home-away-draw choice that British punters are so used to. Far Eastern bookies, in an attempt to offer competitive odds, handicap the favourites, in this case West Ham. So punters there would be able to back Palace at, say, 10-11, with a one-goal start, and stakes are refunded if the match ends all-square (in other words if West Ham win by one goal). This becomes significant when we recall the pattern of the game at Upton Park that night. Palace started superbly and quickly went 2-0 up against a shellshocked Hammers side. For those punters who backed Palace with a goal start, this was tremendous news. They were in effect on a team leading 3-0.

But then West Ham began to take control and in a fantastic start to the second-half hit back to level the scores at 2-2. With the game swinging West Ham's way, the Palace punters must have been understandably nervous. One more West Ham goal and their bet would be ruined. Was it significant, then, that the lights went out within seconds of the Hammers equaliser?

No, say the Hammers. They could have gone at any time. It was just an unfortunate coincidence that they blew just seconds after a goal. John Ball, a former police superintendent, is the stadium manager at Upton Park and he flatly denies any possibility that the lights could have been sabotaged. "After my experience with the police force, I can smell a rat from miles away and there's no way the floodlights were tampered with," he told me.

Ball said the Upton Park floodlights had been installed for five years and something called the 'inhibitors' had worn away – blew a fuse in layman's terms – but insists there was nothing suspicious about the timing of their decay.

West Ham have now installed an emergency generator as back-up should floodlights ever fail again, and Derby have done likewise following the embarrassment of their Pride Park failure in August 1997. Stadium manager David Goodwin also ruled out foul play and blamed an "incorrect setting" on equipment supplied to the new ground only days before the game.

Selhurst Park stadium manager Vic Worrall reported that police had investigated the possibility of tampering but had given the club a clean bill of health.

Said Worrall: "To put it simply, the contacts failed, but the equipment had been at the club since the 1960s, so they could have gone at any time." Worrall added that the power supply to Selhurst Park had now been changed and that the floodlights could blow only if there's a power cut in that area of London.

But although all three clubs ruled out any possibility of sabotage, you don't have to be a conspiracy theorist still to harbour suspicions, especially in the light of the events at Charlton on 10 February 1999. I was told by London Electricity, regarded as the most secure electricity network in Britain because 99 per cent is underground, that it is far from impossible for a villain to target a certain area of London for a black-out. He would almost certainly need the help of an experienced electricity worker to point out which cables need to be cut, but a medium-sized brown envelope would seal that.

It was interesting that, in the aftermath of the floodlight failure at Upton Park, West Ham manager Harry Redknapp reported that much of the area surrounding the stadium had also been blacked out.

The men arrested at Charlton on 10 February 1999 were Malaysian nationals Chee Kew Ong, 49, and Eng Hwa Lim, 35, an electronic engineer, and Wai Yuen Liu, 37, a Hong Kong-born car dealer. A fourth man, Roger Firth, 48, a security guard at Charlton's stadium, The Valley, was arrested but later released on bail.

It was alleged that each of the three men charged conspired with each other and with other people "to obtain for yourself or others a pecuniary advantage, namely by deception to deny persons the opportunity to win money by betting in that you were able to determine the outcome of a match". A second charge alleged that the three men "had electrical devices and other various electrical items intending, without lawful excuse to use the same or to cause or permit another to use the same to destroy or damage the electrical supply, concourse and safety lighting belonging to Charlton Athletic Football Club in a way which you knew was likely to endanger life".

On March 9, two other men were arrested by detectives investigating the blackouts at Selhurst Park and Upton Park. They were bailed until April 20.

The Charlton incident we'll leave - because of legal constraints - to the courts to discuss, but further mention should be made here of the three cases of floodlight failure in the Premiership in late 1997. The evidence I've pieced together suggests the Derby black-out *was* accidental and first gave the idea to Far Eastern figures to sabotage later matches, including the ones at Upton Park and Selhurst Park.

Ian Major, a development manager for Phillips Lighting, Britain's leading supplier, and who had installed the lighting at Selhurst Park, said: "It is extremely unusual for three Premier League games to be abandoned so close together – all the more so with two of them live on TV. The only good news for my company was that there was nothing wrong with the equipment we installed, which means they had some sort of mains power failure. It was surprising for this to happen so suddenly, when they'd had nothing wrong at Selhurst Park in the seven years since the system was put in.

"West Ham's problem was equally surprising. They had been going for around four and a half years without a problem. There are any number of reasons for floodlighting to be knocked out, but the most obvious one is for the power to be halted when one of the many fuse systems is blown. Wanton vandalism could be to blame, but that would obviously be extremely dangerous. What was unusual was that all three were in the same season in the same league. These were relatively new systems – they shouldn't have broken down."

In the aftermath of the Charlton arrests, officers from Scotland Yard's Organised Crime Group flew to Malaysia to in a bid to find the 'Mr Big' allegedly behind plots to sabotage Premiership matches. It was reported at the time that they were also pursuing four other men who fled Britain for Malaysia as soon as news of the arrests broke.

We should not underestimate the significance of the timing of the suspicious Premiership matches referred to above. They occurred immediately after the climax of the match-fixing trial involving Grobbelaar, Fashanu and Segers, which had first alerted British soccer to the threat posed to it by high-rolling gamblers in the Far East. Extensive, and no doubt hugely expensive, investigations were carried out into illegal gambling in the Far East, but the 'not guilty' verdicts for the three footballers sent out a message that its tentacles had not reached British shores. We can justifiably wonder, therefore, whether shady Far East figures, who bet heavily on British soccer, suddenly believed that they were bomb-proof; that they could conspire to 'fix' Premiership matches secure in the belief that British law-enforcers would be highly reluctant to mount another investigation, covering the same old ground, when an initial investigation had proven largely fruitless.

Do not doubt the massive popularity of Premiership football in the Far East, which has three frenetic betting markets – Indonesia, Singapore and Hong Kong. I've been told by a well-placed source that more than 30 per cent of the turnover of a leading British firm on a Monday night live Sky match comes from the Far East. But that is just a drop in the ocean compared to the amounts wagered in Hong Kong and Malaysia, where a bet of £10,000 is as commonplace as a £50 bet in Britain.

It's not that these punters are massive gamblers. The stakes are so large purely because the Far Eastern high-rollers, with access to tax-free accounts all over the world, are past-masters in the art of 'arbing' – guaranteeing a profit no matter what the result.

Let me give you a famous example from the 1994 World Cup in the USA, when Cameroon were so heavily backed all around the world to beat Russia that a fix was the only logical explanation. Incredible sums of cash were wagered on the Africans, who had to win to qualify for the second stage (victory for Russia would have given them only an outside chance of progressing). Hills, who had initially gone 5-4 Russia and 13-8 Cameroon, had been forced to cut the Africans to 4-5, with Russia drifting to 5-2. Those kind of odds changes for a World Cup fixture are almost unbelievable.

Ladbrokes called it "the biggest gamble in soccer history". An Asian-based high-roller told me on the day of the match that a Cameroon victory would cost Far East bookies "many millions of pounds". A Melbourne-based bookie told me that rumours sweeping Australian gambling circles on the day of the match insisted the result had already been determined.

If it had, someone forgot to tell the Russians, who spanked Cameroon 6-1.

My own reading of the situation is altogether less sinister than those rumours of rigged results. In the Far East, Cameroon were posted up in the early betting as favourites to beat the Russians. No doubt bookies there believed that, with little incentive, the Russians would surrender easily (even the 6-1 win wasn't enough to avoid the first plane back to Moscow). A Hong Kong betting syndicate, learning that Cameroon were available at 13-8 in Britain, flooded these shores with big-money wagers on the Africans through a network of representatives. They were, therefore, almost certainly in a no-lose situation. They probably backed Russia with a half-goal start at, say, 11-10, and then backed Cameroon at 13-8 in Britain. All these bets would have been tax-free (their accounts with British bookies are held in tax-free offshoots in Gibraltar). If Russia won or the match was drawn, they were on an 11-10 winner. If Cameroon won, they were on a 13-8 winner. Nice work if you can get it.

A more recent example occurred in February 1999 in the Italian League match between Fiorentina and AC Milan. Fiorentina were available with one British-based firm (with tax-free outlets) at 11-10, while in the Far East, Milan were offered at 11-10 with a half-goal start. A £100,000 bet on both guaranteed a £10,000 risk-free profit no matter what the result. British punters may stare open-mouthed at that last sentence, refusing to believe that any bookie over here will accept bets of that size. Believe me, they do, but only from foreign clients.

Hills, Ladbrokes, Victor Chandler *et al* know that the *real* money is in the Far East, and so desperate are they to grab a slice of it that they will accept massive tax-free wagers from foreign punters. These bookies will not countenance even for one moment that Far Eastern gamblers are more clued-up than their own odds-compilers on Premiership football, and are happy to back their own judgement against them. How long that lasts remains to be seen, especially in the light of a catastrophic run of football results for bookies in the early months of 1999. But more of that later.

The Asian line on a weekend slate of Premiership fixtures is issued on Monday morning. For a game in which both the home and away side would be quoted in Britain at 6-4, the typical market in the Far East would be 1.95 (a shade less than evens) each, draw no bet. Betting in February 1999 on the Leeds v Spurs FA Cup fifth round tie, which in Britain saw Leeds around the 11-10 mark and Spurs 5-2, would in the Far East have been 'level-half', with Spurs around 2.10 (11-10) and Leeds 1.85 (5-6). If Spurs are your choice, half of your stake goes on them off levels (in other words no start) and half on the Londoners with a half-goal start. Therefore if the game finishes 0-0 and you've staked £200, the £100 on Spurs off levels is refunded, the other £100 is a winner. The same stake on Leeds and the same 0-0 result means you lose half your stake.

Once the Far East betting lines are made public on Mondays, agents from syndicates in Singapore, Malaysia and Hong Kong trade with each other and buy up all the best prices. By Wednesday any discrepancies have vanished and it's now time to home in on the British and Italian markets via tax-free outlets in Gibraltar. The aim by this stage is to grab odds that will guarantee a profit no matter what the result. That is why insignificant matches like the Charlton v Wimbledon meeting in mid-February - on the face of it hardly like to grab British punters by the balls - saw huge wads of foreign money for Charlton at 15-8 with Hills, who cut them by kick-off time to 6-4. In Asia, Charlton were the favourites.

One important point to remember amid all the talk of police investigations into the three Premiership matches that in 1997 were hit by floodlight failure: if it emerges that foul play was indeed the cause, surely we should begin to wonder just how many more games were similarly targeted but were allowed to run their course when results were going the way the saboteurs' pay-masters wanted.

Malaysian reporter Johnson Fernandez, who knows more than most about the way betting syndicates in the Far East work, said that he'd been told by underworld figures that both the Upton Park and Selhurst Park matches had been sabotaged, with a gangster known as 'The Blind Man' raking in a £4 million profit.

Fernandez, based in Malaysian capital Kuala Lumpur, where I stayed in January 1999 while researching this book, said: "A single

English League match is worth about £2 million in Malaysia alone. That does not include all the bets made in Singapore, Indonesia, Thailand and Hong Kong. I've heard a syndicate paid men between £30,000 and £50,000 to collaborate with them and rig the floodlights. The man who runs the main syndicate is known only as The Blind Man. I've heard he's blind in one eye."

But another man, a rich Indonesian called Loe Bon Swe, later emerged as the Mr Big behind a syndicate which stakes fortunes on Premiership matches. The 50-year-old's name was allegedly heard during two trials which cleared Grobbelaar and co of match-fixing in 1997.

It was reported three days after the events at Charlton that bookies in Malaysia had changed their betting rules, voiding all bets on matches hit by floodlight failure. But such a drastic rule change would have been practically impossible to implement. Unlike in Britain, where legal bookmakers have hard-and-fast rules, betting in the Far East is all by word of mouth. No cash is placed up front, although welching is not advisable. To change such basic rules and expect them to be adhered to without problems was an awful lot to ask.

In the 1980s, fugitive Harry Rogers claimed in a Sunday newspaper that a daring gang had pulled off two football betting coups by sabotaging the floodlights at matches which were going the way they wanted. At that time even bookies in Britain settled on the score at the time of abandonment.

As Graham Sharpe reported in his book *Gambling On Goals*, "The gang allegedly took Rogers to Brighton for a dress-rehearsal and he watched as they 'poured a can of sulphuric acid over power cables' with predictable results. Claimed Rogers: 'They pulled it off twice. On the second occasion they discovered the football ground had a stand-by generator so they had to sabotage that as well.' John Johnson of BOLA (Betting Office Licensees Association) commented: 'If the bet was shrewdly placed and the football element was included with other events, there's no reason why they shouldn't have got away with it.'"

What Johnson meant by that, I think, was that the gang would have lifted suspicion from their bet if they included the 'fixed' matches with other selections, maybe a red-hot favourite in a horse race.

Looking back, by the way, at all the ballyhoo before, during and after the most sensational match-fixing scandal to hit British soccer, it was only the *Racing Post* which pointed out the absurdity of the case against former Liverpool keeper Grobbelaar, the highest-profile figure of the four men charged in 1994, and who stood trial twice in 1997.

Grobbelaar's alleged involvement in plots to rig the results of Premiership matches was first revealed in *The Sun*, which claimed to have video evidence catching the keeper red-handed. TV news bulletins showed clips of the video which, to these eyes, proved absolutely nothing. Yet football went into shock. It was as though Grobbelaar and his co-accused were guilty without even standing trial.

Before Grobbelaar was officially charged, I suggested in the *Racing Post* that, despite the daily revelations in the mass-selling tabloid, Grob was a 4-7 chance to be cleared. Most experts called me an idiot, but I'd have fancied even myself to have proven successful as the keeper's defence lawyer.

We were told, largely on evidence given by Grobbelaar's former friend Chris Vincent, who seemed to have an axe to grind, that the Liverpool keeper's paymaster was a Far Eastern betting syndicate which bribed him to throw five matches. Yet only the first produced the result the betting syndicate allegedly wanted. Grobbelaar failed to deliver the goods in FOUR subsequent rigged matches.

Were we to believe that a betting syndicate with the muscle to bribe a leading English professional, with the resources to bung him £40,000 (according to Vincent) for his co-operation, would simply shrug its shoulders and say "Oh well, better luck next time" when the 'bought' player reneged on the deal?

To go to the lengths of bribing a high-profile Premiership player suggested that a betting syndicate stood to make massive sums on the game and therefore staked considerable amounts. It just didn't add up that they could forgive and forget so easily. Not once, but

THREE more times. Surely a body wearing cement boots at the bottom of Hong Kong Harbour was a more believable outcome.

We were expected to believe that a Far East syndicate, with Grobbelaar's help, made £3 million on a 3-0 correct scoreline in a Newcastle v Liverpool game in 1993, a match televised live. But that begged so many questions that even now it's difficult to believe the case ever went to court.

1. Why would Grobbelaar choose a game shown live on TV, when all his mistakes would be scrutinised, to give away three goals?

2. How could he give any guarantee that his Liverpool team-mates wouldn't score a goal and ruin the coup?

3. If 3-0 was the desired score, wouldn't it be plain crazy to let in the three goals inside the first half-hour, as Liverpool did at Newcastle, so facing a further neve-jangling 60 minutes?

4. Why did none of Grobbelaar's team-mates, the referee, or the Newcastle camp suspect any wrong-doing?

There was not a shred of evidence, in either *The Sun's* revelations or throughout the two marathon trials, that Grobbelaar had ever thrown a match, still less that he'd ever received money for doing so. Much was made of taped evidence that suggested Grobbelaar had *agreed* to throw a match – Liverpool v Southampton – at a future date. He was by this time a Southampton player. But I've a perfectly plausible theory to explain that, even though no such defence was used during the trial.

I know that if I was Grobbelaar in a similar position, I would hardly have been able to believe my luck. Here was someone prepared to pay him £2,000 a fortnight on retainer, plus another £100,000 on completion, just to throw an end-of-season match – a match Southampton would have been heavily expected to lose in any case. Wouldn't the thought have gone through Grobbelaar's mind that he wouldn't have to do anything wrong and that Saints would still lose, so earning him a bumper pay-packet? Wasn't there the possibility that as an act of good faith, maybe even bravado, Grobbelaar bragged about previous scams merely to show his new-found paymasters just how serious his intentions were and string them along?

In my view, Grobbelaar was guilty all along only of extreme gullibility. He'd put his trust in a so-called friend (Vincent, the man who lured him into the video trap) who held an obvious grudge because of an earlier business deal that had gone wrong, and he willingly believed a betting syndicate would pay him well over £100,000 to 'rig' a result which was almost certain in any case.

You'll notice I'm not dealing here with any of the evidence given in the two trials at Winchester Crown Court in 1997. All that has been well documented. What concerns me here is the initial 'evidence', revealed by *The Sun*, which sullied the good name of a well-respected Premiership footballer. Grobbelaar was never going to be found guilty. The real crime is that the case against him was ever allowed to go to court.

It is pointless here to dredge up the details of the earlier match-fixing scandal which rocked English football in the early 1960s. That belongs to a different era when even the top players, on little more money than the average working man, were far more susceptible to bribes than today's modern-day players on Hollywood wages; and it is impossible in any case to shed any fresh light on the sorry tale of Tony Kaye, Bronco Layne and Peter Swan.

Nor should we concern ourselves here with the many reports of match-fixing with no obvious betting link. For instance, holders Marseille were kicked out of the 1993 European Cup after being found guilty of attempting to bribe French opponents Valenciennes to throw a league match, but there was no suggestion of any betting connections. Similarly, Liverpool, Leeds and Derby were all victims of fixed European matches in the 1960s and 1970s, journalist Brian Glanville reported in his book *Champions Of Europe*; but again the alleged fixers were intent only on further progress in the tournaments rather than plotting a betting coup.

The Derby v Juventus European Cup semi-final first-leg in 1973 sparked one of Derby boss Brian Clough's most memorable post-match comments. Forest lost 3-1 amid reports that Juve's West

German international Helmut Haller followed German referee Herr Schulenberg into his dressing-room at half-time. Derby assistant manager Peter Taylor went in hot pursuit but was blocked by "a group of tough-looking Italians" and a scuffle followed. Clough, quizzed by Italian journalists after the game, said: "No cheating bastards will I talk to. I will not talk to any cheating bastards."

Okay, it's not about betting, but I just had to get that little story in.

Betting on Italian Serie A matches has steadily grown since Channel 4 started showing live games from the Italian League each Sunday, but there's little doubt bookmakers tread warily here. The tale of the unlucky rookie bookie stung for £250,000 on what he remains convinced were bent Italian matches is imprinted on the memory of odds-compilers of the leading firms.

The bookie, now a freelance odds-compiler, was the first British layer to quote odds for Italian League matches in the days before Channel 4 screened live coverage. Aware that the draw was far more common in Italy than Britain, he cleverly, or so he thought, priced the draw up at an incredible 8-11 for some suspicious-looking fixtures – only to be filled in by in-the-know punters who'd seen Italian-based bookies offer only 1-6 for the draw.

"All my clients seemed to know about every fixed game," he said. "In a very short time, I did my bollocks."

He recalled one incident when his fingers were particularly badly burned. Torino had to win at home to Inter and then away to Lecce to avoid relegation. With Inter in superb form after a long unbeaten run, our fearless, perhaps foolish, layer went 9-4 Torino, a pretty accurate assessment on the surface.

"But I was knocked over by a widespread gamble on Torino. Little did I realise that some illegal Italian bookies were going 1-6 Torino. They knew what I didn't – that Inter wanted a big club like Torino to stay in the First Division to attract bigger gates." Torino won 2-0.

Channel 4 viewers were stunned towards the end of the 1992-93 season by the bizarre events in the closing stages of an AC Milan v Brescia clash. Milan, needing just a point to clinch the title, were drawing 0-0 with five minutes to go when Demetrio Albertini scored a fluke goal for them. Such a development in England would have seen the scorer engulfed by his team-mates, but Albertini was shunned. Nobody congratulated him, even though his goal had in effect clinched the title for Milan. It was only when Milan allowed Brescia almost to walk in an equaliser direct from the kick-off that we twigged that here was a pre-arranged result.

Liam Brady, the former Arsenal star now in charge of youth development at Highbury, was the co-commentator at that game and his comments at the time, no doubt built on the experience of six years as a player in Italy, only confirmed our suspicions. When I interviewed him some months later, Brady was refreshingly frank. "I saw it happen on numerous occasions during my time in Italy," Brady told me. "When a draw suits both teams in Italy, the game will end in a draw. It's all to do with the mentality of the Italian people. They see nothing wrong in such an arrangement."

## first goalscorer betting

One of the by-products of the dramatic increase in matches shown live on TV during the 1990s is the growth in popularity of betting on players to score the first goal. Punters seeking a betting interest in a live TV game may not be tempted by odds of 10-11 about, say, Liverpool, but may very much fancy a dabble on Jamie Redknapp at 14-1 to net the opener. These bets are largely placed more in hope than expectation of a pay-out and are generally classed as fun bets. But they are fun only for bookmakers, who use the cash from them to fund their annual holidays in Barbados.

It was possible in the early years of the FA Premiership to argue that this form of betting offered value, with hit-men like Alan Shearer, Andy Cole, and Ian Wright regularly available at around the 6-1 mark. But such golden days lasted only as long as it took to dawn on bookmakers that the infant Premiership had ushered in an era of super-strikers for whom the long-established and once-proud strike-rate of a goal every two games meant absolutely nothing. Now, these master marksman were netting two goals in every three games, sometimes more, and their odds began to tumble.

When England met Bulgaria at Wembley in October 1998, Shearer was just 11-4 to score the first goal. His strike-partner

Michael Owen was 3-1. It is impossible to make money backing such players. The only way to make money from first goalscorer betting is to find an edge. The incident described in Chapter 2 about Riccardo Scimeca for Aston Villa is a perfect example of such an edge. If you discover before bookmakers that a recognised defender has been pushed up front as an emergency striker, then you must lump on immediately.

Such opportunities happen rarely but when they do it's imperative you take advantage. Towards the end of the 1997-98 Premiership season, I was told by West Ham manager Harry Redknapp that then-Hammers striker John Hartson was to be relieved of penalty-taking duties after missing two successive spot-kicks. His replacement, unknown to bookies, was to be David Unsworth, a full-back generally available at around 33-1 or longer to score the first goal.

This was dynamite information and for the next six weeks I backed Unsworth at fancy prices to open the scoring. But isn't it typical of the bookies luck that West Ham never got another penalty!

Before the 1995 European Cup Final between Ajax and Juventus in Vienna, I was tipped off by a mate that Ajax striker Patrick Kluivert was available at 20-1 with one firm to net the first goal. Bookies had clearly done some homework but, crucially, not enough. They had learned that Kluivert, on only the fringes of the first team at the time, was very unlikely to start the game. But they hadn't been informed that on nearly every occasion he'd been given a place in the starting line-up he'd got on the scoresheet.

Thousands of rookie punters are still not aware of one of the golden rules of first-scorer betting: if your selection plays no part in the match, stakes are refunded. Perhaps more importantly, if he comes on as substitute AFTER the first goal has been scored, again stakes are refunded. I'd estimate bookies make a small fortune from punters who mistakenly believe they've backed a loser under such circumstances. So Kluivert at 20-1 that night was manna from heaven. Better still, he came on as sub and netted the only goal of the game. Happy, happy days.

There are two points about first-goalscorer betting that continue to baffle me. First, how has it proved so popular when there is no satisfactory way of solving disputed goals? Second, how has it proved so popular when its half-brother, last-goalscorer betting, logically is a far more appealing medium?

It defies belief that with so much money swirling around the game nowadays no-one has been given the responsibility to adjudicate on disputed goals. Sky TV analyst Andy Gray chairs a Premiership committee that meets sporadically to determine the identity of goalscorers, but their get-togethers are few and far between and quite often will deliver a verdict on a goal scored some three months beforehand. Clearly that is of neither use nor ornament to bookies and punters.

In 1994, BOLA, the Betting Office Licensees Association, asked the Football League, who demand an annual fee from bookmakers for the right to bet on football, to set up a panel to identify the first goalscorer in every live TV match. The League refused, claiming it would be too hard to implement and adding that any official ruling within hours of the final whistle could later be made to look silly. What are they – men or mice? But having said that, surely it is up to the bookmaking industry to put its own house in order.

Bookies are the ones benefiting from the increase in first-scorer betting, so it is their responsibility to devise a satisfactory – I was about to say foolproof, but that would be impossible – system of solving disputed goals.

Elsewhere in this book you will read of my strong demand for the setting-up of a betting ombudsman scheme to arbitrate on disputed bets. If such a figure is ever appointed, it will be his/her duty to adjudicate on first goalscorers. But until then it is vital a solution is found to this thorniest of problems because the current methods of dealing with it are plain crazy. Remember that this does not just involve live TV games. First-scorer odds are advertised nationally for all Premiership matches, televised live or not, and the bigger firms issue prices locally for lower-division games.

Disputed goals happen all the time. A striker's shot may be deflected into the net by a defender, so is it an own-goal or the striker's? Was the shot on target before the defender deflected it? Does that make a difference? Was a striker's shot over the line before his team-mate got the final touch?

Bookmaker methods of settling first-scorer disputes have changed like the wind over the years but even now are far from perfect. Coral used to side with the last player of the scoring team to touch the ball but the weakness of that argument was exposed when Andy Cole raced to the by-line and pulled the ball back across goal, only for a defender to knock it in. It was a definite own-goal, but Coral had to give it to Cole.

Ladbrokes used to employ what they called a common-sense approach, but this left them vulnerable to all sorts of accusations. For instance, is common-sense the first victim when a bookmaker faces huge liabilities? Now Coral and Hills go with the majority verdict in the results column of the following day's national newspapers, while Ladbrokes abide by the verdict of the Press Association, the national news agency which employs stringers to cover league and cup matches at all English and Scottish grounds.

On the face of it that may seem a reasonable solution but again there are huge problems. In roughly 98 per cent of matches (the estimate is from the Press Association itself) the national newspapers adhere to whichever scorer PA decides, even if those national newspapers have their own reporters present. What this means of course is that one man, the PA representative, holds ultimate power over bookmakers and punters. If he believes, say, Michael Owen failed to get a touch on Robbie Fowler's shot before it crossed the line, then the name R Fowler will appear in the results column the next day, even though thousands at the ground will insist the boy Owen was the real scorer.

The Press Association say that if there is still considerable doubt about the identity of a goalscorer the day after a match has been played, they will contact the club involved and get their opinion, abiding by whatever they are officially told by the club. Early in the 1998-99 season, Ipswich full-back Mick Stockwell shot from 25 yards in a midweek match at Tranmere. The ball flashed into the net, but it wasn't clear at the time whether it had touched his team-mate David Johnson *en route*. The goal was credited in the national newspapers the following day to Stockwell, which was a boost to bookies as the full-back is rarely on the scoresheet and would hardly have been backed. But striker Johnson insisted the next day that he got the final touch, Ipswich agreed, and the Press Association amended its records to credit Johnson with the goal. Ladbrokes then had to pay out to punters who had backed the Ipswich striker. But surely this is wrong. Clubs may have a vested interest; for instance if a group of players have backed a team-mate (even though footballers are officially banned from betting on the game) to finish the season top scorer in the League. In some cases – John Fashanu in his later days at Wimbledon, for example – players are paid a bonus for each goal they score.

We must wonder too how open to abuse the current system is. Bookies are happy with it because it puts the onus of determining the identity of a goalscorer on to an independent third party. But while never for one moment would I question the integrity of PA staff, there may in future be a huge temptation for a representative at an insignificant lower-division match to stick £100 on a 16-1 shot to score the first goal and then flash the name of his selection to the nation's newspapers, radio and TV stations and teletext services as first goalscorer. An accomplice could collect the money from the betting shop even before the final whistle, by which time the PA man will have rectified his earlier mistake.

Bookies conceded that they have no safeguards against this and when I put the idea to the Press Association at its Leeds HQ, I was told by a spokeswoman: "That would never happen. Our staff are far too professional." Mmmmm.

I wrote earlier that national newspapers follow the PA line 98 per cent of the time. The exceptions are when it suits their own headline purposes. For instance, in October 1994, Newcastle met Blackburn in a Premiership clash shown live on Sky on a Sunday. The match ended 1-1, with Alan Shearer opening the scoring for Newcastle. Two minutes from time a shot by Newcastle's Steve Howey was cleared off the Blackburn line by Jason Wilcox, only to strike Rovers keeper Tim Flowers and rebound back into the net.

Had Flowers not got in the way, Wilcox's clearance probably would have reached the halfway line so it was a clear own-goal by the luckless Rovers keeper. But the national tabloids had a different agenda. Own-goals rarely lend themselves to great headlines, but Howey as scorer certainly did. So the following day we were greeted by 'Howey the lad' headlines everywhere, with Howey awarded the goal in most result sections purely to justify such a falsehood.

While this had no bearing on first-goalscorer bets, it had huge implications for those punters who prefer to back last goalscorer. With most leading bookmakers (Stanley Racing are the exception) own-goals do not count for betting purposes. They are ignored. This means that had Flowers been credited with an own- goal, Shearer would have been classed by bookies not only as first scorer but last scorer too. And I'm sure there were thousands more punters who'd backed the England striker rather than Newcastle centre-half Howey to notch the last goal.

All this brings me to my second puzzle. Why do punters try to predict the first scorer when they would get a far better run for their money by betting on the last? Such a form of betting, as I've already discussed, is widely regarded as fun, but where's the fun in seeing your bet very often bite the dust in the opening minute? By backing last scorer, however, your bet runs the full 90 minutes. There's just no comparison.

I've a theory here. The punters who snub last-scorer betting in favour of its less appealing half-brother are the same idiots who fancied the dark one in Abba when the blonde was different class.

The problem of solving first-scorer disputes looks set to run and run. It has taxed the best brains in the business and we're still no nearer a solution. Even TV football commentators are well aware of it. Sky commentator Martin Tyler told me: "There ought to be an official adjudicator, a neutral whose decision is final. I am very conscious of this. I know when I am commentating on a game that very often there are huge amounts of money resting on it and sometimes my opinion will be influential, but I try never to let it affect my judgement. I will say something like 'so and so will probably claim it.' I would support the calls for an ombudsman to decide. Certainly clubs should not have the power, particularly with every goal nowadays televised."

It seems certain that before long an independent body will be appointed, whether funded by bookmakers or by football itself. The figure cannot have any links with bookmakers, but at the same time should not be distrusted by those bookies. If football pays for it, the job will almost certainly go to an ex-player, someone like the well-respected Johnny Giles. If bookies pay for it I would venture one name. D McGovern.

## correct-score betting

Like first-scorer, this form of betting has proven popular with punters not attracted to the more cramped 90-minute odds. Arsenal at 2-5 to beat Southampton will make no appeal to the fiver and tenner punters, but Arsenal at 6-1 to win 2-0 will tempt them. It's a form of betting that comes into its own in particularly one-sided matches, like England v Luxembourg at Wembley. Many of you will have noticed that whenever a leading bookmaker advertises his odds for a live TV match in that day's national press, he will highlight correct-score prices. This is no accident. Correct-score odds are framed using a tried-and-tested formula which for years has lined bookmaker pockets and any punter who believes he can make a profit from this form of betting is deluding himself.

Let's consider the odds for the England v Bulgaria European Championship qualifier at Wembley in October 1998. Bookies Hills went 6-1 a 1-0 England win, 6-1 two-nil, 9-1 two-one, 15-2 three-nil, 9-1 three-one, and 14-1 a Bulgarian 1-0 triumph. Their odds for the draw were 13-2 nil-nil, 11-2 one-one, and 22-1 a Desmond (2-2). The percentages for these amounted to slightly more than the magic 100 per cent mark (any book climbing above 100 per cent is automatically in the bookmaker's favour; the more above that mark, the more bookies love it). This meant that bookies theoretically had every other possible scoreline running for them – be it Bulgaria 2-0, 3-0, 3-1, 2-1 and so on.

If England won 3-2 or by any other scoreline, the bookies were laughing. It is not possible long-term to defy those odds – they truly are a licence to print money for bookmakers.

It's my view that the only scoreline in professional football that punters can reasonably be confident of predicting is 0-0. For a start it's one of the few bets you can call a winner the moment you place your bet. Something has to happen, i.e. a goal has to be scored, for your bet to come a cropper, and goals are not easy to come by in top-class football. Just ask Everton. Watch closely matches that go deep into the second-half without a goal. It's as though an invisible shutter clicks in players' minds and from actively seeking a win, their first priority is suddenly to protect what they've got. If someone offers you even-money around the 75-minute mark for a game to remain goalless, bite off their hands.

There are a dozen games per season – be they in Europe or the international arena – in which one team will take to the field determined to hang on for a draw. Their attacking intent will be zero. If such teams are reasonably competent, it's often worth putting cash on the game to finish goalless.

In the early nineties, odds for goalless draws in Premiership matches were generally around 7-1. But 0-0 draws became scarcer in the seasons immediately following the ban on back-passes – the new rule making it more difficult for teams to kill off games; one of the reasons, incidentally, for Liverpool's subsequent shoddy performances in Europe – and odds drifted out late in the decade to around the 11-1 mark. But as professional footballers became more accustomed to performing without the safety net of the back-pass, drab goalless draws became more commonplace and odds have gradually contracted. At the beginning of the 1998-99 Premiership season a spate of 0-0 draws in the early weeks of the campaign saw odds shorten to around 7-1. For European matches 6-1 is the norm.

If you do believe a match is destined to end goalless, there is one very important point to remember. Don't back 0-0: instead back 'no goalscorer' at the same odds. In that way you will be on a winner if the game finishes 0-0, but you will also collect if the game finishes 1-0, or even 2-0, if the goals are deemed to be own-goals. This is because, as I noted earlier, for betting purposes own-goals do not count. Imagine the soon-to-be-puking look on your mate's face if he backs 0-0 in a Merseyside derby and you back 'no goalscorer' and the match is decided by a David Unsworth own-goal. Even better if he's an Evertonian.

I can recall only one incident in which bookmakers were stung on correct-score betting, and even then they acted quickly to plug the loophole. At the start of the 1991-92 season a group of Merseyside-based punters engineered a sting on 3-3 draws. At that time some bookies were offering 80-1 about a 3-3 draw and so, with only 65 matches listed on the coupon, only one such scoreline was needed to yield a profit. Two 3-3 draws meant happy days. The punters sometimes permed their bets in 10p doubles, covering the entire coupon. For 65 matches this meant 2,080 doubles for a stake of £208. A 10p double at 80-1 and 80-1 brings in around £650. By the end of November only four weekend programmes failed to throw up a 3-3 draw. On one occasion there were four and on another weekend three. Realising that these punters were showing a healthy profit, bookies slashed their odds for 3-3 draws to 50-1.

## abandoned matches

It was only the campaigning of the *Racing Post* in the early 1990s, while I was sports editor, that persuaded bookmakers to change their ludicrous policy for settling abandoned matches. For years bookies would pay out on the score at the time of the abandonment, whether it was the third minute or the 83rd. This played right into the layers' hands. The shorter a match, the greater the chance of it finishing all-square (just take a look at the odds on the half-time coupons in British betting shops in which the draw at half-time is generally an odds-on shot). Punters are creatures of habit. When they have a bet on a football match they are seeking an allegiance. They do not want to see a match finish in a draw. Consequently few punters ever back the draw, a point I will pick up on later in the book.

Matches can be abandoned for many reasons – for instance pitch invasion, floodlight failure, or severe weather. We are right to wonder whether a referee is more likely to cut short a game when the two sides are level than when one team holds an advantage.

Further, the shorter the match the greater the possibility of a fluke outcome that will wreck thousands of bets. You've only got to look at snooker for evidence of that. In the shorter first-to-five-frames tournaments, shock results are common; but in the top events like the Embassy World Championship class generally tells in the end.

Most bookies changed their abandoned-match policy in the early 1990s, making all such matches void and refunding stakes. But Ladbrokes and Stanley Racing for some time afterwards refused to follow suit, arguing that they were adhering to the wishes of their punters, although no punters were ever found who favoured the Ladbrokes and Stanley strategy. The *Racing Post* sports betting desk received dozens of letters on the subject, many asking what would happen if a horse race on a Saturday night at Wolverhampton was stopped at halfway through floodlight failure. "Would the horse in the lead at the time be given the race? Of course not," the punters argued, quite correctly.

Paying out on the score at the time of abandonment was also an invitation to skulduggery, as I pointed out earlier. A well-organised gang of punters could feasibly lump heavily on a 0-0 draw in a game and after ten minutes stage-manage a riot so prolonged that the referee would have no alternative but to abandon the game.

It was only following the abandonment after just six minutes of a live TV game between Sunderland and Grimsby because of a waterlogged pitch in February 1994 that Ladbrokes fell into line with other bookmakers. The score at the time, if you have any need to ask, was 0-0. Stanley, who had admitted a month earlier that thousands of Liverpool supporters had complained when an FA Cup tie between Bristol City and Liverpool was abandoned at 1-1 midway through the second-half through floodlight failure, waited until the following season before scrapping their unpopular policy.

Now if a match is abandoned, outright bets are void, although all bookies will pay-out on any bets which at the time of the abandonment have already been decided, like first goalscorer and time of the first goal.

## how the bookies mug us

Not content with forcing punters, lemming-like, into fatal five-timer flutters, bookmakers find many other ways to guarantee a fat profit from football punters. Perhaps the most unacceptable is the steadily growing margins they impose. In the mid-seventies, bookies generally bet to 108 per cent on a football match. Typical odds would have been something like 8-11 for a home win, 7-2 for an away, and 5-2 the draw. By the early nineties the margins had increased to 110, and now they hover between 111 and 112. For a three-runner contest that is totally unacceptable, yet bookies know they can get away with it. The 8-11, 7-2 and 5-2 you may have seen in the mid-seventies will now read 8-11, 10-3 and 9-4.

When bookies upped their margins to 111 at the start of the 1992-93 season, I asked them to explain their motives. These are the responses I got.

**Hills:** "We have increased the margin to 111 per cent but only by tightening up odds for the draw, which is by far the smallest share of the market. We remain very competitive on home and away odds."

**Coral:** "The point was raised recently that our major competitors had increased their margins to 111 per cent and we felt it necessary to bet to the same margin."

**Ladbrokes:** "Yes we have raised our theoretical margin by one point to 11 per cent. But at the same time we have doubled the maximum pay-out on our weekend coupons to £500,000, and introduced free bets. For instance, last week we offered 42 perm bets for the price of 40."

When you've finished laughing, re-read those comments. If Hills believed the draw attracted the smallest share of the market, surely the odds should have been lengthened to attract more money and help balance the books. The Coral response suggests they don't feel it necessary to treat their customers any better than their rivals do. It also reinforces the belief, sparked by the glaring lack of discrepancies in odds on the rival weekend football coupons, that the Big Three operate a cartel when it comes to football betting.

The Ladbrokes comment almost defies belief. I wonder how many punters would have hit the old £250,000 ceiling.

Five years from now there's every chance that bookies will have upped their margins by yet another point. Who's to stop them? They know that 80 per cent of football punters will carry on betting regardless. They wouldn't recognise an increased margin if it hit them across the face 11 times with a wet kipper. The remaining 20 per cent of us may, as a form of protest, withhold our cash but that won't worry the bookies too much. We're the clued-up few – they don't really want our business anyway.

One of the most deadly (for the punter) forms of football betting is on the handicap lists at the start of each season. Manchester United would start off scratch, with mid-table teams getting something like a 20-point start and the weakest teams getting up to 36 points.

With all teams handicapped to finish level, it is incredibly difficult to find a winner but that's not enough for the grasping bookies. Their each-way terms of a quarter the odds for the first three placings are yet another slap in the face for the put-upon punter.

In a horse race, bookies will pay out to fourth place in a handicap of 16 or more runners yet for 20- and 24-runner handicaps in football, fourth place is a loser. But bookies get away with it because the majority of those who bet on football are not the most educated of punters.

## how to make your football betting pay

Though the odds are stacked against us, I honestly do believe that the diligent punter CAN make a profit from betting on football. It's not easy, mainly because bookies as I've already explained have so much in their favour, but there are areas of vulnerability we can exploit.

No matter how skilled the odds-compilers of the leading firms are, they do make mistakes. It is up to us to identify them, and capitalise on them. What works in the punter's favour is the very term 'fixed-odds' betting (bookmakers prefer to use the term 'individual odds'). The odds for football matches are 'fixed' days in advance. When you walk into a betting shop on a Tuesday you will find a coupon listing the odds for all the matches that weekend. And these will rarely, if ever, change. An entire squad could go down with a flu bug on the Friday before a game, but the chances are you'll still be able to get 7-4 about their opponents on the Saturday.

This is because bookmakers hate to make alterations to their coupon prices. They know from experience the problems it causes for their hard-pressed betting shop staff. It is a huge step for a leading bookmaker to make alterations. Indeed, in my long experience in sports betting it is mostly only matches covered live on television (and therefore attracting massive turnover) that are ever altered by weight of money or, very rarely, by significant team news.

It is crucial, then, to find out as much team news as is humanly possible – players suspended, those nursing injuries, the kind of factors bookies may not have built into their odds. I happen to believe that many teams have one key player, without whom they are far less potent. Bookmakers in Britain tend to ignore this fact but their counterparts in America consider it of the utmost significance. I will deal with this subject in depth in a later chapter.

Odds-compilers are handicapped too by the cruel deadlines they must meet. Weekend odds are issued on Monday, giving them no chance to revise their opinion following a slate of midweek fixtures. For instance a month into the 1998-99 season, Blackpool were given at the beginning of the week a 7-4 quote by Hills and Ladbrokes to win at Lincoln the following Saturday. But the next night both teams were in league action – Blackpool at home to Notts County, Lincoln away to Millwall. Blackpool won convincingly, while Lincoln slumped to a miserable 2-0 defeat. Given the chance, bookies would love to have shaved Blackpool's odds for the Saturday encounter, but they were snookered. And it came as little surprise to see Blackpool win 2-1 on the Saturday.

With most national newspapers giving in-depth coverage to matches in Britain, bookies make few mistakes, apart from those caused by early deadlines, when it comes to pricing up domestic fixtures. But they are nowhere near so foot-sure on European ties.

One Cup-Winners' Cup match in 1991 still gives Hills nightmares.

Third Division side Swansea were playing French giants Monaco at Vetch Field in the first-round. Monaco by this stage had won nine of their first ten French League matches to go clear at the top of the table, well ahead of the mighty Marseilles who a few months earlier had been beaten in the final of the European Cup.

Swansea, on the other hand, were struggling to keep tabs on teams like Torquay. Bookmakers Coral understandably went 7-1 Swansea, 4-11 Monaco, 3-1 the draw. But Hills, for some bizarre reason, gave Monaco an outstandingly generous 4-5 quote. Monaco at such odds were the bet of the decade, but there was further crucial information punters learned that made them the bet of the century. To meet UEFA requirements on the number of foreign players in their side, Swansea had to sideline many of their regular English and Scottish players and instead field a team largely made up of untried Welsh youngsters. They didn't have a prayer and Monaco won 2-1 without breaking sweat.

I've been told by a Hills insider that the company flashed urgent messages to their betting shop staff at the beginning of that week to watch out for lumpy Monaco bets. They were hoping that their huge mistake would go largely unnoticed and decided not to take the unwelcome step of altering their coupon odds. No such luck. On the Tuesday, the day of the match, I pointed out in the *Racing Post* the scale of the Hills rick and a betting landslide began, with Hills having to slash the Monaco odds to 8-15.

Some years later, in October 1996, Dutch champions Ajax were stunned as they arrived at Glasgow Airport after a 1-0 win over Rangers at Ibrox to be roundly applauded by Rangers fans. Newspapers reported that the Scottish fans cheered and waved betting slips in the air after costing Hills their biggest-ever pay-out on a match played north of the border.

Hills had made Ajax 11-10 shots to beat a Rangers side with a diabolical recent record in Europe. Rangers fans, recognising better than bookies the limitations of their side, lumped on Ajax, who had reached the previous two European Cup finals, with the result that Hills paid out £600,000.

This incident fuelled the belief in some quarters that bookies can be beaten on football by fans in different parts of the country who pool their knowledge. The die-hard Exeter City fan will perhaps know more about his club than bookies ever could; if he contacts a rival Mansfield fan and the two share their knowledge on the eve of an Exeter v Mansfield match, they are surely, the argument goes, in an ideal position to bet. An Internet site was planned for season 1997-98 to carry out this plan but to date it hasn't put any bookies out of business. In principle the idea is sound, but there's a huge danger natural fan bias will upset all calculations.

We've seen how punters are hamstrung by the minimum trebles and five-timer rulings but there are a couple of ways to skirt around these. The first I believe takes more effort than it's worth and reduces any semblance of value there may be in a bet, but the second really does give punters a chance to pull a fast one on the bookies.

Though singles are not allowed on League matches, those that aren't televised live at any rate, punters can have what amounts to a single on any game they choose by betting on the three possible half-time/full-time outcomes. For example, if you fancy, say, Leicester at 6-5 to win at home to Spurs but cannot back them singly, you can instead split your intended stake three ways and bet as follows: Leicester to be winning at both half-time and full-time (best odds for a team rated 6-5 are usually 5-2); Leicester to be drawing at half-time and winning at full-time (best odds 5-1); and Leicester to be losing at half-time but winning at full-time (best odds 25-1). But the problem with this policy is obvious.

First, it's a monumental pain in the arse to carry out; second, the rewards are disappointing. Stick a tenner on Leicester at 6-5 and if they win you are due a return of £22. But by splitting your £10 stake three ways to guarantee a pay-out of roughly equal proportions no matter what the half-time score (£5.80 on Leicester-Leicester; £3.40 on Draw-Leicester, and 80p on Spurs-Leicester), you'll have to accept diminished returns. The best you can hope for is £20.80; the worst £20.30. And for all that effort.

My tried-and-trusted method of beating the dreadful minimum

five-timer ruling clicks into operation during spells of severe British winter weather when snow, frost, or heavy rain causes widespread postponements on the weekend fixture list. If you strongly fancy one particular team in Division Three for a home victory, simply couple them with four other teams whose matches have been postponed. Very few betting shop cashiers, normally very lowly paid, are motivated enough to keep tabs on the spate of postponed matches so it's a long odds-on chance that your bet will slip through the net. You've therefore abided by the minimum five-timer rule but in effect your bet is a single. All it has to do then is win!

Football punters should always be conscious of the background to a game. If both sides in the same game can benefit from a particular result, then that's the way to bet. In the 1974 World Cup, West Germany and Austria would both qualify for the second round if the Germans won their final group game against Austria. Germany scored early – and both sides then camped out in their own halves, much to the disgust of the entire viewing world.

Similar tactics were used in the closing stages of a Champions League match in December 1998, but because one of the teams involved was Manchester United, there was only token criticism on these shores. United took on Bayern Munich in their final group match at Old Trafford knowing that a victory would definitely take them through to the last eight and that even a draw would very likely be good enough for them to qualify alongside their German opponents, so long as results elsewhere did not go horrifically against them. With just ten minutes to go and the scores level at 1-1, the German bench got wind that the results elsewhere meant that both United and Bayern would go through if no further goals were scored at Old Trafford.

United manager Alex Ferguson revealed afterwards that Bayern players were telling his United players to keep the ball in their own half, a thinly-disguised promise that 'if you don't try to score, neither will we'.

This cosy-cosy set-up made you wonder where soccer authorities draw the line on fixed matches. If this wasn't a fixed result, what is? If the United and Bayern players weren't bringing the game into disrepute, then God knows how a player feels when he's hauled before authorities for reacting angrily, maybe by putting two fingers up, to crowd abuse. I pity the poor punters who backed either United or Bayern to win that night. Through no fault of their own they didn't have a cat in hell's chance.

Three years earlier, in the 1995 Champions League, both Panathinaikos and Nantes would qualify for the lucrative last-eight stage if they drew against each other in their final group encounter. The result? 0-0. With barely a shot on target.

Punters must be wary, too, of backing teams with little to play for. Consciously a professional footballer will always give his all, that's the nature of the beast. Sub-consciously, though, his foot will come off the gas a little. What's the point of thundering into a 50-50 challenge when there's no reward? For the player whose team is fighting against relegation or for promotion, however, every tackle will carry added bite. Look at the bizarre results on the final day of the 1997-98 First Division campaign for proof of that.

Port Vale and Portsmouth, who'd each won only three of their previous 22 away League games, both needed three points from their final-day fixtures to avoid relegation. Port Vale were at mid-table Huddersfield and Pompey at Bradford, another side with absolutely nothing to play for but who until then had lost only three home League games. Vale won 4-0 and Pompey 3-1. The case rests.

Ever since I was a football-mad kid I've always thought the importance of home advantage in professional football was over-rated. It's just a football pitch after all, with the same 11 men against 11 men, yet bookies drastically alter their odds depending upon venue. For instance if Chelsea were playing at home to Leicester on a Wednesday night, the odds would be something like 4-7 Chelsea, 9-2 Leicester, 12-5 the draw. If those two teams, by a curious quirk of the fixture list, were due to meet again at Leicester three days later, the odds (framed before the Wednesday match) would be 6-4 Leicester, 6-4 Chelsea, 11-5 the draw.

Instinctively I know that such a huge discrepancy is wrong, but for years I've struggled to find anyone to share that view. Then Steve

Coppell came to my rescue. The former England winger, now suffering another spell as Crystal Palace manager, firmly believes that the venue should have no direct bearing on a result.

"If players have prepared properly, if they are aware of what will greet them at a certain ground, then they should not be inconvenienced in the slightest by playing away from home," said Coppell, whose Palace side won only two home matches (against six away) during the 1997-98 Premiership season.

"Of course it's different if they turn up at an away game to face 100,000 screaming fans hanging from the rafters, but in domestic British football, players from one week to the next know what to expect.

"Sure they will be barracked by certain sections of the home crowd, but the home fans can often work in the away team's favour too. They will get on the backs of their own players if things aren't going well, and then the home team's confidence vanishes."

Coppell accepts that bookmakers frame their odds with one eye on statistics and are clearly influenced by the fact that there are more home wins than either away victories or draws season after season. But this is a throwback, he believes, to what was commonly regarded as championship form – win your home matches, draw your away ones.

"Teams playing away from home, rightly or wrongly, lower their sights. They regard a draw as not a bad result. But in terms of points, it's better to win one match and lose one than to draw both. Maybe away teams would benefit from raising their ambitions."

Coppell didn't mention that referees, no matter how competent, are likely to give the home side the benefit of the doubt on debatable decisions, for instance penalties, but even this perceived advantage for the home team may be lessened if those horrific proposals to introduce video replays to assist officials are ever implemented.

It's worth noting at this juncture that of 68 red cards in the 1997-98 Premiership season only 22 were for home players. A charitable soul's explanation of those figures would be that away teams are generally under more pressure and therefore more likely to make rash challenges or get frustrated enough to question a referee's parentage. The more cynical would suggest that a referee is far more likely to send off a visiting player for a dodgy challenge than a home player in front of 30,000 baying fans. Maybe that's one of the reasons for such a discrepancy between home and away odds.

You'll have gathered so far from this section on football betting that punters face an uphill battle to make it pay. But in the opening months of 1999, it was the bookmakers who cried for mercy as result after result went against them.

Bookies make huge profits on football because the sport is so unpredictable, but from Christmas 1998 to the start of the Cheltenham Festival 1999, followers of footie form had a field day. Weekend after weekend, bookies would lick their wounds on Saturday night and pray the results on Sunday baled them out. Weekend after weekend, the Sabbath turned into Sunday Bloody Sunday.

It was around this time that Manchester United, Arsenal and Chelsea, the Premiership giants who spearhead most weekend football accumulators, began to find their very best form and walk all over the opposition. Yet it took odds-compilers an awful long time to wake up to what was happening.

The gulf between these three teams and the rest was widening almost by the week, but the odds did not reflect that, with compilers sticking by formulae they'd used for the previous six years of the Premiership, when even the Arsenals and Uniteds could safely be expected to slip up from time to time against the weakest opposition.

Take a look, for example, of the weekend of 16-17 January 1999. Chelsea, at that stage top of the Premiership, were at home to struggling Coventry; Arsenal visited Nottingham Forest, almost certainly the worst side in the Premiership; Manchester United, in superb form, travelled to a disappointing Leicester; and, for good measure, Liverpool were at home to relegation fancies Southampton. Victories for the four Premiership giants looked not merely possible but bloody likely, yet United could be backed at 11-10, Arsenal 8-11, and Chelsea and Liverpool each around 1-2.

Furthermore, Aston Villa, at that time second in the Premiership and still bang in the title race, were due to play an awful Everton side at Villa Park in a live Sky match on the Monday night. Villa, incredibly, could be backed at 8-13. A couple of seasons ago, bookies could bank on at least one of those 'good things' slipping up; but in the early months of 1999, a 'good thing' in football truly was a good thing. All five went in. A very good source in the industry told me that the results that weekend alone cost one of the Big Three bookmakers £4 million.

Industry insiders point to Sunday 31 January as another day of agony, one made particularly hard to swallow by the events in the dying minutes of two of the matches. There were four fixtures live on TV that day, with Manchester United playing at Charlton in a fifth high-profile Sunday clash. Thousands of punters whose weekend accumulators dip on the Saturday traditionally attempt to recoup losses on the Sunday, and on this particular day it was not hard to see which teams they would back.

The four live games, in chronological order, were Birmingham (best odds 6-5) at home to Bradford, mediocre Bari at home to title-chasing Lazio (11-10) in the Italian League, Arsenal (11-8) at home to Chelsea, and Celtic (4-7) playing host to St Johnstone in the Scottish Premier. United, near-certainties at Charlton, were available at 8-13 in a match with a 4pm kick-off, the same as at Highbury.

There looked nothing for the layers to worry about at 2.45pm that day when Birmingham were drawing 1-1 with Bradford deep into injury-time at St Andrews. But with barely seconds to go, the home side were awarded a penalty and Paul Furlong netted the winner from the spot. Good things Lazio thrashed Bari 3-1 and bookmaker backsides began to twitch, particularly with well-backed Arsenal leading 1-0 against Chelsea thanks to a first-half Dennis Bergkamp goal. But news from The Valley was good – Charlton were holding the day's bankers, United, 0-0.

I'll let a bookmaker whose one-shop business collapsed on this day take up the story.

"Birmingham and Bari were evil results but so long as United didn't win, I knew I'd be okay. Every coupon I'd taken had United included in trebles, four-timers and five-timers, and defeat for them would have made me a nice profit. I sat down to eat my dinner while watching the closing stages of the Arsenal-Chelsea game on Sky Sports, knowing that Sky would announce any score from the United match as soon as it happened.

"It was getting on for six o'clock when my son, who'd been listening to the radio, came in and said Dwight Yorke had just scored for United. I've never felt so sick in my life. Honest to God, I felt like throwing my dinner up. There was just a glimmer that the little bugger was lying just to get me going, but even that hope lasted barely a few seconds – in the top right-hand corner of the television screen Sky showed Yorke heading in the winner for United. The goal ruined me. You can take defeats but there was something brutal about this."

It was estimated by a well-placed bookmaking source that Yorke's goal cost the industry £1 million.

Ron Wadey, who owns five betting shops in the north of England, said that instead of making an expected £4,000 profit on football over the first two months of 1999, his business lost £20,000. When you consider that Ladbrokes and Hills own substantially more than 1,000 shops apiece, it gives you some idea of the scale of the industry's losses.

Said Wadey: "You only have to look at the Manchester United v Liverpool FA Cup clash on January 24, shown live on Sky on a Sunday afternoon, to get an idea of how things went for us during that period. It was a massive betting game, with nearly everyone on United at 5-6. With five minutes to go, Liverpool were leading 1-0, which was a good result for us. Deep into injury-time it was 1-1 – a fantastic result for us. At the final whistle, it was 2-1 to United – an absolute disaster. Last-minute goals cost us a fortune. It became impossible to win on the live TV games. We were waiting for late goals to happen, and when they did, they were never in our favour."

A similar United recovery in May 1999 on that unforgettable night in Barcelona to win the European Cup was to cost the bookmakers even more dearly.

Without actually saying it, Wadey seemed to blame the odds-compilers of the leading firms for the huge losses sustained by bookmakers throughout Britain. It is not cost effective for small firms to produce their own coupons and so they pay a fee to use the lists compiled by Hills, Ladbrokes, Corals, or specialist football betting operators like Super Soccer. The small firms, therefore, depend for their very survival on the accuracy of the prices issued by the big boys. But these prices, Wadey maintains, were hopelessly inaccurate.

He said: "Their job is to come up with odds for a football match that will attract three-way support – for the home team, the away, and the draw, although I accept that the draw will never be popular with punters. Yet in a match like 9-2 Charlton, 8-13 United, 9-4 the draw we wouldn't see a penny for Charlton. It was all United, United, United. It was the same story with Arsenal and Chelsea, too. But why go 8-13 United? They could have gone 2-5 or even 1-3 and still taken plenty. Going 8-13 was an unnecessary risk and it's bookies like me who have to pay for it."

Wadey has a point. In early January 1999, Inter Milan, perhaps the Italian equivalent at the time of Liverpool (talented but inconsistent under-achievers), were at home to Venezia in the Italian League. Inter were fifth in Serie A at the time, way adrift of the leaders, and though Venezia were bottom, they were just a point behind a group of four teams, with a game in hand on each of them. Inter were a prohibitive 1-5, while Venezia could be backed at 14-1. Yet a fortnight earlier Manchester United, arguably the best team in England, were at home to Nottingham Forest, by common consent the worst team in the Premiership. United were surely more likely to gain three points against Forest than Inter against Venezia, yet Alex Ferguson's men were allowed to start at 2-5, with Forest 13-2.

In the Far East, where betting on the Premiership as we've already seen is a multi-billion pound business, bookmakers woke up to the domination of the Premiership giants far earlier than their British counterparts, and that caused further damage to the likes of Hills and Ladbrokes. In their calculations Far East bookies would have made United something like a 1-4 or 1-5 shot to beat Forest, would almost certainly have taken huge sums of money at those odds, and would therefore have been falling over themselves to take advantage of 2-5 offers over here, using their tax-free facilities in Gibraltar of course.

It took until just before the 1999 Cheltenham Festival, after almost three months of sustained losses made worse by a run of predictable triumphs in live Sunday evening games for Scottish giants Rangers and Celtic, for bookies to take serious evasive action. Manchester United, though with a crucial Champions League showdown against Inter Milan four days later and almost certain to rest their star players, started at a prohibitive 1-4 to beat Southampton at Old Trafford in a Saturday afternoon Premiership clash. United won, as expected, but those odds when compared to the 2-5 available just weeks earlier against Forest (a far worse team than Southampton) showed that bookies were no longer likely to take any chances on the Premiership class acts.

Another window of opportunity was slammed firmly shut on punters.

One of the reasons I was itching for many years to write this book was the discipline I knew it would instil in me to carry out exhaustive research on football betting. For years I believed I had identified a foolproof way of taking money from the bookies, but needed the results of studious research before I was willing to risk a shilling. That research has now been carried out – and guess what? I was badly wrong. I will deliver the bad news first, and then follow up with the good news, the very good news. There IS a foolproof way to beat the bookies on football.

Bookmakers freely admit that few punters back the draw in football matches. Punters want an allegiance in a game; to shout on a given team. Backing the draw is almost an admission that they can't make up their minds.

Up to mid-March of the 1998-99 season, roughly 30 per cent of matches in the top two English divisions finished all-square, yielding odds of 9-4. Yet very often 12-5, 5-2 or even 11-4 is available about the draw in a top-flight game. Bookies can get away with offering over the odds for the draw because they know it will attract little money, and it allows them to tighten even further odds for the home and away sides. Where I reckoned a loophole could be exploited was in matches in which bookmakers could not split the two sides, for instance offering 6-4 the home win, 6-4 the away win and 11-5 the draw.

For years I swore, without the statistics to back me up, that in such games the only logical bet was the draw.

Bookies were saying, I argued, that there was absolutely nothing to choose between the two sides, that an away win was just as likely as a home win. But by doing that they were also implicitly admitting that the draw was an equally likely result. Indeed you could argue that if two sides are so evenly matched, a deadlock is the likeliest of all three outcomes. Therefore, the true odds of each outcome must be 2-1, 2-1, 2-1, translated into 7-4, 7-4, 7-4 once the bookmaker's in-built margin is taken into account.

If you could consistently get 11-5 or more about a 2-1 chance, my reasoning went, profits were inevitable.

Results early in the 1998-99 season seemed to back me up. On Saturday 29 August, four of eight Premiership matches ended in deadlock and a staggering eight of ten Division One games were also all-square. Five of those 12 games were 6-4, 6-4, 11-5 jobs.

Then on the weekend of February 19-21, Sky Sports broadcast live three English League matches. All three were 6-4, 6-4, 11-5 affairs and all three finished in draws, giving bookies their only respite of a bleak, bleak winter.

"Aha," I thought. "This system is a winner."

Sadly it's not. In the 1997-98 season, 271 League matches in England and Scotland featured odds from at least one bookmaker of 6-4, 6-4, 11-5. Very often it was possible to get 9-4 or 12-5, or on occasions 5-2 about the draw. But of those 271, only 80 were drawn. That's roughly 30 per cent, making the true odds around 9-4. In other words, bookies were pretty much spot on and there was no loophole to exploit.

It was a similar story in the 1998-99 season. By 3pm on Saturday 20 March, 300 League matches in England and Scotland had featured odds of 6-4, 6-4 and 11-5, and 90 (again 30 per cent) had finished in deadlock.

Before the 1990 World Cup in Italy, I outlined in the *Racing Post* a strategy I described as "almost a licence to print money". Back the draw in every match in the first stage of Italia '90, I told punters, and you will almost certainly come out ahead. In each of the previous two World Cups, the 36 first-phase matches yielded 12 and 11 draws respectively. As the average best price for the draw in those games was slightly more than 3-1 (the 9-5s and 15-8s were more than made up for by the 7-2s and 4-1s), a healthy if unspectacular profit would have been made.

"Draws are always a sound bet in the opening exchanges," I wrote, "with teams more concerned with avoiding defeat than going in search of victory. And in a tournament (Italia '90) which sees a mere eight nations eliminated after 36 first-phase matches, three successive draws will probably be enough to take a team through to the later stages, just as it was in 1982 for Italy, who went on to win the tournament."

The logic was sound, but it all went horribly pear-shaped. Incredibly, the first eight matches of Italia '90 yielded not a single draw and though results later improved, the damage had already been done. A foolproof plan, I'd said, but in the end it was me who was proved the fool.

I must add a happy footnote to this sad tale. For France '98, armed with redundancy money, I followed the same back-the-draw policy in all the first-phase matches and came out comfortably ahead.

On 1 January 1994 something very strange happened. I got my leg-over. Then later that day something even stranger. Of 11 Premiership matches that memorable New Year's Day, EIGHT yielded away wins. Though eight away wins had been recorded in an English division on three previous occasions, this was the first time in the top flight. The fabulous eight, some reasonably predictable, were: Aston Villa 0 Blackburn 1 (7-4 Ladbrokes), Everton 0 West Ham 1 (7-4 Hills), Ipswich 1 Liverpool 2 (7-4 Ladbrokes), QPR 1 Sheffield Wednesday 2 (7-4 Hills and

Ladbrokes), Southampton 0 Norwich 1 (11-8 Coral), Swindon 1 Chelsea 3 (7-4 Ladbrokes), Spurs 1 Coventry 2 (10-3 Coral), and Wimbledon 0 Arsenal 3 (11-8 Coral).

I mention this first to reinforce my earlier theory that playing away from home is not the disadvantage many punters seem to think, and second to lead neatly in to my one-and-only foolproof method of making football betting pay.

Quite simply it is this: back away teams in the Premiership at odds of 3-1 or more, but not at Old Trafford, Highbury, or Stamford Bridge.

As I mentioned earlier, Manchester United, Arsenal and Chelsea now inhabit a different planet from the rest of the Premiership clubs. A defeat for any of the three away from home is noteworthy enough; a reverse on their home soil almost unthinkable. Indeed by March 20 of the 1998-99 season, the three Premier giants had lost a total of just two home League matches between them. But there is no such gulf in class among the other 17 top-flight clubs. All, even the likes of Nottingham Forest and Everton, are well capable of snaffling three points from an away trip – as the following figures show.

In the 1997-98 season, there were 162 Premiership matches in which the away team started at 3-1 or longer. This may seem an astonishingly high figure but you have only to glance at an average weekend coupon to see how many Premiership teams on any given Saturday are allowed to start at fancy odds. Of those 162 matches, 32 away sides were victorious at odds ranging from 3-1 to 10-1 (Barnsley at Liverpool).

A £100 stake on each of those matches would have cost £16,200, returning £16,930. Now that kind of paltry profit is hardly worth getting worked up about, particularly as I haven't taken the damaging impact of paying tax into account (more of that in a moment).

But when we exclude all the matches involving Manchester United, Arsenal and Chelsea, the picture for punters becomes far more appealing. Now there are 109 matches for a total stake of £10,900, and the return is a much more healthy £14,230 - a profit of more than £3,300, or around 30 per cent.

It's a similar story in the 1998-99 season. Up to 20 March 1999, there were 131 Premiership matches offering odds of 3-1 or more about the away team. The £13,100 stake would have returned only £12,640 (a slight loss) when we include the Big Three, but take United, Arsenal and Chelsea out of calculations and once again the maths become much more punter-friendly. Now we consider just 89 matches, and the outlay of £8,900 brings a return of £11,300 - a profit of £2,400, or slightly more than 25 per cent.

These impressive figures are easily explained. Premiership football is no place for mugs. Those players plying their trade at such a rarefied level are accomplished performers, who more often than not can be trusted by their managers to do a job. They are fit, strong and talented, and there is precious little to choose between any of the 17 Premiership sides struggling to keep the Big Three in their sights. And all of these sides, whether they are European challengers or relegation candidates, have at least one player capable of winning a match with a moment of magic.

In 1998-99, Nottingham Forest were the least impressive side in the Premiership yet in Dutch World Cup star Pierre Van Hooijdonk they boasted a player who on his day could trouble any defence. Teams in lower divisions do not have such a luxury – that is why they operate at a lower level and why this strategy of backing away teams of 3-1 or more must be limited to the top flight.

You will by now have identified two major snags.

First, the impact of tax; second, bookmaker restrictions. I will make clear later in this book why punters should always pay tax up front on their bets rather than have it deducted from winnings. But there are dozens of illegal operators out there who will lay you bets tax-free. If you are reading this book, chances are you're a regular punter who will have several acquaintances willing to lay you tax-free wagers. Take advantage whenever you can. This back-the-away side strategy is only really worthwhile under such circumstances.

It's highly likely that any illegal layer willing to offer you tax-free betting facilities will also offer you unrestricted singles on football matches. I know of half a dozen such operators. It's no good finding a likely winner at 7-2 if you have to find two more selections to satisfy the dreaded minimum-trebles ruling.

Bear in mind, too, that singles are allowed for live TV games, and that you can also back doubles so long as one of the legs is a live TV match. So Sheffield Wednesday at 4-1 to win at Derby might not appeal if two more selections are needed, but the Owls become far more attractive at those odds if they can be lumped in a double with, say, Rangers at 2-5 in a live Sunday night Sky game from the Scottish Premiership, or Parma at odds-on at home to Perugia in the Italian League.

Betting is never easy – bookmakers will always see to that – but here you have an undeniably profitable strategy. Don't waste it.

## the rise and fall and rise of football betting

It has become accepted fact that betting on football came of age during the 1990 World Cup in Italy. Yet while we should recognise Italia 90 as the tournament that saw football turnover sky-rocket, we should also be aware that betting on football was practically a way of life in Britain for much of the first half of the 20th century before dying a slow death in the early 1960s.

Indeed as early as 1914 the Anti-Gambling League estimated turnover on football that year at an incredible £10 million, and throughout the 1920s and 30s several proposals were put forward to rid football of the evils of betting. Such a part of the fabric of everyday life was betting on football that to the punter of the day the prospect of it disappearing must have been as laughable as an asteroid warning to a stegosaurus.

But in 1964, Chancellor Of The Exchequer Reginald Maudling wiped out football betting in Britain with a move almost as devastating to bookmakers as the asteroid was to the dinosaur. At the time bookmakers William Hill boasted a turnover of £50 million, around a third of which was fixed-odds betting. Hills had a file of five million football clients, from whom they received an average of two million coupons per week. We are talking here big, big business.

But this was in the days following the match-fixing scandal that had rocked Britain, and the link between betting and football was under the microscope. What's more, pools promoters, disturbed by the effects on their business of the burgeoning interest in fixed-odds football betting, began earnestly to lobby high-ranking government figures, urging them to reduce the tax on pools betting from 25 per cent to enable them to take on the fixed-odds boys on level terms.

The Chancellor listened carefully to the gripes of the pools promoters, but his next move surprised even them. Instead of reducing the pools tax from 25 per cent, he increased the tax on football betting from seven per cent to 25 per cent, sounding the death knell to one of the most popular pursuits in Britain. Turnover on fixed-odds, an estimated £65 million in 1963, according to Graham Sharpe in his book *Gambling On Goals*, fell to £15 million in 1965 and £5 million by 1968.

William Hill himself complained: "The pools promoters will be celebrating and thanks to their lobbying they will be drinking wine mixed with blood – bookmakers' blood. Fixed-odds are finished."

One of William Hill's top executives, director Charles Layfield, even speculated in June 1965 that it was the imposition of the 25 per cent tax on football betting that cost the Conservatives the General Election. "He (Maudling) antagonised millions and killed an industry in three months."

I should perhaps point out here that to disguise the massive tax increase on football betting, bookies didn't pass the full payment on to punters (they knew few would be prepared to fork out a pound and four shillings for a £1 bet). Instead they slashed the odds on offer, hoping few punters would notice. Although I have perhaps been a little unkind to the punters of the day, it is to their credit that they did not accept such massive reductions to the odds and turned away from football betting.

In 1972, a few years after William Hill had tried to make a comeback in the fixed-odds world, Chancellor Dennis Healy increased the tax to a whopping 42 per cent, the final *coup de grace*. Football betting was dead.

Two years after its death, however, it was miraculously

resurrected, and the man bookies, and millions of punters who love to bet on football, should thank is a canny Scot called John MacFarlane, then the managing director of the 22-shop Scottish firm Queen Bookmakers.

MacFarlane, in a meeting with Minister of Finance John Gilbert, explained that he intended to produce a football betting coupon that would qualify for general betting duty of seven per cent.

Sharpe wrote: "He explained to the Minister that the new-style coupon differed from the traditional fixed-odds coupon in that it quoted a separate, flexible price about each individuality – home, away and draw. This would make it 'individual odds' betting and therefore no different from any other type of bet."

Remember that, until then, football coupons were nothing like the ones you can pick up in betting shops today. Although a full weekend fixture list would be printed, there were no odds available for individual matches. All bookies would do is print the minimum pay-out for, say, eight homes, or five draws, or four aways.

MacFarlane's coupon, charging seven per cent betting duty, was predictably challenged in court by Customs & Excise.

The case, which lasted a day, was won on a unanimous verdict (three Law Lords voted) by Queens Bookmakers. Within months individual-odds coupons appeared throughout Britain.

Customs & Excise later explained in a public notice the difference between fixed-odds betting and individual-odds betting.

"Fixed-odds betting is where bets are invited by the issue of a coupon, a blackboard list, or a newspaper advertisement. It is a type of bet not usually made without such an invitation and not usually made with a totalisator. The betting offers the punter stated odds for a choice of bets (eg 30-1 for three draws). Fixed-odds coupon betting is liable to pool betting duty.

"Individual-odds coupon bets vary from fixed-odds coupon bets because the coupons provide sufficient variety of odds to give different accumulative results. For example, if two punters place bets of, say two home wins, two draws and two aways they must be able to obtain different odds if they bet on different teams. Bets made on individual-odds coupons are liable to general betting duty."

MacFarlane, virtually single-handedly, had resurrected the football betting industry. He is the man responsible for what today has become a multi-million pound monster.

The 1994 World Cup officially eclipsed the Grand National as the biggest betting event of all time, with industry-wide turnover conservatively estimated at £60 million. But it was the World Cup four years earlier in Italy that first woke Britain up to the fact that football betting was gaining ground hand over fist on traditional market leader horseracing. Turnover hit the magic £50 million mark, and confirmed to bookies that, with aggressive marketing, football was a certain cash cow.

Extensive live TV coverage, the continued progress of England and the Republic Of Ireland, and early attention-grabbing shock results like Argentina 0 Cameroon 1 will go down as key reasons for the betting explosion during Italia 90, but of equal significance was the marketing strategy of the big bookmakers. For the four weeks of that tournament the only companies to take costly adverts on the back pages of the national daily tabloids were Hills, Ladbrokes and Coral. They recognised that the nation, for the first time since 1966, had gone World Cup crazy. Goodness, even the women were entranced, hooked perhaps by the lethal combination on BBC of Des Lynam and *Nessun Dorma*. It was a bold marketing ploy by the Big Three, but it paid rich dividends. Betting on football has never looked back.

# chapter 4

## the importance of
## team news

In America it's regarded as the key to successful bookmaking and punting; in Britain it is barely considered. Team news. In America the motto is, "Don't bet without it"; in Britain it's, "Who gives a monkey's?"

Yet to make your betting pay long-term, it is essential to keep tabs on factors like injuries, suspensions and low morale, and be prepared to change your intended bet to take such factors into account.

Punters in Britain are in an ideal position to make a killing. Odds-compilers here may insist that they keep one eye on team news when framing their prices but I know from experience that it is often pointless for them to do so.

For instance the early odds for Manchester United to beat Aston Villa at Old Trafford on a Saturday may be something like evens. The day before the game Villa may lose, let's say through a flu bug, the services of Paul Merson, Ugo Ehiogu, Dion Dublin, Gareth Southgate, and Julian Joachim. They are significant losses, especially to a club of Villa's strength in depth, and will surely lessen their chances of getting a result at Old Trafford. But will bookies shave United's odds? Will they hell. As sure as eggs is eggs you'll be able to get evens United on the day of the game.

Let me give you an example from the 1998-99 season. In late September 1998, Blackburn Rovers took on Lyon in France in the first-round, second-leg of the UEFA Cup, having lost the home leg 1-0. Lyon were given a top quote of 8-11 to win the return. Then the news broke that Rovers were travelling to France without a recognised striker, Chris Sutton, Kevin Gallacher, Kevin Davies and Martin Dahlin all having failed fitness tests. Inexperienced Damien Duff, all ten stone of him, had to lead the Rovers front-line.

To give you an idea of the size of Blackburn's task, Duff was the most prominent Rovers player in the first-goalscorer betting lists – at a massive 14-1. But were Lyon's odds cut to compensate for the weakened Blackburn threat? No, they weren't. Half an hour before kick-off, 8-11 was still available. As it turned out the game ended 2-2, but in my book it was a match Blackburn could not possibly have won.

In late November 1998, Everton hosted Newcastle in a Monday night Premiership match, screened live on Sky. Everton had scored just one goal in six previous home League matches, while Newcastle had netted only six times in six away matches; so goals, it was easy to predict, would be in short supply.

Independent bookmakers Stan James regularly offer 5-2 that there will be fewer than two goals in a Premiership match but there was surely a case, given the poor scoring record of both teams, for going 9-4 or even 2-1. But Stan James freely offered 5-2 – and still offered 5-2 even after it became clear that Newcastle striker Alan Shearer and Everton striker Duncan Ferguson, the two players most likely to break the deadlock, were not playing. To nobody's surprise, the game yielded just one goal – and that from the penalty-spot – from Everton youngster Michael Ball.

Though football is a team game, I have played it long enough, and at a high enough level, to know that the absence of a certain player can seriously weaken a team's chances. Yet bookmakers seem reluctant to acknowledge this. Their view seems to be that, however talented or influential the absent player might be, his understudy is perfectly capable of filling his shoes. Perhaps 90 per cent of the time this is true, but for the other ten per cent they are badly under-estimating the impact of the key player's absence.

For instance I rate Steve McManaman as one of the best players ever to have worn a Liverpool shirt and until the 1998-99 season, when his form dipped alarmingly because of injury and his impending move to Real Madrid, would have always been prepared to back Liverpool, so long as the odds weren't silly, with him in the line-up. But without him, I reckon Liverpool are only half as effective. The ideas dry up, the option of "giving it to Macca" when a ten-man defence bars the way is no longer there, and Liverpool suffer.

To check whether this theory held water, I asked Dave Ball, the stats-man at Anfield, to find out Liverpool's results whenever McManaman was sidelined since the start of the 1991-92 season (when Macca became a regular first-teamer). Of the 282 league games Liverpool played from then up to the start of the 1998-99 season, McManaman missed only 40. Of those 40, Liverpool won only 13 and lost 16, a 40 per cent losing rate. Their loss rate in the 242 League games featuring McManaman was only 24 per cent. For the record, here are the Liverpool statistics for league matches, with and without McManaman, from the beginning of 91-92 to the beginning of 98-99:

| | | | | |
|---|---|---|---|---|
| **With Macca** | played | 242 | won | 114 (47%) |
| | drew | 69 (29%) | lost | 59 (24%) |
| **Without Macca** | played | 40 | won | 13 (32.5%) |
| | drew | 11 (27.5%) | lost | 16 (40%) |

Of course all this is being a little unfair on British odds-compilers. Clearly they would recognise in the Manchester United v Aston Villa example above that United's chances of victory are increased by the growing Villa injury-list, and in a ideal world they would react. But, for odds-compilers, football betting is not an ideal world. As I've pointed out already, they are hamstrung by the early deadlines they must meet. The big firms would rather absorb a medium-sized loss on such a game than alter prices on pre-printed coupons. Coupon odds therefore are set almost in tablets of stone.

One odds-compiler of a leading firm told me: "We just have to bite our lip and pray. We know we're going to lose money in such circumstances, all we can do is pray the damage is limited."

On no account feel sympathy for bookies in these circumstances. As we have already seen, they have adequate protection in the form of their minimum-trebles and five-timer requirements.

It's difficult for bookies, and punters too, to know how much trust to put in news of injuries and illness. Increasingly nowadays players make apparently miraculous recoveries to line up in matches they were days earlier given no chance of playing in. England coach Glenn Hoddle, in his infamous World Cup diary in 1998, admitted asking players to lie about their injuries to wrongfoot opponents. But bookmaker reluctance to take a manager's words as gospel has, on occasions, given punters a real chance to cash in.

Think back to October 1997 and the third round of the Coca-Cola Cup. Manchester United manager Alex Ferguson had made no secret of his contempt for the tournament, treating it as a hindrance to United's chances in the Premiership and the Champions League.

A year earlier he had fielded a severely under-strength side at the same stage and his threats to do likewise against Ipswich at Portman Road were largely ignored by bookies, who offered an incredible 9-2 about the East Anglians. On the night, United fielded a side of reserve team players and, not surprisingly, were tonked 2-0.

On the day of the 1998 World Cup Final between Brazil and France, I could not contemplate defeat for Brazil. France were the host nation, admittedly, but they'd rarely set the pulse racing *en route* to the final, and whenever has a team won the World Cup without an outstanding striker? Fifteen minutes before kick-off, however, my money went on the French at 5-2

The reason for the about-turn was the remarkable Ronaldo incident. When you're told half an hour before kick-off that the best player in the world is unfit to play in the greatest game of all, then 15 minutes later you're told that he is fit after all, you should begin to wonder about his team's preparation. When you then see that team fail to come out for a pre-match warm-up – for the World Cup Final for God's sake – you know they've lost. France, under the circumstances I've just described, became one of the bets of the year. We did not need subsequent newspaper reports to tell us how divided the Brazilian dressing-room must have been in the minutes leading up to kick-off.

If you're in any doubt about the importance some bookies and punters attach to reliable team news, consider this. I was once offered £500 a week by a Singapore-based bookie to pass him genuine information on injuries and likely line-ups in the Premiership. Such information, he said, was gold dust. But I told him that most of the time I could give him snippets no better than he could learn from dialling Clubcall and reluctantly declined his offer.

To my mind an insider at a Premiership club, perhaps a physio with first-hand knowledge of team plans and direct access to counterparts at rival teams, could supplement his income by something like £1,000 a week if he was prepared to divulge key information not freely available elsewhere. If there's such a figure reading this, perhaps I can be of assistance in arranging a deal – for the usual agent's fee of course!

One more point: I know of a punter who pockets a steady income from betting on matches in the Scottish lower divisions. Although they don't admit it, bookies price up these games almost entirely on current form and League standings. This punter, though, has cultivated a network of contacts north of the border; reliable informers who will tell him the players who make their teams tick and whose absences are most keenly felt.

Remember at this level, unlike the Premiership, the standard of deputy is unlikely to be too high.

American odds-compilers treat team news with the utmost seriousness, perhaps not surprisingly given that the country's two most popular team sports – American Football and baseball – feature pivotal positions. In soccer there is no equivalent of the gridiron quarterback, nor of baseball's pitcher. They hold the key to success and failure.

Indeed, in baseball, the identity of the pitcher is the most important single aspect in setting the odds. If a regular pitcher is injured, the match odds will change dramatically.

Bert Randolph Sugar in his 1991 book *The Caesars Palace Sports Book Of Betting* illustrates just how dramatic an impact the pitcher has on the betting.

He uses as an example a match between LA Dodgers and Houston Astros, with the Las Vegas line looking like this:

LA Dodgers Belcher     −105 (7)
Houston Astros Forsch    −110

The visiting Dodgers (the away team are always listed first, one of the more annoying aspects of betting in America) have Tim Belcher as pitcher, with the Astros, the home team, relying on Bob Forsch.

Sugar wrote: "The Astros opened a slight favourite in the money-line at −110, with the Dodgers right behind at −105, which means that if you like the Dodgers, you must bet $105 to win $100; if you favour the Astros, you will wager $110 to win $100. The '7' is the over/under number; as in other games, you may bet on whether the total runs scored by both teams will exceed or fall short of this number.

"Let's say the Astros' Bob Forsch slips on a cake of Lifebuoy in the shower and is unable to start. Houston manager Art Howe is short of starters and has to press a little-used long reliever into service for his first start in nine years (we'll call him John Doe). The situation has changed radically, and the betting line must move to reflect it. The new line might look something like this:

LA Dodgers Belcher     −105     −200 (8)
Houston Astros Doe     −110     +185

"That's a dramatic move. From being a slight underdog, the Dodgers have moved to strong (1-2) favouritism and the over/under spot has been upped to eight. Ordinarily you would be sitting pretty, secure in the knowledge that your bet on a strong favourite had been made at a very attractive price. Unfortunately that is not the case here. Because of the overwhelming importance placed on starting pitching, the baseball bet is the only bet subject to change.

If at the time you make your wager you specify 'pitchers must go', then your bet is off when a pitching change is made. If you do *not* specify this, then your money will be at risk at the revised price. An over/under wager is similarly affected. Of course, ordinary changes in the line, not brought about by a pitching change, will not change the bet."

To British punters such a rule comes as something of a shock to the system. It's like backing England at 11-4 to beat the Australians in a Test match, learning that Aussie opening bats Matthew Elliott and Michael Slater have pulled out injured, and then discovering we must swallow a reduction in England's price to something like 15-8. Or like backing England at 11-4, specifying that "opening bats must go" and then finding that our bet is voided because Taylor and Slater have pulled out.

But Sugar explains: "The emphasis on pitching is not misplaced, for this is the single most important factor in the game of baseball handicapping and, arguably, in the game itself. It has been said – perhaps too often but it is true – 'good pitching beats good hitting.' This has always been true, but with the passage of time it becomes even more so. The arm seems to get stronger. This is no illusion. Improved training methods and facilities, a better grasp of the science of pitching, better coaching in colleges and in the minor leagues, the development of relief specialists, and even new pitches – like the split-fingered fastball, unheard of a few years ago – combine to keep the pitchers ahead of the hitters. The linemakers (odds-compilers) are acutely aware of all these factors, hence the anomaly of the change in the rules of (Caesars Palace) sports-book betting."

Clearly then, as highly as I regard Steve McManaman, his absence from the Liverpool team can never hope to have the same impact on betting as the absence of a regular baseball starting pitcher. And if you need any more evidence that pitchers are demi-gods in the States then consider this: in December 1998, the Los Angeles Dodgers, owned by media mogul Rupert Murdoch, agreed to pay star pitcher Kevin Brown $63 million over seven years.

The importance of the quarterback in American Football is well known and an injury to a star QB will of course force a change in the betting, although not quite so dramatically as a star pitcher's absence in baseball. But one respected gridiron handicapper has an altogether different viewpoint, one which I think is complete bollocks but which has gained currency Stateside.

George Ignatin, known in America as The Professor (he taught a course on the economics of gambling at the University of Alabama), believes you should bet on the team missing its star quarterback. He argues that to compensate for such a telling absence, the rest of the team tries that much harder, and that his star rating may not be entirely justified in the first place.

As an example, he points to the end of the 1990 NFL season when San Francisco QB Phil Simms sprained an ankle and missed the last few weeks of the campaign. The injury should have been a massive blow to the 49ers but back-up quarterback Jeff Hostetler played magnificently to sweep them to a Super Bowl triumph. It's a fine example but surely the exception, all logic dictates, rather than the rule.

While we're on the subject of American sports, perhaps I should deal briefly with ice hockey, or plain hockey as it is known in America. My view of this game can be summed up by the joke heard regularly in the acts of mediocre stand-up US comics. "I went to a fight the other night and a hockey game broke out."

Top class US comic Milton Berle tells the story of a punter who, after losing ten straight bets on American Football and ten more on basketball, called Caesars Palace to find out what betting action was available that night. "All we've got tonight is hockey," he was told. A short silence and then the punter's protest: "Hockey? What the hell do I know about hockey?"

But minority sport though it is in the States compared to American Football, and baseball, it is treated very seriously by odds-makers in Nevada. They know that on ice hockey they are vulnerable to the clued-up punters who make the sport their living. Sugar wrote: "Hockey betting attracts only those in the know. Many of these wise guys come from back East and know hockey the way Bo knows baseball, often better than the odds-makers. They lurk around the sports-books (in Vegas) like foxes around chicken coops, looking for soft spots."

In Britain, bookmakers Stan James bet regularly on the Superleague, televised live on Sky, with teams like Manchester Storm and Nottingham Panthers, but don't look here for any betting tips. I'm sure the die-hard ice hockey follower with a betting knowledge will more than hold his own, but ice hockey for me has all the appeal of a three-in-a-bed session with *Birds Of A Feather*.

Injuries to key players apart, there are other occasions when teams in any sport can be opposed with confidence. I call it the 'morale victory' and it comes into play whenever off-the-field events affect the well-being, the spirit, the morale, of a team on the pitch.

Two glaring examples from the second half of 1998 spring to mind.

The contempt at Nottingham Forest for bad-boy striker Pierre Van Hooijdonk was not disguised. The Dutchman had committed the cardinal sin of bad-mouthing his fellow players in public, and went on strike when it became clear Forest would not release him from his contract.

Team-mates made it clear that Van Hooijdonk, despite his undoubted talent, would not be welcome back in the Forest dressing-room. But the East Midlands club, hardly awash with cash, could not let their star asset idly kick his heels back home in Holland. They needed him playing, they needed him in the shop window to tempt other clubs into buying a player with an unsavoury reputation for disloyalty, and so Van Hooijdonk returned in early November 1998 to the City Ground in Nottingham, much to the disgust of his team-mates, and then-manager Dave Bassett.

It was obvious to anyone with a morsel of intelligence that team spirit would not be a Forest strong suit when Van Hooijdonk made his reappearance against Wimbledon on November 7 (and given the paucity of talent at the club, team spirit was about all they could normally call upon). Bassett, in his pre-match programme notes, slated the Dutchman and admitted he was astounded that Van Hooijdonk had had the audacity to return without an apology. Under such circumstances, and given that Forest were already struggling at the foot of the Premiership, Wimbledon looked very good things at 13-8. They duly won.

In the late summer of 1998, Glenn Hoddle's ill-conceived World Cup diary betrayed the confidence of his England players. Hoddle blew the lid on the behaviour of Paul Gascoigne after Gazza had been told he'd been axed from the England squad; and, more shockingly in my opinion, implied that the most important member of the whole England World Cup set-up was faith healer Eileen Drewery. No England player rushed into print to criticise his tell-tale manager and this was seen by many as a sign of acceptance, that the players saw little wrong in their coach breaking the No.1 rule of professional football by leaking dressing-room secrets. But the more clear-thinking punter, however, could suspect that the only reason they hadn't slated their coach was that to do so was to commit international suicide, certainly as long as Hoddle kept his job.

Hoddle's revelations were a clear sign that England could be opposed in their next international. Why would players fight tooth and nail for a coach so ready to bad-mouth them in public? That Sweden beat England 2-1 in a crucial European Championship qualifier in the very next international should have surprised no-one.

It's perhaps a good time here to expose a betting myth. Many punters of my acquaintance will blindly lump cash on a football team who have just appointed a new manager, the thinking being that the players will be anxious to impress their new boss and therefore results, in the short-term at least, will improve. It's a persuasive theory, and when you consider how Spurs improved at the start of the 1998-99 season under George Graham, after he'd replaced the unfortunate Christian Gross, it's easy to understand how it has gained currency.

But the facts simply do not back up such an argument. A survey published in 1998 by the Institute Of Economic Affairs said analysis of more than 42,000 matches between 1972 and 1993 showed sides do not significantly improve immediately after their manager is dismissed, whether or not a new boss is appointed right away.

Research showed that while the number of wins per 18 matches (the win ratio) improved slightly after a manager was sacked - from 0.42 before his departure to 0.46 afterwards, this was not a viable comparison because of a natural tendency for results to improve after a lengthy poor run "because no team carries on losing forever". Not counting Everton of course. The report claimed that the ratio for clubs which hung on to their manager despite a slump in form was a more healthy 0.49.

It is important in individual sports to keep tabs on injury news. There's a saying in sport "beware the sick golfer". This is not meant as a warning to punters; rather it's to rival players who may subconsciously under-estimate the threat of a golfer suffering flu, tonsillitis, or some other illness, and who are then made to pay for their complacency. The saying had often puzzled me until world No.1 Tiger Woods explained its logic midway through the World Matchplay Championship at Wentworth in 1998. Woods, himself suffering from flu, nonetheless polished off a bang-in-form Lee Westwood, and then explained why the illness may have helped his victory chances.

"When you're ill you don't expect to play well and that eases the pressure on you," said Woods.

Woods has a fair point, but punters should never confuse illness with injury. A golfer under the weather with a heavy cold is still capable of winning a tournament; the golfer with a rib injury that restricts his swing has no chance.

A day before the 1998 Volvo Masters, the final event of the European season, Westwood revealed that he had damaged a rib midway through his World Matchplay defeat by Woods, an injury that severely hampered his normally wonderful swing. Under those circumstances, Colin Montgomerie, like Westwood chasing the European money-list first prize in the season-ending event, had to be a great bet at around 5-6 to finish ahead of his great rival over four rounds of the Volvo Masters. The bookies did not react to news of Westwood's injury; shrewd punters did and collected when Monty finished third, six shots ahead of Westwood.

Clued-up punters were also quick to cash in on inside information before a Mercantile Credit Classic snooker match between James Wattana and Gary Wilkinson in January 1992. Wattana was the 6-5 underdog on the morning of the match, but by the time the action began he had shortened to 8-13 with Coral, who had on-site betting facilities at the Bournemouth venue. Punters who follow the snooker circuit closely discovered mid-afternoon that Wilkinson was struggling to shake off a severe bout of flu. Steadily, cash piled on Wattana but bookies were spared a massive pay-out by a chance conversation overheard by a Coral representative in Bournemouth.

Wilkinson's father mentioned to a friend that his son was so ill that it had been touch and go whether he would be well enough to play. The Coral mole quickly alerted his bosses who reacted swiftly by slashing Wattana's odds. The Coral move alerted rival firms and they too cut Wattana. By then some hefty bets had already been laid but bookies managed to avoid serious damage as Wattana strolled to a 5-3 win.

Woods had the flu but won; Wilkinson had it but lost – how can the poor punter make sense of that, you may well ask. There is no rhyme or reason to it. Well, actually, there is. Given a dose of flu, I reckon I'd much sooner play golf in the fresh air than be cooped up in a grimy, smoky snooker hall, where the debilitating effects of the virus would be more keenly felt.

I've played five-a-side with flu and felt one hundred per cent better afterwards; I've played snooker, similarly under the weather, and afterwards felt a thousand times worse. Note, too, the different degrees of illness suffered by Woods and Wilkinson in the above examples. Woods was never in danger of pulling out of the Matchplay so we can assume he was troubled by only a mildish dose of flu. Wilkinson, on the other hand, sounded almost at death's door.

I will argue long into the night that one of the best-value bets I've ever placed was on Jan Siemerink at 2-1 to beat Greg Rusedski in the third round of the US Open in September 1998. Rusedski, having reached the final the previous year, was a red-hot favourite at 4-11.

Now, you may have believed that Rusedski was one of the greatest players in the world, and was therefore a good thing to beat his Dutch opponent. You may even have taken that 4-11. If you did, then you are a half-wit. The more diligent punter would have watched Rusedski struggle in his earlier two rounds against Wayne Ferreira (who wasted two match points) and Bohdan

Ulihrach (who wasted one match point); would have clocked that Rusedski was still troubled by a nagging ankle injury that had wrecked his Wimbledon and put him on the sidelines for two months; and would certainly have noted with great interest that Siemerink had won the last three hard-court meetings between the two players.

Under those circumstances, even if you fancied Rusedski for your life, the only logical call was Siemerink at 2-1. He was undoubtedly the value bet. Guess what? Siemerink won in five sets.

Rusedski had admitted all tournament that his ankle was still a problem, yet bookies priced up that game as though he was 100 per cent fit. Absolutely crazy. It's essential if you are a punter to build injury doubts into your calculations. You may beware opposing "the sick golfer" but backing against the *injured* golfer, and the *injured* tennis player is a sound, almost certainly profitable punting strategy.

Of course there are other factors besides injury and illness which will impinge upon a player's performance. We saw in the opening chapter of this book how Jimmy The Greek made a killing by opposing the college basketball team whose captain had just been dumped by his long-time girlfriend, and there are numerous other instances where events away from the heat of battle have seriously influenced results.

Australian golfer Stuart Appleby bore up heroically well to the tragic death of his wife just after the Open Championship at Royal Birkdale in 1998. On his return to the golf course at the US PGA Championship little more than a month later, the whole world wanted him to do well. But it came as no surprise to see Appleby miss the cut and struggle throughout the remainder of the season.

Steffi Graf has been plagued over the last few years by injury but her loss of form could also have had much to do with the worries about her father Peter, who for so long was under the scrutiny of tax investigators in Germany.

Arsenal clinched the Premiership title by beating Everton 4-0 at Highbury on 3 May 1998. It was their tenth consecutive victory in a startling end-of-season run and the players, we can easily imagine, celebrated long and hard. Three days later, possibly still hung over and with nothing to play for, they went to Anfield for their final League game, just ten days before their FA Cup Final date with Newcastle. Liverpool were 5-4 to win that game and were, as I told everyone who would listen, the bet of the year. Liverpool won 4-0.

Eric Bristow was red-hot 2-7 favourite to beat Gary Mawson in his final group match in the WDC World Darts Championships in January 1997. He lost 3-1, a result that came as no surprise whatsoever to more-informed punters. The single set gained by Bristow, who had won his earlier group matches, was enough to see him through to the last eight, and the Crafty Cockney admitted afterwards that once he'd chalked up that first set he lost interest.

Andre Agassi, magnificently talented, lost his head over Hollywood actress Brooke Shields, later to become his wife (even later to become his ex-wife), and for the first year of their relationship Agassi was a player any punter would happily have opposed.

Many have argued that the true reason for Brazilian striker Ronaldo's near nervous breakdown during the 1998 World Cup, which had a massive impact on his country's performance in the final, were fears that his beautiful girlfriend, Suzanna Werner, was on the verge of running off with another man, a Brazilian sports commentator.

And who, apart from those aware of his illicit liaisons with blonde teenager Brenda Cepelak, young enough to be the 40-year-old's daughter, could have predicted the startling decline during 1997 and 1998 of the former world No.1 golfer Nick Faldo?

All of these off-the-field disturbances had a negative impact on the sports stars involved, but punters should also look out for positive developments too, although these are much rarer.

Swiss tennis player Marc Rosset, at one time ranked ninth in the world, was very much a player to oppose in 1998. From the end of February, Rosset's form nosedived catastrophically and he was a safe bet to make an early exit from every tournament he entered. I'll admit here that a large portion of my gambling winnings in 1998 came from opposing Rosset. Then, in September, Rosset narrowly escaped death in amazing circumstances.

He made his customary early exit from a tournament, this time the US Open, and booked a flight back to Geneva the following day. At the last minute, Rosset decided to change his mind and stayed on in New York for further practice with his coach. The Swiss-Air plane he should have caught crashed, killing all 229 passengers.

I'm deeply ashamed to admit here that one of my first thoughts on hearing of Rosset's near-miss was to make a mental note to keep tabs on his future results. How would he react? That so many people had perished took second place to thoughts of making capital out of Rosset's brush with death. That is unforgivable, I know, but it's the way a punter's mind works.

For the record, Rosset, perhaps suddenly realising how precious life is, was a rejuvenated performer and reached a quarter-final and three semi-finals before the end of the season. His good form continued into 1999 with a victory in St Petersburg and a quarter-final appearance in the Australian Open in the first two months of the season.

You will see from all this that to be a successful punter we must not only have a comprehensive knowledge of the sports on which we bet, but a keen grasp of current affairs too. In betting there is no substitute for information. If we know things the bookies don't, things that can have a bearing on a result or a performance, then that is the time to strike. You can not be a successful punter with a half-hearted attitude. Read as much as you can. Take notes. Surf the Internet. If we're well-read, we'll stay out of the red.

# chapter 5

## poker – the real deal

The only way this chapter can make you a better gambler is for you to accept one unpalatable truth: however good a poker player you think you are, you are in fact only half as good.

It's true of us all, whether a small-timer playing at a mate's house every Friday night, or a world champion. When we win, it's all down to skill; lose, and it's rank bad luck. I know my limitations at football, tennis and golf. Particularly golf. But in poker, I'm king. There's absolutely nothing those know-it-alls at the World Series in Vegas can teach me. I know all about the tells, the semi-bluffing, the terrors of the tilt. I know the odds. I know the lot. I do. And I'd be making a fortune from poker, if only I didn't keep getting crap cards.

You don't have to be a genius to recognise that all of the above is bollocks; or to give it its Latin name, *bollockus sheerus unadulterati*. I could fill three books on what I *don't* know about poker, barely a chapter on what I *do*. But the words of wisdom you are about to read over the next few pages are the result of many years of losing in pub card schools, plus interviews and tips from some of the world's top poker players.

Quite probably your introduction to the twilight world of poker was hit 1965 movie *The Cincinnati Kid*, in particular the fabulous climactic scenes when The Kid (Steve McQueen) loses out to Lancey Howard (Edward G Robinson). This was how poker was meant to be. Two of the best, most fearless poker players in the world, locked in combat until a fight to the death in the shape of two 1,000,000-1 hands.

Actually, that's all bollocks, too. The big hand that climaxes the movie is, according to acclaimed poker player and author Anthony

Holden, "still laughed to scorn in card rooms the world over."

The Kid's full house of aces on tens was beaten by Lancey's queen-high straight flush. It's been calculated that the odds about *any* full house being beaten by *any* straight flush in a two-handed game of five-card stud are 45,102,784-1. The odds about these two particular hands, given that The Kid's contained two tens and Lancey's a further ten, are an astronomical 332,220,508,619-1 – or well over 300 billion-1.

According to Holden in his superb 1990 book *Big Deal*, the two could play 50 hands of five-card stud an hour, eight hours a day, five days a week, and the same two hands would appear about once every 433 years.

The Cincinnati Kid, all the evidence screams, was a half-wit to allow himself to be cleaned out by Lancey. Lady Fingers (the dealer) must have been in cahoots with Lancey.

"Why didn't the Cincinnati Kid start screaming foul when he got beat?" asked columnist Michael Weisenberg in the *Poker Player* magazine. "If you got beat like that, would you just walk away shaking your head, muttering to yourself 'Well, them's the breaks'?"

We're perhaps being a little hard on The Kid here. Actually it was Lancey Howard who played like a novice. Any professional player worth his salt would have folded long before filling that straight flush.

There are around eight million poker players in Britain. All eight million think they're better, far better, than they actually are. It's a golden rule of the game. Another is: "If you haven't spotted the chump in the first half-hour, it's you."

How many of that eight million, it's worth wondering, know that poker is a game of odds and strategy more than chance?

How many know, for instance, that it's an even-money shot that they will be dealt not even a single pair straight off in a game of five-card draw poker? That it's a 508-1 chance against them pulling a flush? Or that the odds against being dealt three of a kind are 46-1?

How many of that eight million know that it's just over an 11-1 chance that two pairs will turn into a magical full house on the draw? Or that it's 9-2 about four diamonds (or hearts, clubs or spades) improving into a flush?

Very few, I would wager. But any professional player who cannot repeat these figures parrot fashion will very soon be penniless.

It's an 11-1 chance that you'll fill an inside straight. To you and I those odds may seem acceptable. Come on, we've all tried it. But a pro never will. What's the point in going for an 11-1 chance when there's no chance of winning at least 11 times your stake?

If you're going to make your poker pay, it's essential you know your odds from your elbow. The table below refers to ordinary five-card draw poker. It shows the odds against improving your hand on the draw.

| Cards kept | Cards drawn | Improved hand | Odds against |
|---|---|---|---|
| Ace on its own | Four | One pair | 4-1 |
| Ace on its own | Four | Three aces | 63-1 |
| One pair | Three | Two pair | 5.25-1 |
| One pair | Three | Three of a kind | 8-1 |
| One pair | Three | Full house | 97-1 |
| Two pair | One | Full house | 11-1 |
| Four straight (open-ended) | One | Straight | 5-1 |
| Four-straight (inside) | One | Straight | 11-1 |
| Four-flush | One | Flush | 4.5-1 |
| Three-flush | Two | Flush | 23-1 |

There are 2,598,960 possible five-card poker hands. In every one thousand deals, the ranking hands will theoretically appear as often as follows: no pair: 503 times; one pair: 422 times; two pairs: 47 times; three of a kind: 21 times; straight: 3.9 times; flush: 1.9 times. The table opposite illustrates the odds about pulling certain hands before the draw.

But if all poker pros are wizards of odds, surely it's pure luck that separates the great from the good. Well, luck does play a part, as it must do in every card game, but strategy and psychology are the deciding factors. First, the strategy.

| Quantity in deck | Hand | Odds against |
|---|---|---|
| 4 | Royal flush | 649,739-1 |
| 40 | Straight flush | 64,973-1 |
| 624 | Four of a kind | 4,164-1 |
| 3,744 | Full house | 693-1 |
| 5,108 | Flush | 508-1 |
| 10,200 | Straight | 254-1 |
| 54,912 | Three of a kind | 46-1 |
| 123,552 | Two pairs | 20-1 |
| 1,098,240 | One pair | 1.25-1 |
| 1,302,540 | No pair | Evens |

Former world champion Doyle Brunson was, during his days at the top, from the Poker School of Aggression. These were his tactics: "By playing aggressively, you'll be able to break a lot of players because you're in there gambling all the time. And because of that you'll get a lot of your real good hands paid off. Tight players don't get the real good hands paid off because they make a move so rarely that their hands are an open book whenever they do. But you'll be out there betting, betting, betting – all the time. Your opponents will see you're an aggressive player. They'll know you're out there trying to pick up all those loose pots, so they'll sometimes give you a little loose action. And since you'll sometimes hold the best hand, you'll break one or two of them. After that they'll be scared to get involved with you."

As for the psychology, the tale of esteemed US professional Jack Straus, who once said "If the Lord had wanted you to hold on to your money he'd have made it with handles on", is perhaps the best illustration. Straus was playing Hold'em Poker, a form of seven-card stud in which each player is dealt two hole cards (face down) with which he must improve on five communal cards gradually revealed in the centre of the table. There are four rounds of betting.

The first comes after the first two hole cards have been dealt; the second follows the unveiling of the first three communal cards (the flop); the next after the fourth communal card (fourth street); and a final round after the fifth (fifth street).

This was how Anthony Holden, in *Big Deal*, saw the hand.

"Straus was dealt 7-2 not suited, the worst hand in the deck. But he was on a roll at the time so he raised anyway, and only one other player stayed with him. The flop was dealt - 7-3-3, giving Straus two pairs (7s and 3s). He bet again, but as he did so he saw his opponent's hand reach quickly for his chips, and he knew he had made a mistake. The other guy, Straus guessed, had a big pair in the hole (it was in fact two jacks); with great confidence he raised Straus' $5,000.

"At that point the logical move was to fold since Straus was certain he was beaten and only a bluff could save him. But he called, thereby sowing doubt in the other player's mind.

"The dealer turned over the fourth card - a deuce. It paired Straus' second hole card but did not improve his hand since there was already a communal pair of threes on the board. In other words he knew he was still losing. Without hesitating, Straus bet $18,000. There was a long, long silence while the other man considered the implications of the bet. Then Straus leaned forward, smiling his most charming, lop-sided smile. 'I'll tell you what,' he said. 'You give me one of those little $25 chips of yours and you can see either of my cards, whichever you choose.' Another silence. Finally the man tossed over a $25 chip and pointed to one of the cards in front of Straus. Straus turned it over: a deuce. Another long silence. The only logical explanation for Straus' offer was that the two cards in front of him were the same, so the flop gave him a full house of deuces. The other man folded his winning hand."

Straus explained later: "It's just a matter of simple psychology."

Straus, by the way, is the man who was reduced by a long, lousy run to his last $40 in the whole world. No thoughts of quitting. Instead, priced out of the poker game, he upped his $40 to $500 on the blackjack table, ran it up to $4,000 in a medium-stakes poker game, and then hit the magic $10,000 playing blackjack again. But even this wasn't enough. He put the whole $10,000 on Kansas City Chiefs at 2-1 to win the Super Bowl, converting his $40 to $30,000 in less than 24 hours.

Big-league poker players are a breed apart, with a language and a style all of their own. When a journalist asked poker-pro Amarillo Slim why a Texas oil millionaire who could not be scared out of a pot would not eventually see off the professionals, he was told: "Son, that millionaire would have as much chance in a game with us as you would of getting a French kiss out of the Statue Of Liberty."

Two-time world champion Johnny Chan had an unusual trademark. Quite apart from wearing stylish sweatsuits that allowed maximum comfort in marathon games, and often calmly listening to music from a walkman while big-money games were in progress, Chan would place an unpeeled orange among his towers of chips.

Opinion was divided about his motives. Some said it was his good-luck charm, others an air-freshener to combat smoke-filled card rooms, but I have an alternative theory. Can you imagine the effect of that orange on rival players if Chan was way ahead of the game? It would thoroughly piss them off, becoming more annoying the more hands Chan won.

If I was an opponent watching Chan shovel up chips, my chips, I would want to shove that orange down his smug chops. Itching to get back at him, my play would become ragged, and Chan would win even more. And that fucking orange would still be sitting there, laughing at me.

There's something else that all the top players have in common – an ability, call it intuition if you like, to read an opponent's tell-tale signs, or 'tells' as they are called in the trade.

A blink of the eye, a scratch of the head, a blow of the nose: to you and I, nothing more than normal everyday human behaviour; to the professional card player they're tell-tale signs of strength. A poker-face isn't enough. In a world where a smile betrays a prial, where fortunes are won and lost in a night, and where lives can be wrecked on the turn of a card, an involuntary twitch can spell doom.

Coolness is the god of the card table. Your pulse can quicken at the sight of a mini-skirted blonde but any reaction to a full house and you're a dead man.

One card-table veteran told me: "Every poker player needs an edge, so you're constantly looking for give-away signs in the behaviour of opponents. Some will take a drag of their cigarette, maybe ask for a drink if they've got a good hand. Others may rub their chin. They're all signs. Sometimes they're signs of a bluff, but it's up to you to decide which is which.

"I sincerely believe that I never do anything to betray the strength of my cards, but I'm sure all other players think the same. I've played in games where men have sat with towels around their necks to hide their pulse."

In the excellent *Big Deal*, Anthony Holden wrote: "At the table a player may tend to scratch his ear, or fiddle nervously with his ring, if he is bluffing; or, more subtly, a hollow note in his betting pattern – a raise too aggressive or a call too timid – may betray him. He probably will be the last person to recognise this; it is axiomatic that no poker player, unless of course he is double-bluffing, is aware of his own 'tells'. Once his opponents have isolated them, however, such giveaway habits are worth a great deal – at least as much as they are to the husband or wife who can say 'you were never a very good liar'.

"Whether he likes it or not, a man's character is stripped bare at the poker table; if the other players read him better than he does, he has only himself to blame. Unless he is both able and prepared to see himself as others do, flaws and all, he will be a loser in cards as in life."

The biggest tell of all in this twilight world is known as "the poker tremble". Typically this occurs in hands when the pot is unusually large. But note that if a player trembles when putting in his chips it is usually NOT a sign of fear at a big hand. It is more often a release of tension and a sign that he's pulled a winning card.

There are two kinds of tells – unaware and acting. Unaware tells refer to players who don't realise they are tipping off their opponents. For instance, players who stack their chips neatly in separate piles are invariably tight, cautious players; those who have them strewn haphazardly are quite often reckless players. Acting tells are performed by players who tell us the opposite of what they want us to think. A player acting strong, perhaps by getting ready a pile of his chips before his turn to bet, may quite often have a weak hand. The opposite applies too, of course.

If in any card school you're having trouble working out who the prize mug is, poker wisdom says it must be you. You will probably be guilty of one or more of poker's seven deadly sins.

- Playing too often
- Calling too often
- Rabbit-hunting
- Hesitation
- Recklessness
- Showing cards
- Going for the jackpot

**Playing too often:** If you're going to win money from poker you should figure on playing on average between one in 12 hands. Come on, there aren't that many good starting cards. Players who are in too often just want to see cards. Sure, by playing so few hands you'll get stick from your mates, but flak is much easier to accept when your pockets are full of dough.

If seven-card stud poker is your game, these are the only hands after the first three cards that you should consider playing with: three of a kind (which you'll see rarely), pairs, three to a flush, three consecutive cards to a straight, and three high cards (above ten). So many players stick around with just a couple of high cards, no pair, or two to a flush or straight. These people are stupid. Quite possibly skint, too. Those kind of cards are crap. If you do have a high pair, say queens, from the first three cards, play aggressively if there is no ace or king showing on the table, but play tentatively if there is a higher card showing.

**Calling too often:** Players guilty of this are known in the trade as 'calling stations'. The weakest bet of all is a call. It's not necessarily wrong, but the player who calls persistently is not exploiting his opportunities.

**Rabbit-hunting:** This is the term for asking to see the next card after a hand is over. We've all done it and we've all been sickened when the next card shows us we'd have won had we stuck around and not been frightened out of the pot. There's no point in torturing yourself. This is a trait found only in weak players.

**Hesitation:** Consistent dithering indicates a weak player.

**Recklessness:** Often referred to as going on tilt, an expression borrowed from pinball machines, which 'tilt' when shaken too much. It describes the out-of-control poker player who throws bad money after bad. It's normally brought on by a combination of bad luck, poor concentration or intimidation by other players (Johnny Chan's orange for instance). Those afflicted are normally losing a stack, although big winners are sometimes prone to it in the belief that they are invincible. One minute they are hiding behind a mountain of chips, the next there are just three left.

Nic Szeremeta, of *Card Player Magazine*, says: "Players on tilt do all sorts of irrational things; they raise on the first round with junk cards just in case they catch miracle cards; if they're holding a pair of fives they appear magically to turn into a pair of aces; the bigger the bet an opponent makes the more reasons the tilt victim finds for believing it is a bluff; and inside-straight draws become a matter of course." One of the qualifications a player requires to be capable of going on tilt is to be of a reasonable standard. This is because poor players might be regarded as permanently on tilt.

**Showing cards:** Giving away information unnecessarily is lunacy. The lunatics have two reasons for doing this: first to try to justify their strategy; second, to show off after a successful bluff. All it is telling opponents is: "I'm prepared to bluff, so make sure you see me next time."

**Going for the jackpot:** Instead of folding, the player will go for the impossible, maybe trying to fill an inside straight, or staying in for two last cards to fill out a flush. Crazy. Crazy. Crazy.

If you can avoid these seven deadly sins you've more than half a chance of making your poker far more profitable.

Of course even the best players will struggle on a regular diet of bad cards but these guys have learned to make the best of the worst by using one of poker's most potent weapons – the bluff. No two people will ever agree on the rights and wrongs of bluffing but one fact is irrefutable. Even if you do not have a strong hand, the cards you have showing must make it look as though you have. An extreme example is four hearts, ace high, showing in a game of seven-card stud. You may not have the flush but you have a very real chance of scaring off your rivals.

It's crucial to identify the right time to bluff. Don't do it when rival hands look strong – chances are they'll have pulled a winning card and no amount of bluffing will scare them off. And don't try to bluff several opponents at the same time. Ideally it should be just one opponent or, just occasionally, two.

Know the strategies of rival players, too. When you run a bluff you should do so in the knowledge that your opponent has a fair chance of folding. There is absolutely no point in bluffing against a calling station – a player who will call on anything.

Some players regard bluffing as a mere cosmetic exercise – a ploy to increase their chances of being called when they do have a big hand. These players will quite often reveal their cards at the end of a hand to show what junk they were bluffing with. These players are to be coveted because they are destined forever to be losers. While it is true that a by-product of bluffing is that other players may be more willing to call when you bet, the main objective has always been to win the pot with a bad hand.

An obvious example of a perfect time to bluff in five-card draw poker is when you hit three of a kind before the draw. The ideal strategy here is to raise, and then take one card instead of two. Clearly this will halve you chance of pulling four of a kind but your odds on making the full house are the same as if you drew two cards. If you bet or raise again after the draw, you will be called by players holding two pairs. But if you draw two cards to your three of a kind, those players will pass. You may also be called on the basis that you might be bluffing.

Nic Szeremeta gives a tip to make your bluffing more decisive. It's not one I necessarily agree with, but Nic has been around the block more than me, so his advice is worth noting. "Bluffing," says Nic, "often relies on decisiveness to succeed so anything to make your bluffs more convincing should be welcomed. Say you hold four cards to a heart flush before the draw. If you hit you will obviously bet, but you may also win by bluffing if you miss. The way to decide is to bluff if the card you draw is any picture card which doesn't make your flush. This means that you have nine cards which will make your flush (i.e. the nine remaining hearts) and nine others on which to bluff. The effect is to randomise your betting in such a way that your opponent will have no idea what you are up to."

The very best poker players are expert in what has become known in the trade as 'the semi-bluff'. This perhaps can best be described as a bet which, if called, does not figure to be the best hand at that moment but has a reasonable chance of outdrawing those hands which initially called it. Notice that, by definition, there must be cards to come in a semi-bluff situation.

The semi-bluff gives you two ways to win. First, the opposition may fold; second, your hand may improve to win a big pot. Here's a specific example from Hold'em Poker: You hold Jack and ten of spades and the flop comes eight, seven, two of mixed suits. A bet or a raise here would be described as a semi-bluff. An opponent who calls is likely to have you beaten, with probably at least a pair of eights or sevens. But you still have ten cards which will give you a winning hand; three jacks and three tens would give you a higher pair, and any of the four nines will give you a near unbeatable straight. And remember you still have two more cards to come.

There is also a bonus here because if you have semi-bluffed on the flop and the fourth card doesn't help, your opponent will most likely check to you and let you have the fifth card free.

I cannot finish this chapter without recounting the incredible story of big-time gambler Archie Karas, who won $20 million from virtually nothing, thanks to the most aggressive gambling strategy in the history of betting. Bear in mind before digesting this marvellous tale that even the best poker players get edgy when the stakes are high. Money may play a part in other gambling games like blackjack and roulette, but in those games the money and the outcome are unconnected. The fact that you may have a fiver on the spin of a roulette wheel doesn't influence the path of the ball. But in poker, money is the essential ingredient. Not only does a bet convey information, it also alters the odds.

Take the following, perhaps over-simplified, example. There is £100 in the pot and you hold a straight, with one card to come. Your opponent has four cards to a heart flush and needs a heart to beat you. His odds of drawing that card in Texas Hold'em are 38-9, or just over 4-1. If you bet £100, your opponent will have to bet £100 as well; he'll therefore be betting £100 to win £200, which at odds of 2-1 is not value. However, if you bet £20 (some players might even do this to lure in an opponent) you will be giving him odds of 6-1 (£20 to £120) about a 4-1 shot. In the first case, he cannot call; in the second, he must. Money, therefore, is your ammunition; the bullets in your smoking poker gun.

And it was with such bullets that Greek-born Karas amounted his fortune in Las Vegas in 1994, after a run which prompted one poker veteran to comment: "Playing cards with Karas is like playing Russian roulette. If I use a gun with two bullets and I give you one with one bullet, you're a big favourite to live longer than me. But are you going to play? It's suicidal."

With a bankroll of $50, Karas first headed for the poker room at the Mirage Hotel and somehow persuaded a fellow gambler to loan him a stake. Within a few hours he had rolled it up to $20,000 – the start of what Vegas insiders now refer to simply as The Run. He returned the borrowed money to his benefactor, with a $10,000 thank you present.

Next on his hit-list was a high-rolling casino boss who fancied himself as a pool-room shark. Karas' offer of $10,000 a frame was eagerly accepted; what the would-be shark didn't know was that the Greek had been pool-hustling since he was a teenager. By the time the marathon session was over, Karas had hit the casino boss for $1 million.

Now bosses of Las Vegas casinos, however high-rolling they might be, do not take kindly to dropping a million, so this one, who also happened to be a former world poker champion, suggested a big-hitting poker session. Just the two of them. Head to head. Winner takes all. Karas once again was the winner, relieving his rival of another $1 million. Suddenly the Vegas grapevine was buzzing. Who was this new kid (Karas was actually 43) on the block? It was surely only outrageous luck that had taken him so far; only a matter of time before he squandered his newly-won $2 million.

So Chip Reese, another world-class poker player, was the first to throw down the gauntlet. Within a fortnight he was $2 million down. As he got up from the table after the final, stamina-sapping session, Reese allegedly told Karas: "Greek, God made your balls a little bigger. You're too good."

Former world champions queued up to take a pop at the new Vegas Goldenballs. In succession he had Stu Ungar, Doyle Brunson and Johnny Chan waving the white flag and was $7 million richer. With a multi-million dollar fortune burning a hole in his pocket, Karas took on the legendary Horseshoe Casino, home of the World Poker Championship, in downtown Vegas. This time the game was different – craps – but the result was the same, with the Horseshoe handing over $12 million. Pretty soon, no-one wanted to play with Karas any longer.

But what was the secret of this incredible run? In a word, fearlessness.

"I'm the biggest gambler in the history of the world," Karas said at the time. "All other gamblers win a bit and then stop, but I'm fearless. I just carry on until I think I've won enough for the time being. Even as a kid I always played against the best, and I always bet everything I had.

"If I lose it's like a kick in the stomach. It makes me feel sick. But while I'm at the table, I concentrate very hard on what I'm doing.

"When you play poker you're taking on human beings. They're only flesh and blood. They can be scared easily..."

# chapter 6

## in the line of fire

Gambling is responsible for the two most terrifying episodes I've ever experienced.

Four days of round-the-clock punting in the casinos of Las Vegas was finally to be relieved by a light-aircraft flight to the Grand Canyon. Come on McGovern, the idea was, grab a bit of culture. You can play blackjack anywhere, but a bird's-eye view of one of the world's geological wonders does not come around often. So my mate John and I stumbled – reluctantly perhaps; bleary-eyed most definitely – from the gaming tables of the MGM Grand to the taxi rank outside for the short trip to the airport. Big mistake. Huge.

If you learn nothing else from this book learn this: never ever fly in a light aircraft over the Grand Canyon. Particularly when it's windy. Death said a cheery hello as brutal air currents tossed us around like a schoolboy's paper aeroplane. One minute we were gliding majestically, kings of all we surveyed; the next, our stomachs exited through our mouths as the aircraft plunged like a stone. It was only later, in the sanctuary of the casino, that we learned such trips to the Grand Canyon had caused dozens of deaths and that concerned Vegas residents were campaigning to outlaw them.

Yet that Vegas episode registered barely a shiver on the Richter Scale of fear compared with the sheer paralysis of being caught in the middle of an armed betting shop raid.

That was real fear.

It was a William Hill betting shop in Liverpool, early afternoon on an Easter Monday. A strange time, you'd have thought, for a raid, given that only a few races had been completed and the tills were unlikely to be bulging. But the two robbers seemed not of the patient kind. And that made them a thousand times scarier.

The black balaclavas they wore were bad news. The shotguns they carried were worse.

"Get against the wall. Now!" Balaclava One screamed at 20 or so punters who moments earlier had been tearing up betting slips after an unfancied 16-1 shot had won the first.

At first I thought it was a wind-up. Someone would burst out laughing in a minute. But nobody did.

"Move," he screamed again, and suddenly the barrel was pointing straight at me. Why me for Christ's sake?

Cleverly I managed as I hurried towards the far wall to manoeuvre another punter between Balaclava One and me, but how could I be sure a bullet wouldn't blast through his body and still hit me?

It was then I became aware of Balaclava Two. He was standing at the pay-out desk, shotgun pointed at the white-faced manager, who was virtually throwing banknotes at him, while one of the two female cashiers was crying hysterically. I can't remember what the other was doing – possibly still painting her nails.

"Move it, you gobshite," he screamed at the manager with the politeness of a betting shop regular.

Two more fears now. Some of the punters, incredibly as it seems, began shifting impatiently from one leg to the other, seemingly annoyed that their afternoon of punting had been interrupted. What to me was the most terrifying moment of my life seemed to them a mere irritation. Surely they weren't about to have a go, were they? For God's sake, lads, you might fancy one in the next but it's not worth getting killed for. How many of us would die for an act of foolishness disguised as heroism?

Then an even bigger fear. Ten minutes earlier, I'd left my dad in the pub with his mate. "I'll see you over there in a minute," he'd said to me. Now there was a hammering on the betting shop door, bolted shut by the Balaclavas.

Balaclava One whirled around. He'd been getting more edgy by the second and the commotion outside seemed to panic him. The banging got louder and more urgent. Balaclava One screamed at his mate to get a move on, but his body language spoke more eloquently. He was about to blast a hole in the door, and anyone, my dad probably, standing behind it. Oh no. Oh fucking no.

His eyes darted between the pay-out window and the door and you knew what was going through his tiny, warped mind. "Please," I silently urged the poor, terrified betting shop manager. "Please, get a move on and let them be gone."

Then in a flash they *were* gone. Out the back. For a few seconds, nobody moved, the only sound the sobbing of the hysterical cashier and the comforting words of her colleague, nails by now completed. "It's okay Tracey. It's okay. They've gone."

A real man would have gone to check that the staff, clearly in more peril than the rest of us, were okay. But there were no real men in the Hills shop that day.

One of the more daring punters had unlocked the door and as a fresh wave streamed in, wondering why they'd been barred, we traipsed out and went our separate ways, like Henry Fonda and his fellow jurors at the end of *Twelve Angry Men*. My dad was still in the pub.

Betting shop robberies are one of the chief concerns of the country's leading bookmakers. The numbers may have decreased over the last ten years because of a number of deterrents introduced, but the levels of violence have most certainly increased. In the last ten years, two betting shop workers have been killed as a result of bungled raids.

Chris Bird is the head of security at Hills. Reluctant though he is to estimate the scale of betting shop crime, he recognises its seriousness and the effect it can have on employees.

"It is a very traumatic experience for any victim of a betting shop robbery," said Bird. "Some may never be able to work in such an environment again."

He insists that the crime prevention techniques taught by the leading firms have helped halve the number of betting shop robberies in the last ten years.

There are four steps bookies take to cut crime.

- **Strict cash controls.** Bird would not explain what this phrase meant, but a betting shop manager of 20 years told me quite often it means banking any excess cash. That may lessen the risk of the cash being stolen in the first place – robbers are more likely to strike inside a betting shop than in broad daylight in the High Street – but it surely increases the risk of the employee being harmed when a villain does decide to pounce. Managers in larger shops will also use a floor safe – a secret vault hidden beneath the floor in addition to the regular safe normally targeted by villains – to house wads of banknotes. But again villains are wise to these tricks.

- **Staff training and alertness.** Always keep the counter door locked; be alert when venturing on to the shop floor alongside customers, that kind of thing. Hardly crime-busting stuff, you'd have thought.

- **Bandit screens.** These were acclaimed as highly effective deterrents when they were introduced in the 1980s but many shops, preferring to concentrate more on customer relations than staff safety, scrapped them in the early 1990s, following the example of banks and building societies. Said Bird: "You have to be selective about which shops should and should not have bandit screens. For instance, you're not going to take them down in, say, Brixton, but you might in the wilds of Devon." But bandit screens are effective only in deterring the opportunist raider who would otherwise vault over the counter and threaten staff with, say, a knife. The screens, far from being bullet-proof, shatter beneath a hefty blow and you can imagine the terror that would provoke in victims. Further, there's little to stop raiders booting down the door which separates staff from punters.

- **Closed-circuit TV.** Probably the most effective deterrent but again a long way from being villain-proof. Bird says CCTV is effective not only in terms of preventing crime but also in detection. He pointed out that many raiders, hard though it is to believe, wear no disguise and even those who do often have tell-tale physical characteristics. I mentioned that it is not beyond the wit of villains either to disable the machinery or demand from staff the video tapes, but Bird claimed that in most cases the staff are not told where the tapes are and raiders are unlikely to waste time, crucial in a robbery, in a search. Some would suggest that keeping such information from employees heightens the risk of those employees being hurt by an armed gunman refusing to believe their protestations of ignorance. It should also be noted that closed-circuit TV is costly and not financially viable for every betting shop.

Bird did not mention panic buttons – a device for staff under attack to contact police discreetly – presumably because he does not want to alert villains to their existence. But I would suggest that only the most greenhorn of robbers is unaware of panic buttons, and I would also suggest that any employee facing the barrel of a sawn-off shotgun would be mighty foolish to even think of pushing one.

I asked both Hills and Ladbrokes to give some indication of the scale of betting shop crime – how many shops are hit, what levels of violence are used, that kind of thing – but, fearful of encouraging further robberies, both firms were reluctant to comment.

Sean Boyce, public relations manager of Ladbrokes, responded to my queries with a polite, though not very revealing, letter.

"We do not want to comment on all of your specific queries," he wrote, "partly for security reasons and partly because we believe that staff and shop security is an area where we have made considerable progress and prefer to concentrate on the positive in relation to an issue that is very important to all of us in this business.

"Ladbroke Racing Ltd has a policy of not commenting directly on individual criminal incidents. As well as making sure that we do not compromise security it is also vital to us that our staff are, as far as possible, protected from any threat of pressure or intimidation by those involved in such activities.

"Like any other cash-based high street business, a betting shop can be a target for criminals. Without being complacent, it is very important that the scale and impact of this issue is kept in proper perspective. The fact is that the number of incidents of shop robbery has been in decline for some years now, as improved security techniques have come into effect and better practices employed.

"As responsible employers our prime concern is the health and safety of our employees, and in this area in particular Ladbrokes has made considerable progress during recent years. It is company policy to ensure that any member of our staff who has been affected by any such incident receives all the help and support that they require. It is now accepted practice that an experienced colleague will be directly appointed as a one-to-one 'buddy' for any affected member of staff.

"The appointed 'buddy' will know the personality and needs of their individual colleague well, and will be empowered to recommend whatever help and support they themselves deem to be necessary. In dealing with the needs of an employee in these circumstances, it is the views of their immediate colleagues and workmates that carry the most weight and their recommendations will be heeded by line management and department heads."

I have a sister, Jean, who has managed betting shops for more than 15 years. It was a job she enjoyed, until a particularly violent raid on her Ladbrokes shop in September 1995 left her traumatised and off work for six months. Today she still has nightmares.

"It was two men in their twenties," she recalled. "They didn't wear masks or balaclavas but one had a gun, one of those with a long barrel like something out of a Clint Eastwood film. The shop was pretty full, probably around 25 punters, but they were all glued to the TV screens watching a race. The two men – one of them looked a druggie type, really spaced out – vaulted the counter and one put the gun to my cashier Dave's head. 'Where's the money? Where's the money?' they demanded."

As the unarmed, druggie robber stuffed banknotes into his pockets, his accomplice tortured the young cashier for fun, first putting the barrel of the gun to his ear and then, hideously, in his mouth. By now the televised race was over and it had begun to dawn on punters exactly what they were witnessing. No-one moved a muscle.

When it became clear to the raiders that the amount of ready cash was substantially less than they had anticipated, they grew more violent. "Where's the rest of it?" Druggie demanded. Despite repeated denials that there *was* any more, the raiders grew uglier. "Shoot him. Go on. Do it now. In his mouth."

Jean had all this time stood, frozen, in the corner, unable to move or even talk, but something inside her suddenly snapped.

"WE HAVEN'T GOT ANY MORE!" she screamed at them.

With that they were gone.

Someone on SIS said the hare was running at Hackney and punters, the ones who moments earlier had hardly dared to breathe, rushed to get their bets on, as though the previous five minutes had never happened.

Police later asked for descriptions. Dave said the gunman wore a black jacket; Jean thought it was white. The only thing she could remember with any clarity was the shape and size of the gun, and a feeling of absolute terror. Yet horrendous though the experience was, worse was to follow for Jean and her colleague.

The young cashier, on his return to work in a different branch (after just a week on the sick), was attacked once more. This time his assailant beat him with an iron bar. So mentally scarred was Dave (as honest as the day is long, according to Jean) that he flipped. Jean heard months later that he had been sacked after walking off with the day's takings, an offence he did absolutely nothing to conceal.

Jean's return to work after a six-month lay-off coincided with a new cost-cutting policy by Ladbrokes, the company whose gaming division (betting shops in other words) made a profit of more than £100 million in 1997-98. In summer months, betting shops could operate until noon with just one member of staff, they declared loftily.

The traumatic effects of the robbery – the jumpiness, the suspicion of strangers, the terror of being left alone – she had expected; what shocked her most was what she described as the uncaring attitude of her firm.

"I told them, given what had happened, that I was not prepared to work in a shop on my own," she said. "But their reaction stunned me. I remember the exact words they used: 'If you're not prepared to accept it, we suggest you look for employment with one of the independents.'"

After 18 months of seeking alternative employment in a city of few job prospects, Jean, 43, was forced to return to life in a betting shop, although with a company which does not operate the single-staff policy.

"No-one who hasn't been through such an experience can possibly know what it does to you," said Jean. "I know I will never be the same person again. I have chosen to continue to work in this industry fully aware of the risks it carries. I'm not sure betting shops will ever again be safe places; all I ask is that victims of attacks are treated with kindness by their employers."

But whatever Hills and ladbrokes might say, the bad news for Britain's betting shop staff is that robberies will never stop because villains see them as easy targets. Bandit screens, panic buttons, closed-circuit TV – all are mere cosmetic exercises that will never deter the committed criminal.

'Mocko' (as we must call him) is a well-known Liverpool villain. He's done time for raids on security vans and banks, but has never once been caught for robbing a betting shop, even though for the first few years of his life of crime he carried out 40 raids, netting a total of £30,000 from bookmakers.

He used the stock tools of the trade – motorcycle crash helmet, handgun, shotgun – plus an intimidating physical presence and a frighteningly aggressive manner to terrify staff, and met resistance, quickly dealt with, only twice.

"It's easy money," he said matter-of-factly. "If ever I was short of a few quid, me and a mate would just go and do a betting shop. In and out inside three minutes, and the bizzies (police) would never have a chance of catching you."

His biggest haul was £2,000 on a Grand National day, his smallest a couple of hundred quid. "But it was money for old rope."

Mocko, seemingly oblivious to the effect on his victims of his actions, laughed when he told of hitting the same betting shop twice in one day.

"We hit it first in the morning. I knew we wouldn't get much but reckoned there had to be a couple of hundred quid in the float. I steamed over the counter with a gun and the manager, the only one behind the counter, shovelled the cash towards me without saying a word. But can you believe the board marker came rushing over trying to stop me? He must have been about 90. You've got to laugh. He kept going on about being in the war and he was getting on my tits to be honest, so we tied him up. Should have heard him.

"It was one of my local betting shops and for much of the rest of the day me and my mate were betting with the dough we'd robbed. By about 5 o'clock, we only had a fiver left between us, so we did the shop again. Same method, same messing around by the board marker. But this time as we were legging away the manager shouted: 'Bloody hell lads, how about a dropsie for me', so we left him 50 quid. That night I took the cashier who worked there to The Grafton (a Liverpool nightclub widely regarded as a pick-up joint) and gave her one. She was going on all night about her shop being robbed but didn't have a clue it was me who'd robbed it."

Mocko described his typical *modus operandi*. "For an out-of-town job we'd go there in the morning with maybe a grand between us and bet with it. If we won then fine, we'd leave the shop alone. But if we lost we'd be back just before closing time to rob it and get our dosh back. So we couldn't lose really.

"Mostly we hit a shop just before closing time when there were few punters about. We'd dive in, lock the door behind us, one of us would take care of the punters and the other would go to the counter. If there was no bandit screen we'd just leap across the counter and wave the gun at the staff. If there was a bandit screen we'd kick down the door. The staff would always be too terrified to do anything."

The vocabulary of terror was predictable, borrowed perhaps from a thousand B-movies. "If you don't move, no-one will get hurt."

The escape route differed. Out the back way whenever possible; through the front door otherwise. Any unsuspecting punter popping in for a late-afternoon bet was bundled in to the shop by a burly villain carrying a shotgun. Somehow you can imagine a quid each-way on Trap 4 at Monmore losing some of its appeal after such a scare.

In all 40 raids Mocko carried a gun, mostly a shotgun, sometimes a handgun. But he insists that never once did he come close to pulling the trigger. "Not for a betting shop job, no way," he said. "The kind of money we're talking about didn't merit shooting someone. Not once in all those robberies did anybody jump on us. And if they had done, they'd have got a good dig, not a bullet. We weren't off our heads on smack or anything like that. To us it was just an easy way to make a few quid. If any of the staff ever looked like making a move, maybe by edging towards a panic button, we'd just push them in the corner, swear loudly at them and point the gun at them. That usually did the trick."

Mocko said he was surprised, pleasantly, when so many bookies decided to do away with bandit screens. "Look, let's get one thing straight," he said. "If I want to rob a betting shop, a bandit screen's not gonna stop me, but given a choice of raiding a shop with screens and one without, I'll take the one without any day."

But although he conceded bandit screens are a slight deterrent, he argued that they increase the likelihood of further violence.

"If I vault over a counter waving a gun, there's no time for the staff to react, maybe even to panic. But if I first have to kick down a door or smash a screen, they could in those seconds try to press a panic button, or dial the police, and when that happens people get hurt. I think the big bookmakers realised that and is one of the reasons they got rid of the screens. Now they practically throw the money at you."

In the Easter Monday robbery I described earlier in this chapter, neither of the two robbers forced their way behind the jump, but Mocko argued that a raid could never be 100 per cent successful unless the counter was breached.

"If you're standing on the customer side of the counter they might just pass you a bag with a few quid in and say they've got nothing more left. On their side of the counter, you get them to open the safe, and very often there'll be a floor safe, perhaps under a carpet, with the bulk of the money in and it doesn't take you long to find it."

I asked Mocko whether his conscience ever pricked him, whether he ever agonised over the psychological damage his victims suffered.

"No."

What? Not ever?

"Sometimes when I heard that someone had been so terrified that they might never work again it shocked me, because to me it was just a game. I never treated it as some life-or-death gamble. But I couldn't waste my time worrying about them. Only the money mattered."

Mocko, in his late thirties, then told a story about his earlier gambling exploits that perhaps underlines his callousness. After leaving school, he fell in with a shady crowd who, when not on the rob, gambled from morning till evening. Particularly flush after a betting shop job, he bought a couple of greyhounds and placed them with a gambling trainer. On the day of the first dog's debut, with the money down, he gave it a dose of speed. But he overdid the dosage.

"It came out of the traps, got to the first bend, suddenly spun round in a circle as though chasing its tail, jumped over a barbed wire fence and out of the stadium, and I've never seen it since."

The second one was so slow that straight after its first run, Mocko carried it to the river and hurled it in. "I saw its head bob up first time," he recalled. "It was still wearing the trap-five jacket. I'm sure it said to me just before it went down again, 'I'll win the next one …'"

He said he was a gambler as young as 11 and remembers putting the four-bob his mother had given him for a haircut on the first favourite at Newbury. It lost. "I had to ask the board-marker to cut my hair for me," he said. "But he made such a pig's ear of it that when me mam saw it she marched right around to the barber's and gave him a right mouthful. When he told her he'd never seen me before, I got a good hiding."

Mocko, caught during a bungled bank job and sent down for three years, says he's unlikely ever to hit another betting shop because the rewards compared to bank and security van raids are paltry. If a security van raid registers 10 out of 10 for difficulty – "planning has to be almost military precision; you can't be a second out," he said – a betting shop job gets a 1 out of 10.

"There's nothing they can do to stop us," he said, pointing out that closed-circuit television poses no fear to the robber whose features are hidden by a crash helmet. "Those that hit betting shops without a disguise of some sort are most probably smacked up," he said.

"If I ever fall on hard times, I'll probably do another betting shop because even though the money's shit, I know there's hardly any risk. But it really will have to be hard times. When I hit a security van I'm pumped up, the adrenalin is going. But when I hit a betting shop, I'm practically asleep. It's as easy as blinking."

Two weeks after interviewing Mocko, I was told he'd been involved in a pub fight during which he'd given someone a serious pasting. The following night his victim returned and beckoned him outside, where two accomplices with baseball bats, waiting in an alleyway, exacted revenge. A week later, Mocko was spotted in the neighbourhood of his pub victim. He wore a long black coat. Inside it was a shotgun.

Years ago, while at the *Racing Post*, I described my terror at being caught up in a betting shop armed robbery. The article passed without comment, except for complaints from three betting shop managers that I'd tipped off villains that it's more sensible to strike at the end of a day's racing than at the beginning.

Years later, I was told by my editor to cut a paragraph from an article about robbers demanding from betting shop staff video tapes from closed-circuit TV. "You'll just tip them off," I was told. And in the course of researching this chapter, security men at Hills and Ladbrokes were incredibly sensitive about the information they could give me. "We don't want to give villains any ideas," was their excuse.

For God's sake, grow up lads. Do you seriously believe that this chapter is likely to persuade an otherwise law-abiding citizen to hit a betting shop? Do you seriously believe that the villain with the mind-set to plan a raid on his local Ladbrokes or Hills is not already aware of floor safes, of panic buttons, of closed-circuit TV?

In November 1998, a three-paragraph story in the *Racing Post* must have led to sharp intakes of breath in the security departments of all the leading firms. This is what was written: "Detectives are investigating a burglary at the William Hill betting shop in Ascot High Street last weekend in which the safe, understood to contain close to £30,000, was stolen. The theft was discovered on Monday morning when staff arrived for work. With racing at Ascot last Saturday, the shop's takings had been higher than on a normal weekend."

As an incentive to villains to go out and knock over a betting shop, this was top-of-the-range stuff. Bookies have always jealously guarded details of the amount of cash stolen in a betting shop raid. They play down the scale of the theft to discourage copy-cat crimes. But that three-paragraph story must have almost given Britain's villains an erection.

It's formula to conclude here with some solutions for hard-hit bookies, ideas to make betting shops more raid-proof. I only wish I could, especially as I have several relatives working in the industry. Just as vulnerable women are destined always to be victims of rape (sorry, I've given men the idea to commit such a crime), and frail old ladies prey to drugged-up muggers, so betting shops are sitting ducks for the tooled-up villains who see such raids as the training ground for more serious, more lucrative offences.

# chapter 7

## snooker

It's the final of the Embassy World Snooker Championship, live on BBC, with Jimmy White taking on Nigel Bond. Five minutes after the scheduled start time there's still no sign of Bond. BBC bigwigs, as well as the crowd, are getting worried. Suddenly the cameras spot Bond entering the arena – to the opening bars of the world-famous James Bond theme tune. Cameras switch immediately to White, and he's standing there, a look of nonchalance on his face and a fluffy white Persian cat cradled in his arms.

"Aaahh Mr Bond," says White. "We've been expecting you ..."

Far-fetched, perhaps, taking showbiz to the extreme, almost certainly; but in my book it's the only way snooker can save itself from oblivion. Those heady days when a world record TV sports audience watched Dennis Taylor dramatically beat Steve Davis in the World Championship final in the 1980s are now a distant memory. Snooker chiefs can argue as much as they like that the sport still delivers a huge audience but even snooker die-hards know that it's living on borrowed time.

The UK Championship is snooker's second-biggest tournament, yet *The Express* could not find the space for even a one-paragraph preview on the day the 1998 championship began in November. And *The Express* carried 25 pages of sport that day!

Between 1991 and 1995, snooker could boast sponsorship contracts with 32 companies. For the 1998-99 season there were just five sponsors. The effect of such a catastrophic marketing policy can be seen in the pattern of prize-money in the sport. In 1988, Steve Davis pocketed £65,000 for winning the Grand Prix. In 1998, Stephen Lee's first prize was £5,000 less. Doug Mountjoy's

1988 Tennents UK Championship was worth £80,000, yet ten years later John Higgins trousered only £75,000.

When a sport loses its popularity, betting on it is also adversely affected. TV coverage dries up, press reports dwindle, interviews are less and less frequent, and all in all it becomes a right royal pain trying to keep tabs on results and performances. That must have a negative effect on betting turnover.

Snooker was hit during the 1990s by two betting scandals, but I would argue that such stories actually encourage punters to bet on the sport rather than snub it. We all know racing is bent, but that doesn't stop us having a daily flutter. We are happy to accept all sorts of skulduggery in the faint hope that one day soon we will be part of a coup that really does sting the bookies. The same goes for snooker betting.

What is more responsible for turning punters in their droves away from snooker is the emergence of dozens of faceless, grey youngsters who are unknowns one minute, title winners the next. I'm thinking here of the likes of Dominic Dale, Paul Hunter and Stephen Lee, players I wouldn't recognise if they tripped over my left leg in the local boozer but who have seemingly overnight stolen the thunder of the old stalwarts like Stephen Hendry, John Parrott and Steve Davis.

In the good old days, players had to serve long apprenticeships before having a hope of reaching the latter stages of a tournament; nowadays they rub on acne cream before making victory speeches. How can we bet on a sport with any confidence when there are players we've never heard of clinching first prize?

Years ago the clamour was for a new wave of young players to lift the profile of the sport. Viewers were fed up with the same old faces, the argument went. Open the game up to hundreds more professionals and wait for an explosion in interest. But the move backfired.

What the sport's bigwigs had forgotten is that snooker above all is a comfort sport. Roll in from the boozer, switch on the telly, and wallow in the hushed, gentle atmosphere. The whispering tones of the commentator, the stifled coughs in the audience, the odd smile or grimace from the players – all pure theatre.

We were comfortable with Cliff, and Doug, and Alex, and Jimmy, and Ray, and Terry. They were old friends, familiar faces. But where once the wrinklies reigned, we now have only callow youth. Pasty-faced, lank-haired, colourless, drab. Even their very names betray their youth. Dominic, Marcus, Jason, Quinten – surely all apprentice advertising copy-writers, not top-ranked snooker stars.

Something needs to be done urgently to restore the magic, to give snooker, and therefore snooker betting, a much-needed shot in the arm. I confess I've largely lost interest in the sport but I recognise that occasionally it can throw up some of the best betting opportunities around.

Two in particular stick in the memory. In October 1990, Tony Knowles took on Ken Owers in the fourth round of the Rothmans Grand Prix. Knowles, the red-hot favourite with most firms, was on offer with independent bookie AR Dennis (later to be bought by Ladbrokes) at a stand-out 4-5. Owers, as short as evens with Dennis, was a massive 11-4 with Coral, yielding a book of an incredible 82 per cent.

Just to refresh your memory on what that means, if a bookie offered evens 'heads' and evens 'tails' on the toss of a coin, his book would be 100 per cent, meaning that in theory he could neither win nor lose. For a book of 82 per cent, he would have to offer something like 11-8 heads and 6-4 tails.

The result: Owers won 5-4.

Earlier that year, in February, Steve Newbury was 1-6 favourite with Tote to beat unknown Tommy Murphy in the fourth round of the British Open in Derby. At those odds he was unbackable – but Hills offered a stand-out 4-7 and were promptly filled in. Newbury won.

Though few bookies will admit it, they are highly vulnerable in head-to-head sports like snooker and tennis, where they do not have the draw to come to their rescue and where they are very much reliant upon the knowledge and efficiency of their odds-compilers. Snooker betting, therefore, must not be allowed to wither and die, which it will do if the sport continues to haemorrhage both support and sponsors.

It's essential for the sport to jazz up its stale profile. In some ways snooker has been MTV-ed by the influx of so many young players, but you can sense it still clings to its whispering image and this can never be a healthy mix. Opening the floodgates to a mass of faceless youngsters was, as I've said, a mistake. But having taken that step, snooker should now be prepared to go the whole hog.

Maybe snooker should look to darts for its lead. It should scrap once and for all its 'temple of silence' image and instead cultivate the boisterous, boozy, betting appeal of big-time darts. I've sat in the audience for UK Championship snooker matches, and I've sat in the audience for an Embassy World Darts Match. One's *Last Of The Summer Wine*; the other *Men Behaving Badly*.

Darts is dynamite. You can cheer, you can swear; you can bet, you can sweat. You can do pretty much what you like. When you've had a monster bet on Dennis Priestley to beat Rod Harrington, and The Menace needs double 16 to go three sets clear, you don't want to sit there with your finger on your lips. You want to be up there shouting, giving it the large one. And when he does plonk it sweetly in double 16, you want another pint to celebrate. You want it there and then, not two hours later during the interval.

The atmosphere at the Lakeside in Surrey, where the Embassy World Darts Championship is staged, is electric and that comes across vividly to TV viewers. They hear the shouting, they witness the drinking, they see clearly the agonies and ecstasies of the players, and they want a part of it all, maybe by placing a bet. Now switch channels and suddenly there's the snooker on. God, what's happened to the sound? Has somebody died? Why is the audience asleep? Quick, turn back to the darts.

Why shouldn't we be allowed to get up and buy a drink or have a bet during a marathon snooker match? Darts players are expected to cope with such an unruly atmosphere, so why not snooker stars? What makes them so special?

It wasn't so long ago that big snooker tournaments were guaranteed live coverage on BBC and ITV, but those channels, recognising the sport's diminishing appeal, have reduced it largely to highlights around midnight, on a par with *Prisoner Cell Block H*.

Even Ronnie O'Sullivan, the sport's great white hope in the late 1990s, declared himself "bored silly" with the game towards the end of 1998, although his state of mind probably had much to do with his well-documented family problems.

In the 1980s, Tony Knowles figured in a lurid double-page tabloid spread, which detailed his bird-pulling prowess. Alex Higgins was never out of the news for all manner of misdemeanours; later Stephen Hendry was a *This Is Your Life* subject, although only in his early twenties. Somehow we can never imagine snooker being afforded such massive coverage today.

Indeed, it seems the only time snooker wins back-page coverage is when tales of alleged betting coups occur.

The first hint we got that snooker might not be entirely straight came in 1989 when South African player Silvino Francisco was at the centre of match-fixing allegations following his 5-1 defeat by Terry Griffiths in the Benson & Hedges Masters at Wembley.

Punters had plunged on a 5-1 scoreline for Griffiths and bookies, by nature suspicious, withheld payment on winning bets and referred the matter to Scotland Yard. Ladbrokes poured fuel on the fire when they refused to price up Francisco's next match, even though it was in the first round of the massively prestigious Embassy World Championship. Francisco won his first-round match (against Joe O'Boye) and by coincidence faced Griffiths again in the second round. This time both Hills and Ladbrokes opted not to quote odds on that game.

Given that the name Francisco was to figure in a subsequent match-fixing scandal, maybe bookies were perfectly entitled to act the way they did. But it's also easy to share the misgivings of betting guru Mark Coton, founder of the popular Pricewise column in the *Racing Post*.

In his highly informative 1990 book, *Value Betting*, Coton wrote: "Griffiths, a solid, consistent player in decent nick, was inevitably a strong favourite against a badly out-of-form Francisco. There was reported heavy support for a 5-1 Griffiths victory and the correct-score odds were cut from 6-1 to 7-2 before Ladbrokes stopped betting shortly before the match started. Griffiths duly won 5-1 and the bookmakers cried foul. BOLA investigators, the snooker authorities, and even the fraud squad were brought in to investigate alleged 'match-fixing'. No evidence of any malpractice ever came to light.

"To my knowledge the 'unusual betting patterns' reported by the bookmakers were almost certainly caused by a handful of snooker shrewdies deciding there was value to be snapped up on a 5-1 scoreline and acted accordingly. As bookmakers sought to lay off money, a knock-on effect was caused as other punters (most from the bookmakers' own offices) followed the smart money.

"The fact that bookmakers cried foul over the allegedly small amounts involved (£50,000 was the sum quoted at the time) is far more indicative of their mentality than any sickness in the game of snooker."

But the damaging effects on snooker of that betting riddle was dwarfed six years later by the controversy surrounding the Jimmy White v Peter Francisco (Silvino's nephew) match in the 1995 Embassy World Championship.

White won 10-2 – and all hell let loose.

Snooker chiefs immediately launched an inquiry into "unusual betting practices" following one of the most extraordinary betting plunges in the sport's history. Bookmakers throughout Britain reported that six-times World Championship runner-up White was backed to win 10-2 "almost to the exclusion of all other results".

BOLA, the betting industry's watchdog, alerted snooker's governing body, the WPBSA, six hours before the match began on the Saturday evening of April 15, and an inquiry was announced 30 minutes after White, who led 7-2 after the first session, won the three frames required in the second session the following day for the 10-2 triumph so widely predicted.

Bookmakers Hills, who were betting on-site at the Embassy venue at The Crucible in Sheffield, cut odds for a White 10-2 win from 4-1 (by far the shortest price around) to 7-4. Stan James reported one "significant bet" at 6-1, and the odds fell to 5-2. Ladbrokes initially went 9-1 but then cut the odds, first to 6-1, and then again to 3-1 as money poured in.

A Ladbrokes spokesman said at the time: "We laid some small bets at 9s but went 6-1 after we heard Hills were 4-1 on site. That was well laid and even when we went 3-1 we were still well accommodated. Everyone who wanted to back White to win was interested only in a 10-2 scoreline."

A report, later denied by BOLA, suggested it was switch-betting firm Stan James, the same Stan James which blew the gaff on the late kick-off in the UEFA Cup tie between Slavia Prague and Schalke, who alerted the betting industry to the attempted 10-2 snooker coup.

They reportedly set industry alarm bells ringing when one of their 'faces' – a high-staking value-hunter – completely changed his betting habits and asked for £200 at 6-1 for a 10-2 White win. A spokesman said at the time: "It wasn't the size of the bet so much as the identity of the punter involved. Ladbrokes were offering 9-1 about a 10-2 win, so it didn't make sense that he should try the bet with us. We cut the odds to 5-2 but that didn't stop punters trying to get on. When we were informed that there were cash punters in independent shops up and down the country trying to put as much as £1,000 on, we suspended betting and informed BOLA."

BOLA advised bookies, reportedly facing an industry-wide loss of £50,000 (there's that neat, headline-grabbing figure again), to withhold payment pending a WPBSA inquiry into the match.

What was most noticeable in the days leading up to the WPBSA inquiry was that while a host of snooker's top names leapt to the defence of White, few put in a good word for Francisco. And interest in the inquiry was heightened by the admission by top player Willie Thorne, a former high-staking punter himself, that he had been offered cash several times to throw matches.

Said Thorne: "A sport which involves a lot of betting opportunities, like snooker does, is open to this sort of thing going on. Whether it's snooker, football, horseracing or the dogs, there's always someone trying to pull a stroke."

At the first inquiry, in Sheffield on April 19, White was cleared of any part in match-fixing allegations – the player himself called that outcome "the biggest certainty of all time" – but Francisco had to face further questioning on May 8, with the second inquiry banning him from snooker for five years. Such a punishment, the heaviest ever imposed on a professional snooker player, suggested the WPBSA had found that the South African had indeed been up to his neck in match-fixing, yet they made absolutely no mention of any betting involvement. In a masterpiece of a cop-out, the WPBSA said Francisco "had not conducted himself during the match in a manner consistent with his status as a professional sportsman".

That really bowled BOLA a googly. The WPBSA clearly thought Francisco was guilty of engineering the 10-2 scoreline but had neither conclusive evidence, nor the balls, to say so.

BOLA, however, decided that the five-year ban was proof enough for them to advise bookies to declare void all bets taken on the White-Francisco match. In other words, those punters who backed a 10-2 White win would get only a refund of their stake-money.

This was totally unacceptable. First, it sounded a loud-and-clear message that they believed Francisco was guilty of match-fixing, further damaging the player's reputation. Second, it set a hugely dangerous precedent. Although there was no concrete evidence of any betting malpractice – the 'unusual betting patterns' can just as easily be explained by using the Mark Coton argument above, although this instance admittedly requires a somewhat larger suspension of disbelief – BOLA gave themselves the power to deprive punters of their rightful winnings.

One punter told me he staked a total of £300 at 6-1 on a 10-2 White scoreline not because he was privy to any inside information but because he saw the odds shorten from 4-1 to 5-2 while in a Hills betting shop and, fearful of missing out on an inspired gamble, scrambled to get on at longer odds elsewhere.

BOLA were absolutely right to harbour suspicions that the game was not straight (White was pretty scathing about Francisco in his 1998 autobiography), but they had no right to void bets on the strength of mere suspicions.

Francisco, it should be pointed out, was actually paid his £8,750 prize-money as a first-round loser. And it's worth asking that if BOLA believed Francisco played so abysmally by design, how

144 . sports betting and how to make it pay

would they have reacted if the South African had won only one frame instead of two? A 10-1 scoreline would not have been much use to the masterminds of this alleged coup, but would BOLA have advised clients to refund stakes then? I'll leave you to make up your own minds.

I hope all this doesn't sound as if I think snooker is 100 per cent straight. Far from it. No sport (apart perhaps from horseracing) is more open to skulduggery. If 11-man games like football and cricket can be hit so hard by match-fixing allegations, as they have been for much of the 1990s, how much simpler must it be to engineer a result in a head-to-head battle?

Snooker is a game of fractions. Professionals can miss a pot by the narrowest of margins and make it look for all the world like they were trying to sink it. The high-profile snooker players are wealthy men, so it's hard to believe that they would involve themselves in the black art to win the merely moderate sums talked about in the last two snooker betting scandals. But that is not the case with many of the younger, lesser-known pro-players who have burst onto the scene in the last five years. While the likes of Steve Davis and Stephen Hendry can become snooker millionaires, there are more and more run-of-the-mill players who are barely scraping a living on the pro-circuit.

John Parrott has spoken of the young pros who qualify for a single ranking tournament, say the Thailand Open, and must pay the air fare to Bangkok for the prospect of a first-round drubbing from John Higgins. How great a temptation must it be for those players to make a few bob on the side by engineering a correct scoreline?

It's worth noting, by the way, that former WPBSA chairman John Spencer was alleged in 1997 to have advised players that they should bet against themselves as a financial insurance against losing. The story caused a storm, with Spencer denying the allegations, but the insurance strategy was backed by snooker pro Mark Bennett, himself the owner of a betting shop. "As long as players don't back the opposition to win more than they would get for winning the match themselves, then I can't see a problem," said Bennett, a semi-finalist in the 1996 Grand Prix. "But you've got to be realistic - you can't get that much on anyway. Players are playing for ranking points, and if they lose, it costs them more in the long run anyway because they'll drop further down the rankings."

The more cynical among us have always wondered how so many snooker finals in the late 1980s, when the sport was battling to win TV contracts, developed into deciding-frame cliffhangers that would grip the nation's viewers far more than a one-sided walk-over.

It's worth asking if snooker would ever have become so popular if Steve Davis had beaten Dennis Taylor 18-6 in that momentous 1985 World Championship Final instead of losing 18-17 in such dramatic circumstances.

Given the Spencer allegations and the nagging thought that maybe, just maybe, players were sometimes persuaded to allow televised showpiece finals to run their full course, perhaps it would be no surprise if players were nowadays easily nudged into stage-managing a particular scoreline. After all, a cynic would say, the betting culture is already there, so too the tacit approval of the sport's governing body, so why shouldn't a player struggling to make a living earn himself a few quid on the side?

But don't let this put you off betting on snooker. Few matches are likely to be bent because ranking points are so important, and the sport, as I wrote earlier, can throw up some wonderful betting opportunities. So what is the best snooker betting strategy?

First, match betting.

Head-to-head records have some bearing, I suppose, but snooker differs from most other sports in that the actions of your opponent often have little effect on your own game. For instance, if I play Greg Rusedski at tennis, the outcome will be heavily dependent upon my ability, first, to return his serve and, second, to handle the rest of his game – be it passing shots, baseline rallies, or volleys. Rusedski in other words has an influence on every point I win.

In snooker, though, once I'm at the table my opponent ceases to be a factor. All that stands between me and the frame is my ability to pick my way through 15 reds and six colours; and while I'm at the table there is absolutely nothing my opponent can do to stop me, apart from beat me about the head with his cue.

That's why I treat head-to-head records in snooker with a fair degree of suspicion.

Far more important when you're betting on the outcome of a single snooker match is current form. Anyone who has ever played snooker, at whatever level, will tell you it's all about confidence.

When you're playing well, the pockets are huge; when the balls refuse to drop, however, the pockets seem as tight as a nun's doo-dah. Look at that incredible Stephen Hendry defeat in the Liverpool Victoria UK Championship first round in November 1998.

Hendry wasn't playing well in the run-up to that tournament, admittedly, but even if you fancied little-known opponent Marcus Campbell to pull off a shock win, surely it would have been by only the narrowest of margins. So how do we explain this scoreline - Hendry 0 Campell 9? Even the winner was flabbergasted.

But Hendry's words later suggested that such a shock had long been on the cards. "This result has probably been coming for 18 months or so," he said, "My confidence has been going down and down and at the end I couldn't wait to get out of there. It didn't matter who I was playing, I was always likely to lose 9-0. When you get down on a shot and you think 'I'm not going to pot this ball', then it's not a good platform to win a match."

Those words were allowed to pass almost without comment in the press but I thought it was a stunning admission from Hendry. Here we had a five-times world champion almost expecting to be whitewashed by a comparative unknown. I doubt there's ever been a more vivid illustration of the importance of confidence to a professional sportsman, one who six months later went on to regain his world title.

Another crucial factor you must bear in mind before placing a bet is the length of the match. Shock results are commonplace in the shorter best-of-nine-frames matches but rare in the much longer Embassy World Championship. The reasons for this I'd have thought were quite obvious, yet bookies seem to ignore them.

If you ran a Derby winner over five furlongs, he would almost certainly lose out to the specialist sprinters. By the same token the five-furlong speedsters would not be sighted at the end of the 12-

furlong Classic at Epsom. It's the same in football. Manchester United would be massively odds-on to beat, say, Wrexham, in the FA Cup Final at Wembley. But if that final was reduced to 20 minutes, the chances of a fluke result automatically increase.

In snooker the potential for such flukes is even greater. Given what I said about the opponent having no influence once his break is finished, even a run-of-the-mill professional could, with a fair run of the balls, rattle up three or four frames in a row before the hot favourite has even woken up. In a best-of-nine-frames match, that spells curtains for the favourite. Yet despite this, I would confidently wager that the odds for John Higgins v Shokat Ali in the first round of the Thailand Open (best of nine frames) would be little different to the odds for Higgins v Ali in the opening round of the Embassy (best of 19). It's crazy but it's almost as if bookies don't even consider the length of the match when framing their odds.

I picked, purely at random, the opening day of the Regal Welsh Open in January 1997 to see if the underdog is favoured by shorter matches.

There were 15 first round matches on the opening day and seven were won by the underdog. The top odds for those seven underdog winners were: 7-4, 5-2, 7-4, evens, 10-3, 5-2 and 7-2. Had you placed £100 blindly on all 15 underdogs at those odds, you would have netted a pre-tax profit of almost £850.

It's worth noting too that upset results are much more likely in the early-season tournaments – as a rule of thumb, those before Christmas. This is because top-ranked players, short of competitive matches from the end of the Embassy World Championship in April to the start of the new season in late September, are vulnerable to those young guns who all summer long have been battling through the tournament qualifiers in Blackpool, and who will surely have a far keener competitive edge in the early months of the season.

It should pay, therefore, to oppose the favourites in first-to-five matches, particularly those in the early months of the season.

Nick Hill is a 33-year-old former teacher who realised there was more money to be made from a different kind of homework. He packed in full-time teaching and now makes a healthy profit – "a guaranteed second income," he calls it – from betting on snooker. His profits from the game over the 1997-98 season were a so-so £6,000, but as early as Christmas in the 1998-99 season he was already £5,000 up, with another four months of the season to run.

"I hesitate to say it's easy money because it's not quite as easy as it used to be," said Hill, from Epsom in Surrey, "but I find snooker the easiest of all sports on which to win money from gambling."

His secret is attending as many tournaments as he possibly can. "Results, facts and figures are all very well on paper, but they can never give you the whole picture," said Hill. "There's absolutely no substitute for being there. You get to know which players are playing well, who is confident and, just as importantly, who is struggling."

As an illustration he uses the 1997 UK Championship clash (best of 17 frames) between hot favourite John Higgins and little-known Gary Ponting. "Ponting went 5-1 up by the interval and I rushed to the Hills on-site betting booth to check their updated odds," he said.

"There were still offering Ponting at 6-5 which, given that he needed only another four frames to wrap up victory, was daft. Hills may argue that they were adhering to a strict formula which determines what price the favourite will be at any given point of the match, but I don't give a toss about all that. I trusted the evidence of my own eyes and I could see that Higgins was never at the races and had very little chance of coming back." Ponting won 9-4

Hill, whose biggest snooker triumph was backing Peter Ebdon at 100-1 to win the 1993 Grand Prix, confirms that the shorter best-of-nine frame matches offer punters the best chance of profits. "I wouldn't go so far as to say they are lotteries," he said, "but I've shown my best profits by backing selected outsiders in those kind of matches." He cites Fergal O'Brien at an incredible 6-1 to beat John Parrott as the finest example of that strategy. O'Brien won 5-4 in the 1994 Regal Welsh.

Hill says he prices up every game himself – to a 100 per cent book – and will step in if a bookie clashes wildly with his own assessment. "If I make a player 6-4, I'll move if I see a bookie offering 2-1."

The other most popular form of snooker betting is outright tournament betting, for instance backing Ronnie O'Sullivan at 11-2 to win the Embassy World Championship. I would argue here that there is very little value left in this form of betting. Once upon a time it would be easy to study the draw for a tournament, plot a player's likely path to the latter stages, and sometimes find odds far greater than his true chances of winning. But not any more. Bookies do their homework much more diligently now and they will be equally aware if one quarter of the draw is substantially easier than the other three.

For the 1997 Embassy World Championship, the blue riband event of the sport, Ladbrokes unforgivably offered no each-way betting for what was a 32-runner race, in which the favourite (Stephen Hendry) was a 5-6 shot. This was because the Embassy draw was very lop-sided and they did not want to lay heavy each-way bets for players in the far easier bottom half.

Punters should have refused to bet with Ladbrokes for the duration of the whole tournament. In more than ten years as sports editor of the *Racing Post*, I came across several examples of bookmakers taking the piss out of punters but nothing quite so blatant as that Ladbrokes manoeuvre.

In a bid to avoid censure Ladbrokes pointed out that they had framed a separate book on 'players to make the final'. But their odds in this market were stingy beyond belief. All the rival firms were betting each-way one-half the odds the first two, yet the majority of Ladbrokes odds for players to make the final were less than half their advertised odds to win the event. Of the 32 runners, only seven players were quoted longer than half their win-odds, six were exactly the same, and an incredible 19 at vastly reduced odds.

For example, John Higgins was 11-2 with Ladbrokes to win the Embassy, but only 11-10 to make the final; Peter Ebdon was 8-1 outright but only 9-4 to reach the climax. Okay, those two players could not meet Hendry, practically invincible at the time, until the final, but if the Scot was such a stumbling block, surely Ladbrokes offered increased odds about all the runners in his half of the draw? Er, no. In fact three players scheduled to meet Hendry were shorter than half their win-odds.

Absobloodylutely unbelieveable.

# chapter 8

## tennis

First the good news: tennis offers the diligent punter a fantastic opportunity to make money. Now the bad news: bookies have long recognised this, which is why few ever quote prices for tournaments other than the four Grand Slam events.

I love tennis. I also hate it. At its best – Steffi Graf v Jana Novotna in the 1993 Wimbledon final, or Graf v Arantxa Sanchez-Vicario in the Wimbledon final two years later – it is perhaps the most compelling of all sports; at its worst – Pete Sampras v Goran Ivanisevic on the lawns of SW19 in 1998 – it's as gripping as three-hour speech on the euro in the House Of Lords.

The aesthetics of the sport I will deal with later. First, let's consider a far more important aspect – the betting. Like snooker, tennis betting can be divided into two categories – outright and individual matches. And, like snooker again, it's the individual matches that offer by far the easiest route to profit.

Tennis is a difficult sport to keep tabs on. Coverage in the British national press is poor, even in the broadsheets, and unless Tim Henman and/or Greg Rusedski are playing, chances are that a tournament in Colorado or Croatia will receive zero publicity. Bookmakers therefore refuse to quote odds.

They worry that clued-up punters, perhaps acquaintances of a dedicated tennis correspondent who follows the Tour all around the world, will have heard that, say, Felix Mantilla has an ankle injury and is only 50 per cent fit for his first-round clash with Julian Alonso and are ready to lump large on Alonso.

Only Stan James, the Oxfordshire-based switch betting specialists, regularly quote odds for the weekly ATP tournaments, with William Hill generally entering the market at the last-eight stage. But things are improving. As recently as 1994, Ladbrokes did not quote prices for the first round matches at Wimbledon, claiming, would you believe, that there was no interest!

Such gruesome days are now over and most bookmakers will generally price up a stack of first round matches in each of the four Grand Slam events – Australian Open, French Open, Wimbledon, and US Open.

I should reveal here that a very reliable authority has told me that Stan James, the pioneers of tennis betting in Britain, find it impossible to make the sport pay, even though they employ a specialist tennis odds-compiler. Contests with only two possible results have always been an achilles heel for bookies, and their vulnerability is heightened in tennis for reasons I am about to make clear.

If you're wondering why Stan James continue under such circumstances so regularly to offer odds for tennis matches, then I should point out that they consider it a loss-leader. First, it offers their clients a service no other bookmakers can match; second, the clients it attracts may quickly develop a taste for other, more bookie-friendly sports.

If you are to become a successful tennis punter you must evaluate three factors before placing a bet on a match – playing surface, current form, and head-to-head records. The sports betting team of the *Racing Post* seem to have made head-to-head records their god when it comes to analysing a tennis match, but in my book they are far less significant than the first two factors.

Just as some racehorses cannot act on heavy going, so certain tennis players struggle on surfaces alien to them. For instance, Boris Becker, one-time king of Wimbledon and a fantastic player on indoor carpet, would struggle to beat me on clay. Similarly you'd be a fool to risk a red cent on Alberto Berasategui on any surface other than clay, on which he improves by about three stone. Some players seem at home on any surface – Yevgeny Kafelnikov, Richard Krajicek and Andre Agassi, for instance – but these are the exceptions rather than the rule.

Look at Michael Chang. Everyone knows he struggles on grass but what is less well known is his relatively poor record on indoor carpet. The American did not win a single match on that surface in 1997 and of four indoor carpet tournaments he contested in 1998, he crashed out in the first-round in three. To prove that there's always something to cock up even the best-prepared argument, Chang actually won the title in his other indoor carpet tournament in 1998, but that was in Shanghai, where he always performs well. And the field was hardly star-studded, with Chang not meeting a single player ranked in the world's top 60 until Goran Ivanisevic in the final.

Grass and clay, surfaces for Wimbledon and the French Open respectively, could not be more different. Big servers are almost unplayable on the slick Wimbledon lawns, which is why Pete Sampras and Boris Becker have won so many titles and why Goran Ivanisevic has three times reached the final.

But booming serves are rendered almost impotent on the cloying clay in Paris, where the ability and the staying power to slug it out for hours on end from the baseline are all important. Should we be surprised, therefore, that Sampras and Becker have such poor French Open records?

It is imperative that you are fully aware of a player's preferred surface before placing a match bet. Beg, steal or borrow the annual *Player Guides* published by the ATP Tour and available in top bookshops, and invest in a home computer for access to the Internet. Yes, the very word bores me too, but the atptour.com website is absolute gold-dust giving as it does the record of players in every tournament they've contested for the past five years, plus incredibly detailed head-to-head records. Betting without it is betting blind.

If on a scale of 1 to 10, the playing surface gets a 10 for significance, current form merits a 9. Quite simply you should not make a habit of backing players who are making a habit of bowing out in the first round of tournaments. Conversely, those players clearly in form should be backed with confidence until they lose.

In tennis, arguably more than any other sport, form very much goes in cycles. Rarely does a player perform abysmally one week, superbly the next. Improved form will usually be a gradual process, maybe a third round slot one week, a quarter-final appearance the next, then perhaps first prize.

It helps, too, that there are tournaments virtually every week of the season, so that a player gradually hitting form has plenty of chances to take advantage. That makes form in tennis a much more reliable tool than form in snooker, where tournaments are sometimes three weeks apart and a player who reaches the final in one event has sufficient time to lose his edge before the next tournament begins. He's not given the chance, in other words, to cash in on his purple patch.

By rights Greg Rusedski should not have had a prayer of reaching the US Open final in 1997. In three previous appearances at Flushing Meadow he'd bowed out in the first-round every time. But Rusedski arrived in New York in red-hot form and brimming with confidence. In his two previous tournaments, both on hard court like the US Open, Rusedski had reached one semi-final and one quarter-final.

It was a similar story with Pat Rafter, the Aussie who beat Rusedski in the US Open final. In his three previous hard-court tournaments in the build-up to Flushing Meadow, Rafter had reached two finals.

I remember backing Karol Kucera at 80-1 to win the Australian Open at the beginning of 1998. The Slovak had never gone further than the third round in Melbourne in three previous attempts, but he was pure dynamite in the weeks running up to the first Grand Slam event of the season, winning four of his five Hopman Cup matches in Perth before clinching the Sydney title, and in that kind of nick had to be worth a bet.

As it turned out he gave me a fantastic run for my money, beating Pete Sampras in the quarter-final before losing to subsequent champion Petr Korda in the semi.

For a two-month spell at the beginning of 1996, Goran Ivanisevic was almost unbeatable. On February 4 he beat Cedric Pioline to win a carpet title in Zagreb, won another title in Dubai (hard) a fortnight later, and then the following week reached the final in Antwerp (carpet). But that wasn't the end of Goran's golden run. A week later, in Milan (carpet), he dropped just one set in five matches to clinch the crown, and then dropped just one more set in Rotterdam (carpet) the very next week to claim yet another first prize.

The switch to American hard courts the following week could not halt Ivanisevic's incredible charge and he powered to the semi-final at Indian Wells before a week later thrashing Andrei Medvedev, Michael Chang and Pete Sampras on his way to a final appearance (lost to Andre Agassi) at the prestigious Lipton Championship in Key Biscayne on March 31. Throughout February and March that year, Ivanisevic played 35 matches – and won 32.

It was a superhuman run and one that would have given form students huge profits. But then it all dried up for the Croat. A formality of a Davis Cup tie against Ukraine (Croatia won 5-0) halted his momentum and he did not play in another ATP Tour event until Monte Carlo in late April, when he lost 6-2, 6-2 at the first hurdle to Magnus Gustafsson. A first-hurdle exit in Hamburg quickly followed, and the Goran cycle of success was clearly at an end.

The moral of all this is to get behind a player whose form is beginning to show signs of an upturn after a spell in the doldrums.

Tim Henman lost 11-9 in the fifth set of the Australian Open first round to Jerome Golmard in January 1998 and as a result of that shattering blow made first-round exits in each of his next three tournaments. His game was in crisis and only a fool would have backed him. But back on home territory, at London's Battersea Park in late February, Henman hinted that his barren run was coming to an end, beating Richard Krajicek and Rainer Schuttler before losing a tight quarter-final to Yevgeny Kafelnikov, who went on to frank the form by landing the title.

Those punters who'd clocked the turnaround in Henman's fortunes were rewarded soon after when he went to the hotly-contested Lipton Championships in Florida and beat Carlos Moya, Petr Korda and Gustavo Kuerten in quick succession *en route* to a semi-final defeat by Marcelo Rios.

Head-to-head records, although important, should not be over-estimated. While in some instances they illustrate clearly that one player has a huge psychological advantage over another, too often they are not worth the paper they are written on.

At their peak you'd imagine there was precious little to choose between Boris Becker and Andre Agassi, but Becker managed to beat his American rival only once in ten encounters during the 1990s.

Up to the end of 1998, Pete Sampras had met fellow American Todd Martin 19 times and lost just twice, so it would take a huge leap of faith to back Martin whenever these two next met, especially as Sampras had won the last 12 meetings for the loss of just four sets.

Similarly, Steffi Graf has tackled 1998 Wimbledon runner-up Nathalie Tauziat 20 times (to the end of 1998) and has yet to drop a set.

Sampras and Graf are undoubtedly superior players to these two opponents, but you could fancy them to win even if they played only to 50 per cent capacity because there's a real chance that, mentally, Martin and Tauziat are beaten even before they start.

But we could perhaps have made a similar remark about Greg Rusedski before he tackled Sampras in the final of the Paris Indoor Championship in November 1998. Sampras held a 6-0 call over the Brit, but Rusedski made a nonsense of that stat by winning in straight sets.

The following week, Sampras took on Jason Stoltenberg in the second round of the Stockholm Open. This was an important match for Sampras, still bidding at that time to finish the season as world No.1 for a record sixth consecutive year, and all the signs looked good as he had never lost to his Aussie opponent in four previous meetings. But Stoltenberg won in a deciding set.

So head-to-heads should be looked upon as a useful guide rather than the ultimate reference point. And if you're still in any doubt about which factor you should pay most attention to, consider this hypothetical situation.

Tim Henman has met Felix Mantilla six times and has won every one. But none of those matches was on a clay court and the seventh meeting of the two is on the red clay of Barcelona, with bookies going 8-11 Henman, evens Mantilla.

Do you back Henman because he's never lost to Mantilla, or do you back the Spaniard because on clay he's different class?

The answer, ladies and gentlemen, is Mantilla for all you're worth. In 1997, Mantilla played 50 matches on clay and won 42. Henman by comparison can hardly win a game on the stuff, although his form on the surface showed some improvement in the spring of 1999.

Though bookmakers know they are vulnerable on tennis – one of the sports in which quite definitely there are punters with greater knowledge than the odds-compilers – they feel obliged to quote prices on the major tournaments and sometimes leave themselves badly exposed.

I'll never forget the match between Jeremy Bates and Javier Sanchez at Wimbledon in 1992, which threw up perhaps the biggest betting discrepancy of all time. Bates, who earlier in the competition had knocked out Michael Chang, was odds-on favourite with most firms but an incredible 11-4 with one bookie. Sanchez, the Spaniard whose best results had come on clay or hard courts, was 1-4 with the same firm but 7-4 elsewhere. So in a two-runner race you could back one runner at 11-4 and the other at 7-4, yielding an unheard-of book of 63 per cent.

Needless to say these odds didn't last long. Punters who contacted the bookie at 9.30 that morning were told that Bates, who went on to win in straight sets, was now a 4-7 chance. I was one of the few punters to take advantage of this monster rick.

But disappointing though the their actions were, they were nothing compared to the strategy adopted by Surrey Racing later that Wimbledon. Bates went on to play Frenchman Guy Forget, a proven grass-court competitor, and Surrey made the mistake of offering Forget at 5-2 to win in straight sets. When it became clear in the pages of the *Racing Post* that their offer was way above anyone else's, Surrey slashed it to 13-8 without, as they freely admitted, taking a single penny.

Surrey Racing managing director Mervyn Wilson boomed: "We're not guaranteeing prices to anyone any longer. If we see our prices are way out of line with other bookmakers', then it's our prerogative to change them."

Though Wilson's honesty is to be applauded, it was an astonishing admission from a hitherto well-respected firm. One representative of a leading rival firm told me at the time: "I can't believe he said what he did. What a terrible admission for bookmaking."

He was right. Wilson's words were indeed unacceptable. What is the point of bookmakers employing odds-compilers if they're not prepared to stick by their opinion? As it turned out, Bates took Forget to a deciding set.

Betting guru Mark Coton, chairman of the now-defunct National Association For The Protection Of Punters, raged: "Surrey are undermining the whole spirit of betting. The big attraction of gambling is the notion that you *can* win, but Surrey are in effect saying 'thou shall not win and if you try we'll do everything in our power to stop you'.

"If bookmakers are advertising prices they are setting their own opinions so why are they not prepared to stick by them? They want to reserve the right to correct themselves if they make a mistake, but punters don't have that right. We can't say, if we take 8-1 about something that goes out to 12-1, 'Sorry, we made a mistake. Can we have our money back, please?'"

While the whole episode showed up bookmakers in a bad light, it did once again make clear that tennis betting, perhaps more than any other sport, offers the value-seeking punter real opportunities to win. Some of the best bets I've ever struck have been on tennis. Perhaps the best came in November 1997 when Sweden hosted USA in the final of the Davis Cup at Gothenburg. As a little exercise, I'll tell you who was playing for Sweden and USA, and the strength of their form at the time, and you can judge what the odds should have been.

**For USA:** Pete Sampras, ranked No.1 in the world, and Michael Chang, ranked No.3, were the singles battlers, with Todd Martin and Jonathan Stark pairing up for the doubles. Their combined doubles ranking was 1,290.

**For Sweden:** Jonas Bjorkman, ranked No.4, and Magnus Larsson, ranked No.25, were scheduled for the singles, with Bjorkman and Niklas Kulti the doubles pairing, with a combined ranking of 33.

Chang was struggling badly for form in the closing weeks of the 1997 season and a fortnight earlier had been soundly beaten by Bjorkman in the ATP Championship on indoor carpet, the same surface as the Gothenburg venue. Chang and Bjorkman were up first, followed by Larsson v Sampras. Those two had met three times that season, with Larsson winning two. The two singles matches, played on a Friday, were reversed on the Sunday, with the lone doubles match taking place on the Saturday.

So how would you have bet? I'd have thought, given the above information, plus Sweden's home advantage, that 5-6 each of two wouldn't have been far off the mark, but didn't argue too much when Stan James went 8-11 USA, evens Sweden. Then I checked out the Ladbrokes odds and could hardly believe my ears. "USA are 1-3," a female voice said, "and Sweden are 9-4." I swear it's the nicest thing a woman has ever said to me, better even than "Jesus, that's massive" (I wish).

I bet you're dying to know the result now, aren't you? Well, it was Sweden 5, USA 0. Happy, happy days.

It was way back in 1990 that I seriously began to study tennis betting and I didn't have to wait too long for my first maximum bet. It came in the Wimbledon semi-finals, slap bang in the middle of the 1990 World Cup in Italy, and saw Stefan Edberg, king of the grass-court game, taking on Ivan Lendl, whose motto was that grass is only for cows. It's hard to believe, I know, but Edberg was available at 7-4 to beat his Czech rival, even though Edberg had won Wimbledon in 1988 and reached the final the following year. The result? Not surprisingly a straight-sets win for Edberg, who went on to beat Boris Becker in a five-set humdinger in the final.

The following year I latched on pretty early to Michael Stich, who a month earlier had reached the semi-final of the French Open. Selecting him pre-tournament as the best outsider at 40-1, a massive price considering he was seeded sixth for Wimbledon and ranked seven in the world, I managed to steal a few quid on the German in his early rounds, but could hardly believe his odds for his quarter-final clash with Jim Courier.

Corals went 4-7 Stich and 5-4 Courier, which was pretty much spot on. But Tote made Courier the favourite at 8-11, with Stich evens.

At that time these facts were known: Courier held a 3-1 head-to-head edge over Stich and had beaten him 6-2 6-7 6-2 6-4 in the French semi-final. Relevant, admittedly, but what was far more significant, and what had been well documented, was Courier's aversion to grass and Stich's love of it.

I'd watched Stich from courtside several times at Wimbledon that summer and I'd never before seen such supreme coverage of the net. He was virtually impossible to pass, and of course he had that explosive serve, too. Courier had neither of these, which is why he admitted on the eve of that quarter-final: "Michael's game is definitely better suited to grass, so it's going to be very difficult for me."

You weren't far wrong, Jim. Stich won in straight sets before beating Edberg and Becker to clinch the title and set in motion a wonderful summer for this writer, who was a fortnight later to strike it rich again on Ian Baker-Finch at 50-1 in the Open Golf Championship.

It's a fact that all sports become more watchable once there's money riding on the outcome, but I would argue that tennis benefits most of all from a bet. Back Alex Corretja to beat Carlos Moya and you can't take your eyes from the screen. Every single shot matters, every cross-court winner a mini-orgasm, every double fault a kick in the bollocks.

Turf diehards maintain that sports betting will never overtake horserace betting because it does not offer a quick fix. A football match takes 90 minutes, they smarm; a golf tournament four days. Why wait that long when a race can be over in less than a minute? But what these numbskulls don't seem to realise is that in sport the fixes come thick and fast, and in tennis thickest and fastest of all.

Backing a winner in tennis is heaven on earth; even backing a loser has something to recommend it.

I will never forget as long as I live the 1991 Wimbledon final between Steffi Graf and Gabriela Sabatini. I'd had £80 pre-tournament on Sabatini at 10-1 – partly because I reckoned the draw had given her a great chance of clinching the title but largely because I was in love with her.

The gorgeous one strolled imperiously to the final and held a 5-2 lead in the deciding set against Graf. What a wonderful place the world was right then. The hit song *Perfect Day* was written specially for that afternoon. But then everything went arse over tit. Gaby choked. She choked like no-one had ever choked before. She choked big time, lost 8-6, and I wept. I wept for Gaby; I wept because my perfect day had been wrecked; I wept most of all for the 800 snarlers I so nearly had in my grasp. That's what a bet on tennis can do to you.

So much for tennis betting – what about tennis itself? Well, to my mind, it's in trouble. The surge up the world rankings of Tim Henman and Greg Rusedski have given the sport a shot in the arm in Britain, but worldwide it seems to have lost its appeal. The only thing that sticks in the memory from the last few Wimbledons was the attractive female streaker at the men's final between Richard Krajicek and Mal Washington in 1996 – and even that welcome interruption allegedly had a betting link.

The *Racing Post* reported on 8 July 1996, the day after that Wimbledon final, won in straight sets by Krajicek: "A Wimbledon streaker was at the centre of a betting riddle last night. The blonde stunned finalists Richard Krajicek and Mal Washington by dashing naked across Centre Court as they warmed up before yesterday's climax. It was the first time a streaker has been sighted at Wimbledon – and came the day after Hills curiously slashed their streaker odds from 6-1 to 4-1.

"Wimbledon chiefs have criticised Hills for offering such odds, believing that eventually they would encourage punters fearless enough to bare all to cash in. There was no clear evidence last night that the streaker, 23-year-old London student Melissa

Johnson, had taken a slice of the 6-1. But in a twist to the story, it emerged that Miss Johnson may have been put up to her history-making nude dash by a national tabloid newspaper, whose reporters could have helped themselves to the Hills odds.

"Hills spokesman Graham Sharpe denied that they had taken any lumpy bets, insisting that the maximum wager on a Wimbledon streak was £10. 'I figured that Wimbledon was the last major sporting event that has never been graced by a streaker and the law of averages meant it would happen sooner or later,' said Sharpe, explaining why the odds were slashed. But a Wimbledon insider told us: 'Hills may not yet pay up. It's a put-up job.'"

That Krajicek-Washington final, a drab affair, was a further example of how the men's game has been ruined by the potency of the serve. Most matches at Wimbledon and on any other fast surface are non-events. Rallies are a thing of the past, except in clay-court tournaments, which themselves become boringly repetitive with two faceless Spaniards slugging it out from the baseline for what seems six-hour stretches. Any men's rally of more than five shots at Wimbledon is wildly applauded, as though it's a superhuman effort by the two players merely to keep the ball in play so long.

Something needs to be done – and quickly. It would not be so bad if tennis had the colourful characters who could draw attention away from the drabness of the game, but the days of McEnroe and Connors are sadly long gone. Agassi does his best, but can't do it all on his own. Pat Rafter has potential but is beginning to annoy me because so many supermodels want to hop into his bed. The bastard.

Reformists insist that the introduction of the single serve would revolutionise the game and at a stroke usher in a new era of thinking man's tennis in which power would no longer be the chief weapon. They argue that a professional golfer who hooks his tee shot into the trees doesn't get a second chance (well, not without penalty anyway) so why should a tennis star have another crack at a serve if he cocks up the first one? I agree 100 per cent.

It's a shocking indictment of men's tennis that virtually everyone

I've spoken to prefers nowadays to watch the women's game in which the serve, naturally less powerful, is so often just a means of getting the ball in play rather than a sure-fire point-winner.

The top players have raised stern opposition to the single-serve proposal, but they would, wouldn't they? They say it would wreck the fine traditions of the game, but no tradition is worth persevering with if it is ruining the enjoyment of the sport. I have not heard one reasonable argument against the introduction of the single serve.

A report in 1991 claimed that an afternoon-long Wimbledon final might see only 20 minutes of actual tennis action. Some men's indoor matches, traditionally best-of-three-setters, offer as little as ten minutes, said Brian Wicklin of the Swedish Bureau of Statistics.

Wicklin measured the length of matches with a stopwatch and concluded that some of tennis's most dramatic contests may have been determined by time. He argued that the length of points may be more important than technique or temperament in determining a winner. A baseliner's ability to lengthen points – and to shorten the rest period between them – can exhaust a serve-and-volley player.

As an example, he cited the dramatic 1980 Wimbledon final in which baseliner Bjorn Borg defeated the net-rushing John McEnroe 1-6 7-5 6-3 6-7 (16-18) 8-6 in a four-hour match. "Borg won by extending the playing time from 6-7 minutes per set to well over 12 minutes," explained Wicklin, "and by starting serves quickly – 10-12 seconds after points, compared to McEnroe's 25-30 seconds."

I use this report merely as a tool to show how tennis fans can be short-changed by these boom-boom servers who seemingly take ages between points but who complete a point in lightning-quick time with just one rocket delivery

Yet given the massive influence of the top players themselves in the politics of tennis, we're unlikely to see the current serving rules changed. So I have an alternative proposal. Watch any tennis match on TV and an ace is the cue for spectators to applaud. Erm, why? Why should we cheer something that's reducing our enjoyment?

Maybe in years gone by, when tennis equipment was a long way from the hi-tech stuff we see today and serving an ace truly was a commendable achievement, the cheers were justified. But surely not now? On the contrary, we should boo an ace. Boo for all we're worth. Let the players know we want to see guile and grace, not power and pace. Maybe that way they'd get the message.

A final little tennis anecdote to serve as a word of warning against the practice of after-timing, dealt with extensively in Chapter 2.

On the day of the 1991 US Open quarter-finals, Hills reported a flood of money around 3.30 in the afternoon for Ivan Lendl at 6-5 to beat Michael Stich. The wave of support took them by surprise because business until then had been pretty slack. When odds-compiler Richard Browning paged the Oracle teletext service on TV, he was horrified to see that Lendl was already holding a two-set-to-nil lead in a match that had not been scheduled to start until 7.30pm New York time, 12.30am BST.

It looked like the after-timers had struck, until Browning phoned the Flushing Meadow venue in New York for confirmation and was told that the match had not yet started. Oracle later admitted their mistake. A spokesman said that two of their text pages had merged, placing the result of the previous night's match between Jennifer Capriati and Gabriela Sabatini on the Lendl-Stich page.

A happy ending, though. When the match finally got under way, Lendl won in five sets.

I should not close this chapter without explaining the full significance of the different surfaces on a top pro's performance. The surface of a tennis court can drastically affect the way a tennis star plays his game. And often a player's success will to a certain degree be determined by the surface.

As I said earlier, few players would back Michael Chang on grass, while Tim Henman is very much a player to oppose on clay. Just as no serious horseracing punter would place a bet without first checking the going, it's important for tennis punters to be aware of the demands different surfaces make, and the preferred 'going' of the players.

## hardcourts

The most common surface worldwide is the hardcourt and is

usually made of cement or asphalt. A topping such as Greenset Grand Prix, Greenset Trophy or Rebound Ace is applied to the surface to give more grip and flexibility. The texture of this topping will determine the speed of the court. The smoother the topping, the faster the speed of the ball and the lower the bounce.

Two of the four Grand Slams – US Open and Australian Open – are played on hardcourt, as are 30 ATP Tour tournaments.

Pat Rafter, Greg Rusedski, Michael Chang and Andre Agassi are some of the players whose greatest success has come on this surface.

Hardcourts are considered to be a medium-to-fast surface and this means that an aggressive style of play, such as serve and volley, is preferable to playing from the baseline. But the main advantage for the players is that the ball bounces uniformly and therefore a player is more easily able to anticipate where the ball is going to bounce.

Although hardcourts are faster than claycourts, they are not as fast as grasscourts and several clay specialists have been able to adapt fairly easily. One such player is Carlos Moya, who won the French Open, a claycourt tournament, but was also finalist at the Australian Open on hardcourt.

"I have a typical hardcourt style," said Moya after the 1997 Australian Open. After his success the Spanish Tennis Federation built a hardcourt in Barcelona so that their claycourt specialists could practice on it.

Overall if there was to be only one surface, most players would vote for hardcourt.

## indoor courts

Of the 77 tournament on the ATP Tour, 23 are played indoors, including the Mercedes Super 9 events in Stuttgart and Paris, as well as the ATP Tour World Championships in Hanover. Due to the weather, indoor tournaments are particularly popular during the European autumn season, and attention focuses on these events as the ATP Tour World Championship gets closer and the points to be gained at indoor events are of crucial importance to qualifying hopes.

Indoor surfaces can vary between hardcourts (such as Green Set) and carpet. All these surfaces are relatively fast, though classical carpet – the fastest of them – has become less popular recently. To a large extent the speed depends on the under-surface upon which the carpet or hardcourt is laid. It is either wood or cement. Cement is slower, but wood is more frequently used since the locations of indoor tennis tournaments are not used exclusively for tennis and wood is more easily removed.

Serve-and-volley players have the advantage at indoor tournaments. The ball bounces fast and not very high, and therefore the chance to end the point with a winner is far greater than on claycourt. Topspin fiends, on the other hand, are at a serious disadvantage. They usually have a huge backswing, for which there is no time on fast surfaces.

Basically, big servers do well indoors, particularly on carpet. This is not only due to the speed of the surface: wind or sunshine do not inhibit service movement, which makes it easier to serve well.

An exception to this rule was the Guardian Direct Cup in London in February 1999, when high winds played havoc with the huge marquee venue on the opening day and big servers like Marc Rosset complained bitterly.

There is otherwise clear statistical evidence that big servers should always be followed indoors. Boris Becker has by far the best record on carpet. Up to the start of the 1999 season he had collected 26 titles on the surface, which put him way ahead of two other aggressive players – Pete Sampras on 15 and Goran Ivanisevic on 14.

Two other big servers were in the top ten of carpet titles, too, by the end of 1998 – Switzerland's Rosset at six, and Richard Krajicek at five.

The best baseliners on the list were Michael Chang (eight), Yevgeny Kafelnikov (six) and Andre Agassi (four), all of whom serve well and have aggressive groundstrokes without much top-spin.

## claycourts

While grasscourts are fading in popularity, the claycourts which are common in Europe and South America are becoming more popular. Though the term 'clay' is used, claycourts are actually made of well-packed and rolled dirt with sand-like granules of brick or ash on the surface. By far the slowest of the surfaces used in top-flight tennis, there are variations of claycourts depending upon the type of material used and the size of the compacted granules.

The finer the granules, the faster the speed of the ball on the court. There are three main types of claycourt: European or red clay, found mainly in Europe and Latin America; American green clay found mainly in the States; and the less-common shale of the United Kingdom.

Clay is slow and high-bouncing and it is therefore much easier to play a defensive game. And spin can be used more effectively than on any other surface. Players raised on claycourts learn to use topspin and slice to keep opponents under pressure. They also tend to have large backswings on their shots.

The relatively high bounce gives more chance to retrieve balls. It also means that when a player approaches the net, his approach shot must be very good because his opponent has much more time to prepare for a passing shot. Because so much of the play is defensive, with a slower moving ball and a higher bounce, rallies on claycourts tend to be far longer and extraordinary patience is often needed by a player merely to win a point. This might explain why Thomas Muster, who has won countless titles on clay, was for so long regarded as one of the fittest players on Tour.

The French Open is the only Grand Slam to be played on clay but there are 28 ATP Tour tournaments, including three of the Mercedes Super 9 events, played on the surface. Indeed, wherever you are in Europe in spring, you can switch on satellite channel Eurosport and be almost guaranteed to see two clay-court players slugging it out.

## grasscourts

By far the fastest surface, grass has become increasingly less popular on the ATP Tour. At the start of the Open era, three of the four Grand Slams were played on grass, as were many other tournaments. Now only Wimbledon and five ATP tournaments are on grass. It is, as I'm sure everyone knows, a fast surface where the ball has a low bounce and tends to skid off the surface. As a tournament progresses, the bounce of the ball becomes more unreliable.

Because of the speed of the game on grasscourts an attacking serve-and-volley game is important. Speed gives players little time to recover and a well-placed volley invariably wins the point. Drop shots are another potent weapon because the ball will not bounce high enough for an opponent to reach it.

Most Wimbledon champions have been serve-and-volley players, although baseliner Bjorn Borg was a notable exception. Andre Agassi was crowned Wimbledon king in 1992 but was helped by a dry summer which baked the courts and allowed the ball to bounce higher.

Though serve-and-volley is king at Wimbledon, increasingly a power serve alone is good enough to take players through to the latter stages. If the likes of Greg Rusedski, Richard Krajicek and Pete Sampras find their best ace-serving form, there is little opponents on grass can do to stop them.

# chapter 9

## athletics

The only way to make a small fortune from gambling, they say, is to start with a large one. That's not strictly true. We've seen already that the best way to make gambling pay is to attack bookies where they are most vulnerable - and nowhere are they more vulnerable than athletics.

Bookmaker tales of woe in athletics are legendary. In 1972 they were filled in by a clued-up gang of Swedish punters – still operational even now – who knew that a little-known runner named Lasse Viren was well-nigh unbeatable in long-distance races and who cleaned up when the Finn took Olympic gold in Munich in both the 5,000m and 10,000m at 6-1 and 9-1.

The brains behind that scam was a man called Peter Andersson, later to become boss of international bookmakers SSP Overseas Betting. Andersson said he knew of dozens of Swedish punters who that year flew to England specifically to back Viren. "We must have won close on £1 million between us," he recalled. "Even at the Montreal Olympics, four years later, British bookies still hadn't learned their lesson and still didn't have a clue what they were doing on athletics. We cleaned up again."

His recollections were confirmed by William Hill spokesman Graham Sharpe, who said he vividly remembered a set of shrewd Swedes pocketing tidy sums on Viren's golden runs. "Sophisticated punters would have had a big advantage over us in those days, when 95 per cent of our ante-post department was geared to horseracing alone," he said.

Sharpe's words imply that bookies today are much more clued up, but that just isn't true.

In the 1991 World Athletics Championships in Tokyo, bookies were surprised to see heavy, sustained support for a Russian unknown called Tatyana Dorovskikh for the women's 3,000m.

Dorovskikh was backed down from 50-1 to 14-1 before bookies decided to do a spot of belated homework – and to their horror found that Dorovskikh was none other than reigning Olympic 3,000 metre champion Tatyana Samolenko, now running under her married name. The Russian, who under the name Samolenko would have been no longer than 11-8, duly won gold.

The final of the women's 400m hurdles at Atlanta in 1996 was due off at 5.25pm live on BBC. But coverage on the Beeb, still live so everyone thought, did not begin until 5.30pm. Bookies did not close their books until the cameras showed the athletes lining up, allowing punters who'd listened to the race live on Radio 5 five minutes earlier to cash in on 9-4 winner Deon Hemmings.

In 1991, Peter Andersson, as head of SSP bookmakers, took out a full-page advertisement in one of the trade racing papers to publicise a wide list of odds a week in advance of a major athletics championships.

Andersson knew that rival bookmakers, less informed on athletics, would rip off the odds of a company widely recognised as athletics shrewdies. So he deliberately left out of his lists the names of several fancied runners. He anticipated, correctly, that when he asked one of these copycat rivals to quote odds on the 'overlooked' runners, they would offer him inflated prices in the belief that these runners were there merely to make up the numbers.

"It's the same as a fisherman using live bait to attract the big fish," said Andersson, whose company at the time had few British clients and who, therefore, were taking only a small risk in publicising their odds in the racing press.

The problem bookmakers face is that athletics becomes big business only once, maybe twice, a year, with the Olympics, the World Championships, European Championships and, to a lesser extent, the Commonwealth Games the only events punters are interested in. It is therefore not worth their while to train a close eye on the sport – the rising stars, the fading big names, that kind of thing – when they would be better employed keeping tabs on the weekly golf and tennis tournaments across the world. But there are punters – maybe athletics correspondents who follow the circuit all around the globe – who know everything there is to know about the sport; new world record marks, the number of silvers Ecuador won at the last Olympics, even the dimensions of Linford's lunchbox. What a fantastic opportunity they have every year to make that inside knowledge pay.

Of course the leading firms pay athletics insiders to advise them before big events, but these specialists very often know nothing of odds and, fearful that a wrong opinion will cost the bookies, their occasional paymasters, dearly, they play safe and talk up the chances of the favourites.

Bookies react by giving those same market leaders far shorter odds than they deserve, thus allowing live outsiders to start at really fancy prices. Ladbrokes, for instance, still shudder at the £200 bet they laid in the Seoul Olympics of 1988 on Paul Ereng at 80-1 for the 800m.

Bookmakers accept that they are vulnerable to athletics experts, which is why they adopt totally unacceptable defensive measures.

For the Barcelona Olympics in 1992, Surrey Racing were the only firm to offer each-way betting on the top track events, even at the first-round stage when theoretically there were still several runners in with a chance of gold. If we were talking about contests with a red-hot odds-on favourite, that would just about have been okay. But look at the pre-Games' odds that year for the blue riband event, the men's 100m. Leroy Burrell was favourite at 5-2, with Frankie Fredericks 4-1, Linford Christie 9-2, Olapade Adeniken and Dennis Mitchell 8-1, and Mark Witherspoon at 10-1. That's perfect material for each-way betting, yet bookies insisted on win only.

"We may quote ten runners but very often there are only two who can win so why should we bet each-way?" they said.

Yet the Seoul Olympics four years earlier had thrown up a string of surprise winners and that trend continued in Barcelona, with hardly a good thing obliging. Christie won 100m gold at 9-2 and earlier that year, before a golden mid-summer spell, had been available at 50-1. The second most important event, the 1,500m, was won by 20-1 outsider Fermin Cacho. It was a similar story in the women's events, with 50-1 chance Gail Devers capturing 100m gold and 20-1 longshot Hassiba Boulmerka leading them home in the 1,500m. Britain's Colin Jackson was a cert for 110m hurdles gold but that went to 25-1 outsider Mark McCoy. Goodness, even Michael Johnson, the 200m god, blew out and failed even to qualify for the final, with gold going to Mike Marsh, a 7-1 chance.

What gives bookmakers most headaches when it comes to framing prices for athletics is the lack of a starting line-up.

So often fancied runners make 11th-hour withdrawals, maybe because of injury, or perhaps they're double booked and don't want to ruin their chances of, say, 1,500m gold, by tiring themselves out in the 800m first. Until bookies see the runners on the starting blocks, very often they have no concrete idea who will be in the field and that will always hamper the development of athletics as a betting medium.

The best advice I can possibly give athletics punters is this: when the big championships come around, you can safely ignore all the times recorded in run-of-the-mill grand prix events that litter the summer months. These may offer rich prize-money, but they are totally irrelevant as form guides to the Olympics and World Championships.

Allowing times recorded in, say, Nice, to influence your betting two months later at the Olympics in Sydney is like taking into account Manchester United's form in the Worthington Cup before a Champions League clash seven days later. The top athletes don't care about grand prix events: they are mere opportunities to warm up for the truly big races.

All that matters in athletics betting is the evidence of your own eyes, and that is why it is crucial when the Olympics and World Championships come around to study closely the qualifying heats. I am not talking about the times set in those heats; rather, it is the manner in which the races are run that is all important.

A woman athlete clocking 3:57.92 in winning her 1,500m first-round will not necessarily be a better bet than a rival running

4:01.20 in a later heat, if the winner of the earlier contest was flat out while the later winner was easing up.

Punters must judge how much more there is to come from an athlete in the final; how much more she has in reserve. This can never be an exact science and this is where bookies can come unstuck.

Gary Burton and Athos Christodoulou are the men charged with setting athletics odds for William Hill, the market leaders in the sport. They were forced to give athletics more attention once Hills, in 1998, clinched a contract to post odds for domestic events covered on TV by Channel 4 and, with the help of trusted athletics advisors, are probably the most informed of all odds-compilers on track events. But they readily admit that their individual interpretations of form in qualifying heats can differ wildly.

Burton may believe an athlete has been running well within himself; Christodoulou will swear he was flat out. It all boils down to their opinion, and who is to say their opinions are any more worthy than ours?

Burton says he video-tapes all qualifying heats and watches them again and again, in the manner of a steward at a racecourse studying the validity of a jockey's objection to the winner.

In 100 metre races he looks for giveaway glances at rival athletes that suggest a runner has plenty left in the locker. The more a sprinter's facial expression wobbles, the more relaxed he is and the greater the potential for a faster time in the next round, he says. A runner finishing seventh in a heat from which the first eight qualify for the final can be just as dangerous as the winner, he insists, quite correctly.

The two best athletics bets I have ever struck came as a result of performances in qualifying heats. In the 1996 Olympic Games in Atlanta, Russian athlete Svetlana Masterkova picked up a gold medal at 800m before beginning her bid for 1,500m glory two days later. I'd already marked down the Russian as a live bet pre-Olympics at 8-1, as leading up to Atlanta she could boast the fastest time in the world over three and three-quarter laps.

In the first-round heat Masterkova, confidence flying with a gold medal already in her locker, cruised home in first place without breaking sweat. I'm no athletics expert but even this untrained eye could see that the Russian girl could have won by half the length of the track had she really been trying.

By contrast, Hassiba Boulmerka, the reigning 1,500m Olympic queen and hot favourite, could only stutter into third place in her heat. Boulmerka had folded in a grand prix event in Nice three weeks earlier and again looked deeply ill at ease in the 1,500m heat, unleashing a late spurt to snatch third place.

With no other real dangers, I rated Masterkova next door to a certainty to clinch her second gold medal, and could not believe my eyes when Ladbrokes gave her a 9-4 quote, behind 11-10 favourite Boulmerka. Masterkova won gold doing cartwheels.

Then in 1998, in the European Championships in Budapest, Wilson Kipketer was by all accounts a stone-cold certainty for 800m gold. He'd recorded all the fastest times at the distance, and no-one could live with him. But Kipketer had been struck down by malaria earlier in the year, had been sidelined for six months, and there was no clear evidence that he had fully recovered before the heats got under way.

At this time bookies had not even bothered to frame odds for the event, so certain were they of a Kipketer gold. But the Kenyan, running under the Danish flag, looked decidedly sluggish in finishing second in his semi-final heat.

Yes, of course he could have been taking things easy, qualifying with room to spare and saving his energy until the final. But instinctively I knew all was not well with Kipketer. There were signs of distress in his expressions, his stride was far from fluent, running all of a sudden seemed a huge effort.

Bookies were immediately aware that Kipketer was perhaps not the sure thing they had at first reckoned, yet still opted to play safe with a very tight 1-4 quote. But punters who now knew that the Kenyan-born athlete was beatable, also recognised that there had to be value elsewhere.

I watched the heats again on tape and was struck by how well German runner Nils Schumann finished in taking his heat. If

Kipketer was below par, Schumann looked the man most likely to take advantage, so the 4-1 quote about the German was a gift. The result is history, Schumann winning in superb style.

I've always believed that athletics has massively undersold itself. Its grand prix circuit is endlessly repetitive; top athletes were for so long allowed to treat the sport almost with disdain, pulling out of engagements for the merest sniffle; and the evil spectre of drug-taking has turned away sponsors and fans in their thousands.

As recently as 1997, Michael Johnson, one of the finest athletes God ever put on earth, was introduced at some showbizzy razzmatazz in track-ignorant America as Michael Jordan; at another, as Michael Jackson. Yet athletics, drug-free athletics, is sport in its purest form. There is no high-performance car to rely on, no powerful thoroughbred between your legs (Linford apart), no team-mates to let you down. On the track, you are in charge of your own destiny.

The effort the athletes put in, the tearing lungs, the pumping muscles – all make a huge impression on the impartial spectator. We know that we could never have made it to the top in tennis, or golf, or football. But athletics. Well, maybe with a bit of training ...

It's a sport with massive potential to involve the ordinary man. The bell that signals the last lap also quickens the pulse of the viewer – even if we haven't had a bet.

We saw the future of athletics, a brighter, higher-profile sport, in May 1997 in the Challenge of the Champions in Toronto. Purists frowned upon this gimmicky contest between 100m king Donovan Bailey and 200m master Michael Johnson over 150m, but I could hardly wait for it to start. This at last was giving us what we wanted. Two brilliant athletes clashing head-on over a distance familiar to neither – a real journey into the unknown.

Leading runners had previously made a career of ducking the real issues, of side-stepping contests with their main rivals unless it was for Olympic gold, but here we had two of the very best prepared to put their reputation on the line. So what if they were each getting $500,000 to turn up, with a further $1 million going to the winner? We weren't paying. For us it was all free.

And what made this contest all the more appealing was that it was a pure head-to-head. Just two runners, no bit-part players liable to gatecrash the party.

Twice before, athletics had bowed to public pressure and staged what should have been head-to-head humdingers. Twice they were damp squibs, wrecked by unwanted interlopers. Carl Lewis and Ben Johnson were overshadowed by Dennis Mitchell in Lille in 1991. And then Jon Drummond stole the thunder of Lewis at Gateshead in 1993 when it was he, rather than superstar Lewis, who pushed Linford Christie so close.

Incidentally, the odds for that Toronto showdown illustrated how bookies, and indeed most of the betting public, can easily be brainwashed by facts and figures. In the weeks leading up to the race, we were constantly told how Johnson's times for the second 100m of his best 200m runs was as fast as anything achieved by sprint king Bailey. So if Johnson was as fast as Bailey at 100m and guaranteed to stay the 150m trip, unlike his opponent, he must therefore be a red-hot favourite, the thinking went.

Bookies fell for it and made Johnson 1-4 favourite, with Bailey 11-4. Punters were duped too, with hardly a bean wagered on the underdog. It was only when I pointed out, in the *Racing Post*, an obvious fact seemingly overlooked by all these track experts that Bailey began to attract support.

"Bookies seem to have read too much into Johnson's time over the second 100m at the Atlanta Games last summer," I wrote. "Clocked at 10.12secs for the first half of that world record run, he ran the second half in 9.20sec, significantly faster than the world record of 9.84sec Bailey set for 100m. But it's a daft comparison. Bailey ran 9.84sec from a standing start; Johnson, by comparison, was fired by catapult."

It reminded me of the almost scientific analysis of the finish of the 1986 Derby at Epsom, when Dancing Brave's late, late run narrowly failed to overhaul winner Shahrastani. In the days leading up to their next clash in the King George at Ascot, clock experts explained comprehensively why time studies showed that Shahrastani would uphold the form. Punters were taken in, even though all the evidence screamed at Epsom that given a more sensible ride the beautiful Brave would have coasted home.

I spent the Friday night before that Ascot return in a pub explaining heatedly to assorted knobheads why Brave was a certainty. Had he lost out the next day, I would still be broke today. He won. As if there was any doubt.

The Johnson-Bailey circus was ultimately wrecked when Johnson pulled up mid-race with an injury, leaving Bailey to waltz home alone, but the publicity it had garnered had surely shown athletics the way forward. The two athletes had played their part even before donning a vest, displaying their intense dislike for one another in a series of TV appearances in the way boxers hype a world title showdown. For the brash Bailey, read Hamed or Tyson; for the more serene Johnson, read Lennox Lewis or Evander Holyfield.

As we've seen already in this book, head-to-head events are an Achilles heel for bookmakers, who would much sooner lay an eight-runner race to a book of something like 130 per cent than a two-runner contest at 108 per cent. But privately they acknowledge the appeal and the potential of contests like Bailey v Johnson which, properly marketed, can give a kiss of life to a sport dangerously close to terminal illness.

Perhaps I'm guilty of slight exaggeration but I see no reason why, given the right protagonists – for example Coe v Ovett in the distant past, Lewis v Christie more recently – one-on-one athletics showdowns should not become as feted as world heavyweight title fights.

I will explain in the next chapter how boxing has become a frustrating sport on which to bet because antiquated scoring methods make the draw such a likely verdict.

Yet in athletics, when athletes are consistently running to within one-hundredth of a second of each other, judges always manage to provide a definite result. It seems that in athletics a dead-heat is taboo, which is great news for punters who have always regarded that phrase as nothing more than two offensive four-letter words.

I remember vividly the controversy following the women's 100m final at the World Championships in Stuttgart in 1993. Well-backed

4-6 favourite Gail Devers and 9-4 second-favourite Merlene Ottey breasted the tape together at the climax of a thrilling race, with TV cameras suggesting that Ottey may just have got up on the line. But judges awarded the race to Devers, leading to a high-level objection from Ottey's Jamaican camp and a dramatic change to Devers' official time.

World Athletics Championship officials initially gave Devers a winning time of 10.81secs, with Ottey a hundredth of a second behind in 10.82. But a jury of appeal met to re-read the photo-finish and decided to revise Olympic champion Devers' time from 10.81 to 10.82, the same as Ottey's.

They did not, however, alter the placings, arguing that it had been possible to confirm that Devers had won while awarding the athletes identical times. It was further proof that athletics officials are notoriously reluctant to give dead-heats, with Alan Wells v Mike McFarlane in the Commonwealth Games 100m in Brisbane in 1982 the last in major competition.

Dave Moorcroft, BBC analyst at the time and the man now in charge of British athletics, insisted that judges had a duty to call a dead-heat. "If hundredths of a second can't separate athletes, then it has to be a dead-heat," he said. "What's wrong with having joint-champions?"

And athletics correspondent Mel Wattman, consultant editor on *Athletics Today* and a keen punter himself, said at the time: "Officials pride themselves on being able to separate two athletes. They look upon it as a defeat if they can't give a definite result."

Punters loathe dead-heats because if you back an odds-on favourite which dead-heats for first place, you actually lose money. For instance, an £11 straight bet on a 10-11 winner will earn you a return of £21.00. If, however, it dead-heats, your return is £10.50 for an £11 outlay, even though you've backed a winner (dead-heat bets are settled at half your stake to full odds).

I should point out here that the somewhat puritanical view of athletics chiefs towards betting in the early 1990s has now softened, the sport's rulers perhaps recognising at last that anything that offers heightened publicity, as betting so often does, is to be welcomed. Before Atlanta in 1996, Australian Olympic chiefs launched a serious bid to ban betting on the Games. They claimed that punting would "demean the Games and divide the nation" and feared that races would be thrown by athletes trying to land betting coups.

AOC president John Coates, who also called for a betting ban for the Sydney Games in 2000, said: "You'd have a question mark over form reversals at the Olympics. People would ask whether races had been thrown. It would also put extra pressure on the athletes."

A couple of years earlier the British Athletics Federation had voted against moves to allow bookmakers William Hill to open betting booths at major British tracks. Hills spokesman Graham Sharpe, in an appeal to the BAF, said: "Betting on athletics has not come anywhere near to its full potential. When you have things like the Linford Christie v Carl Lewis showdown of a couple of years ago you realise the sort of potential, and it's still there."

But Arthur Gold, president of the Amateur Athletics Association, warned that a betting link would encourage athletes to perform below par. "It offers opportunities for grave abuse," he said. "The sport seems to be thinking only of material advantages. There is no thought being given to the long-term consequences."

Continental bookmakers had been allowed to operate at the 1994 European Championships in Helsinki, where odds were very publicly flashed up on the stadium's giant Diamond screen. And Rob Denmark, who won a 5,000m silver in Helsinki before becoming Commonwealth champion, said: "Personally I do not see a problem. It could add more spice to meetings, attract more crowds and generally make the sport more popular. I was aware of it in Helsinki but it certainly did not affect my performance in any way."

Athletics chiefs did not object to William Hills odds appearing prominently on the Channel 4 coverage of domestic meetings during 1998, and the logical next step is for Hills to operate betting facilities trackside at high-profile European meetings.

As a final example of how bookies can get their athletics sums hopelessly wrong, take a look at the betting in 1990 for the race to stage the 1996 Olympics. In Britain, Hills and Ladbrokes each made Athens the red-hot favourite at 4-7 and 4-6 respectively, yet the Greek capital was a 7-2 chance with American bookies.

Athens had everything going for it, the layers in Britain insisted. The Greek government had pledged massive sums on facilities, and the city could boast an 80,000-seater Olympic Stadium, plus an indoor arena with 20,000 seats built specially for the following year's Mediterranean Games. Above all it had history – the 1996 Games was to mark the centenary of the modern Olympics held 100 years before in - where else? - Athens.

Yet American layers insisted Atlanta was the true favourite, even though its opponents pointed to the city's inexperience in staging multi-million dollar extravaganzas. Atlanta was 7-4 with Ladbrokes the day before Olympic committee members cast their vote.

Atlanta, as we all know, got that vote, although given the controversy late in 1998 over reports of Olympic bigwigs being bribed into awarding the Winter Games to Salt Lake City in 2002, we should perhaps wonder just how straight that vote was.

Although I mentioned earlier that run-of-the-mill meetings on the athletics grand prix circuit are rarely top of a leading athlete's priorities, I still see no reason why bookmakers do not bet on them, particularly as most are televised live on TV.

Agreed, it's devilishly difficult to find reliable news about line-ups, and the ever-present threat of undisclosed injuries will always worry bookies, but Hills for one clearly recognise the sport's betting potential – which is why they were so delighted to win the Channel 4 contract – and it's amazing how quickly a sport can grow as a punting medium once bookies put their weight behind it.

For instance, it wasn't until the mid-1990s that bookies began regularly to bet on the weekly American golf tournaments, and they have quickly become a part of everyday punting life.

Bookies may argue that to quote prices on grand prix events is too risky because they will never know which athletes are 'off' (betting terminology for committed) and which are there purely for appearance money. But the same applies to punters, too. We're just as much in the dark as the bookies. Okay, punters like Peter

Andersson of SSP may seek to take advantage of inside knowledge, even though Andersson says he has scaled down his athletics betting because, "It is now no longer about which athlete is the fastest, more which pharmaceutical company can produce the strongest drug." But bookies are happy to leave themselves open to clever money in many other fields (next England manager, Booker Prize, etc) because quite often such clever money accurately marks their card. So why should athletics be so blatantly snubbed?

It's surely absurd that bookies can bet on insignificant contests like the Shark Shoot-Out in golf, or the manner in which Alec Gilroy leaves *Coronation Street*, yet refuse to consider the sometimes highly-competitive athletics grand prix circuit. Remember too that, in 1998, the grand prix circuit received a much-needed shot-in-the-arm when serious prize-money was offered to win races. Athletes now have a greater incentive to treat these competitions far more seriously.

Much of athletics – hammer, discus and javelin for example – is a sick joke. Indeed I've always resented the massive publicity enjoyed by British triple-jump ace Jonathan Edwards because in my book there are only about seven people across the globe interested in that discipline (which kid in his right mind wakes up one morning and thinks "I know, I'll become a triple-jumper"? If I started training now, at 38, I reckon I'd make the world's top ten in a couple of years). But at its best, the sport has the capacity to lift the spirits like no other. Call me sad, but I keep a list, updated regularly, of sport's most uplifting moments.

Right up there at the top, as it has been for several years, was Liz McColgan's victory in the 10,000m at the World Championships in Tokyo. It wasn't such McColgan's victory, against the odds though it was, and in stamina-sapping humidity, that tugged at the heartstrings as the reaction it provoked in BBC commentator and old-pro Brendan Foster. Foster, voice quivering, croaked: "This is the greatest performance by any British athlete anywhere in the world. Anywhere, any time, ever." On the page those words perhaps lose their poignancy, but at the time they had me blubbing.

Perhaps it's a good time here to complete my top-ten list of magic sporting moments that make me go "aaahhhh"!

**1.  The tearful embrace between Seve Ballesteros and Nick Faldo after Europe clinched victory at Oak Hill in the 1995 Ryder Cup**

*Two men of vastly different personalities, who had little apart from their chosen profession in common but who recognised the sheer guts the other had displayed to help claw victory from what had looked certain defeat. It was easy to understand Ballesteros, who wears his heart on his sleeve, reacting like that. But what made the moment extra special was the show of emotion from the more aloof Faldo. Seve played like a pig at Oak Hill, yet in that moment Faldo acknowledged the importance to the side of the inspirational Spaniard.*

**2.  Gary Lineker's infectious grin when David Platt scored THAT goal**

*Platt's epic volley in injury-time against Belgium put England into the quarter-finals of the 1990 World Cup but Lineker's reaction will live longer in the memory. As England players dived in jubilation on Platt, Lineker's head turned momentarily towards the TV cameras and his face wore a grin that perfectly summed up the feelings of a nation. Unrestrained joy.*

**3.  *Nessun Dorma***

*The song that made Italia 90 so memorable. I can't hear it without thinking of that World Cup; I can't think of that World Cup without hearing that song. I haven't a clue what the words mean, but they make me blub.*

**4.  Liz McColgan and Brendan Foster**

**5.  Aldaniti's Grand National**

*For the horse itself, for Bob Champion, for a story that even now is almost impossible to believe.*

**6.  Kevin Keegan's TV tantrum**

*We loved it, we just loved it when an emotional King Kev lost it in front of the live Sky cameras during the epic Newcastle and Manchester United championship run-in. Ever-popular Keegan* launched a tirade at Alex Ferguson that every non-United fan endorsed. This was one of the game's biggest stars speaking our language, the language of the fans.

### 7.   Dancing Brave's Arc

And I was there to see that beautiful animal in his finest moment. On TV it may not have been that special but Longchamp that day was electric. The French could see no further than Bering but we knew the Brave was pure class. Even when he wasn't sighted three out, we still knew he'd do it. And then that incredible surge up the straight ...

### 8.   Hayley Baker-Finch's ice-cream

As BBC's Steve Rider interviewed leader Ian Baker-Finch after the third round of the 1991 Open, little daughter Hayley hilariously mistook the microphone for an ice-cream and started licking. Baker-Finch was a superb champion and Hayley a delight. It made the Aussie's subsequent decline, and the thought of what it must be doing to his family, so hard to bear.

### 9.   Stuart Pearce's penalty

Not the one he so famously missed; but the one he scored during Euro 96. It wasn't ball hitting net in that shoot-out against Spain that brought the tears, it was Pearce's totally uninhibited show of jubilation. Only when he punched the air so violently and mouthed obscenities at Fate did we realise how deeply he had been scarred by that missed penalty in the World Cup six years earlier.

### 10. Michael Dickinson's famous five

To get five steeplechasers fit enough to run in the same Cheltenham Gold Cup was a magnificent achievement for one trainer; to get them to fill the first five places one of the greatest feats in 20th Century sport. As Dicko's No.1 fan, I put money on the great man pulling it off. And when Peter O'Sullevan picked up on what the BBC cameras hadn't yet shown, that Dicko's weak link, Ashley House, had moved into fifth place, the tears rolled. Not because of the bet, but because at last Dickinson would be recognised outside racing as a true sporting genius.

# chapter 10

---

## boxing

---

It wasn't the biggest upset in just boxing - it was the biggest in sporting history. When Buster Douglas knocked out Mike Tyson in the tenth round of their world heavyweight title fight in Tokyo in 1990, the result shook the world. David was given a better chance against Goliath than Douglas against the invincible Iron Mike. A Douglas victory was just not an option.

One American boxing correspondent was asked after landing at Tokyo Airport how long he expected to work in the Japanese capital. "About a minute and a half," he said, showing more charity to no-hoper Douglas than his odds-making countrymen in Las Vegas, where wags on the Strip joked that Tyson was not taking his opponent lightly enough.

As it turned out, Tyson had indeed taken his opponent too lightly. We hadn't believed the tall tales of pre-fight indulgences – women, women and more women – by Tyson for two reasons.

First, because he was a professional boxer, surely too dedicated for such weakness; second because the thought of him bedding all those lovelies while we were getting none was too painful to bear. But suddenly, as he laboured against the merciless Douglas jab, the truth of those rumours became horribly apparent.

It is commonly reported when writers refer to this Tokyo shocker that Douglas was a 42-1 underdog, but that betrays a lack of betting savvy. Tyson was indeed the 1-42 favourite in Vegas, but Douglas was never longer than 34-1.

Those Douglas odds are a damning indictment of bookmakers on this side of the Atlantic. So one-sided did Hills and Ladbrokes see the fight, they refused to quote odds for Tyson. Fair enough, but in that case why was Douglas a mere 7-1 chance?

You may have noticed that bookmakers in Britain rarely refer to the Tyson defeat whenever they talk of insurmountable odds being defied by apparent no-hopers. The reason? They're ashamed of those miserly odds they offered, and so they should be.

The Tyson-Douglas fight was staged around the same time as the opening of the new sports book at the luxurious Mirage Hotel in Vegas. Mirage chief odds-maker Jimmy Vaccaro, in a bid to attract the big players to his casino, opened with Tyson at 1-31, comfortably the best odds around.

He recalls: "The first bet we took was a guy laying $62,000 on Tyson to win $2,000, so I moved the number to 35-1 (1-35 in Brit-speak). Five days later, a guy laid $70,000 to win $2,000. Then, a day and a half before the fight, another man walked in with $98,000 to bet on Tyson and the line moved to 42-1. People were betting against Buster Douglas like he was crippled. But in a way you couldn't blame these guys. After all Tyson had done the business for 15 previous wagering fights. Can you walk into a bank and walk out two minutes later with $2,000? I've had people say, 'If you've got $60,000, why would you want $2,000 more?' and my answer is, 'People always want more.'"

Tyson's pre-fight training regimen of wall-to-wall babes apart, how else can that incredible Tokyo result be explained? Bert Randolph Sugar, the doyen of boxing betting in America, has a credible theory.

In his book *The Caesars Palace Book Of Sports Betting*, Sugar wrote: "The student of styles could have seen it coming, for it was the difference in styles that had done it as much as Douglas himself. Mike Tyson's calling card always had been his baseball bat of a left; he would just lower his shoulder and let it fly. What Buster Douglas did to counter this was simplicity itself: every time the 5ft 9in Tyson set up to let fly, the 6ft 4in Douglas would take a half-step backward, taking him out of Tyson's range, while the shorter man remained in his range. There, Douglas would double-jab him, catching him repeatedly. By mid-fight the champion's right eye was closed; all the better for Douglas to hit him again. And again."

Bookmakers take huge amounts of money on world heavyweight title bouts – betting on the two Frank Bruno fights against Tyson went through the roof – but the sport in my eyes can never fully grab British punters by the balls for four reasons.

First, betting-friendly fights are so few and far between that there's no chance for the punter to play catch-up.

Lose on your Saturday football treble and there's another slate of games on the Sunday, a further live TV match on Monday, and virtually a full fixture-list Tuesday and Wednesday. All offer a quick chance to recoup losses. The same is true of most sports, and especially true of horseracing.

Lose on a boxing title fight, however, and you'll sometimes wait three months for the next one. There is no incentive, therefore, to become an authority. Why waste all those hours of study and research for something that offers so few opportunities to strike it rich?

Second, so many title fights, generally the only contests bookies ever bother to price up, are mis-matches that punters are forced down an alley towards the perils of round-by-round betting, where the layers enjoy a massive advantage. Yes, we all remember fights like Hagler v Leonard, Leonard v Hearns, Eubank v Benn, Lewis v Bruno, and Tyson v Holyfield, not only because they offered rich sport but also because betting was pretty much two-way. There was no massive odds-on favourite to deter punters. On the contrary, all the boxers had healthy bands of supporters. But 90 per cent of the time a title fight, no matter what the weight, will feature a near unbackable jolly.

The man in the street is not going to get worked up about a 1-8 chance, and so he will have no alternative but to try to pinpoint the exact round his favoured fighter will win, and even the most naïve punter should know instinctively that this form of betting is sport's equivalent of the National Lottery.

Let me give you an example of how bookies cash in whenever a punter backs a boxer to win in a designated round. Tommy Hearns was 11-4 with Hills for his 1989 re-match with Sugar Ray Leonard, a full eight years after their first unforgettable contest in Vegas, when Leonard knocked out the 'Hit Man' in the 14th after suffering 12 rounds of fearsome punishment. But if you backed Hearns to win in each of the 12 rounds, with a 13th bet on a Hearns points victory - in other words, covering all eventualities - you'd have got no better than 11-8 for your money.

Bookies know that punters who indulge in specific-round betting are by nature ignorant and prepared to accept whatever odds are posted, no matter how tight.

Naseem Hamed has made a habit in the late 1990s of predicting the round in which he will stop his opponents. Only once has Hamed's forecast been accurate and yet still punters take his boasts seriously. It makes you wonder whether bookies have entered into some secret sponsorship deal with the arrogant Sheffield-based fighter.

Third, there's something intrinsically barbaric about the sport that disturbs the more sensitive among us. I must confess here that my views on whether boxing should be banned have changed like the wind over the last few years.

Two dangerous men punching each other senseless is not the most edifying of sights, even the most fervent boxing fan will admit, and the cloud cast across the sport by the mental deterioration of its finest-ever exponent, Muhammad Ali, after years of absorbing wrecking-ball blows will take some time to pass.

When we think of our pathetic wagers on Chris Eubank's fight with the tragic Michael Watson, and Nigel Benn's ill-starred contest with the equally tragic Gerald McClellan, we are rightly repulsed. "Hit him harder," we screamed, pound signs in our eyes. "Put him down." Both men went down and are now living what some would call slow deaths.

In the aftermath of those two wretched fights, bookmakers - at least one or two of them - showed they do sometimes have a heart. Torquay independent bookmaker Nic Szeremeta, deeply affected by Watson's sad fate, banned betting on boxing in his shops and called upon the major firms to follow suit. "Let's just say I find it difficult to justify making money out of a sport when there is a man lying in hospital, possibly dying," said Szeremeta after news broke that Watson was on a life-support machine. "If all bookmakers in the country followed suit and banned betting on boxing, there would be considerably less interest in the sport, and considerably fewer risks."

When it was put to him that horseracing throws up more casualties than boxing, Szeremeta said: "The difference is that in racing, accidents are precisely that. In boxing the main aim is to knock someone unconscious."

It was no surprise, however, when the leading firms adopted a more hard-hearted approach. "The public demand prices on boxing matches and we have to compete with other firms," a Coral spokesman said. And his Hills counterpart said: "As Mr Szeremeta says, the main aim of boxing is to knock someone unconscious, but that has always been the case and I would be more impressed if he had always refused to lay prices on boxing. Both fighters knew the risks they were taking when they stepped into the ring and they did so of their own free will."

Four years later, in 1995, spread betting firm City Index said they were considering scrapping boxing betting as McClellan fought for his life in a London hospital hours after his title fight with Benn. "We lost money on the fight but I'd rather have lost double if you could tell me that McClellan was going to be okay," chairman Jonathan Sparke said. "It was a sickening end to the night and I'm going to have to sit down and think very carefully about whether we'll price up boxing again. Money doesn't come into it after such a tragedy."

Soon after the fight, the *Racing Post* canvassed leading boxing experts for their opinion on the future and the safety of the sport. At the time it was a very contentious issue – it still is - and their replies are worth recalling here.

The question was: "In the wake of the McClellan tragedy there have been renewed calls for boxing to be banned. What are your views?" This is how they answered:

**Frank Maloney (Lennox Lewis manager):** "At the end of the day boxing offers more good than bad. There is a far bigger health risk in smoking and I'd like to see it banned from all public places, but you don't see calls for cigarettes to be outlawed."

**Jim Neilly (BBC boxing commentator):** "I don't think boxing will or should be banned. You cannot deny the intrinsic nature of boxing and anybody who gets in the ring knows the risks. It is a mature choice."

**Hugh McIlvanney (esteemed sports writer):** "Strangely the sufferings of McClellan have not removed my desire to watch fights. It is at times an appetite as worrying as an addiction. But most addicts pay with their own health. It seems worse when the cost of a high is met by others."

**Barry McGuigan (former world champion):** "The abolitionists cannot play God. The bottom line is that we live in a democracy and people have the right to choose to do what they want. If we banned boxing it would merely go underground and the consequences then wouldn't bear thinking about."

All four men made valid points but McGuigan's comment about the dangers of the sport going underground, repeated by several other knowledgeable observers, somehow rankled. What does it mean, this "going underground"?

No-one knows for certain that boxing, if outlawed, would flourish as an unlicensed sport. It is merely an argument trotted out whenever a ban is called for after every particularly bloody bout. Its advocates maintain that young men with fighting in their blood could not give up the sport if it was banned. Instead they would slug it out in the anything-goes savagery of underground fighting, where butting and gouging are legitimate ploys and where referees are mere token gestures. Your average rugby union international in other words.

For these bouts there is little, if any, medical presence. An underground boxer suffering the kind of injuries sustained by Gerald McClellan would surely die. Yet underground boxing is already with us. Anyone who watched a gruesome documentary on ITV a few years back will be fully aware of it.

Fighters banned from licensed bouts, maybe because of eye or head injuries, go underground to earn a living at what they do best. And those not quite good enough to make it big in pro-boxing, or perhaps lacking the necessary self-control, find their niche in the more brutal environment. How could a ban on boxing, therefore, *create* a twilight underworld when this twilight underworld already exists?

Quite possibly it may not even expand it. For while it's true that some young men take up boxing for the smell of blood and others because it's the only way out of the ghetto, and while it's also true that such characters will very likely gravitate underground if boxing is outlawed, a great many others dream of world titles, of fabulous riches, of fame and women. Take away such dreams and those early-morning slogs, the incessant pounding of punchbags, the sit-ups, the skipping, and the sweat just won't seem worth it. They'll look elsewhere.

I'm not saying here that boxing should be banned, even though I can see the logic in the arguments of the anti-boxing lobby. All I'm suggesting is that as this anti-ring faction gains more support, as it will do every time a fighter is put in a coma, the sport will have to come up with stronger resistance than the threat of an underground explosion.

But what perhaps most deters punters from betting regularly on boxing is the maddening frequency of the draw. The draw, as I've pointed out in previous chapters, is the bane of the punter's life. Most of us seek an allegiance when we bet, a team or individual to cheer on. The draw, an admission perhaps that we can't make up our mind, appeals to few of us. For years we regarded it as the sporting equivalent of the zero in roulette – rarely a factor but an absolute skinner when it does crop up. But the draw in boxing has become a serious player over the last ten years.

In the early 1990s, the draw in big boxing bouts was regularly quoted at anything between 66-1 and 100-1. But clued-up ring punters cashed in at these fancy odds after identifying much quicker than bookmakers two very significant factors. First, the archaic scoring system in boxing meant that a drawn bout was always a semi-strong possibility; second, as the sport began to splinter, with various governing bodies like the WBO, WBA, WBC, and IBF all offering world titles, greedy promoters recognised that a drawn fight would automatically spark calls for a money-spinning re-match. How easy it is to believe that such promoters, some with tremendous clout in the sport, would bring pressure to bear on judges to get the verdict they desired.

Suddenly, drawn bouts were no longer the skinner for bookies that they'd previously been. Gradually the odds shortened and by the late 1990s it was not uncommon to see the draw posted at 25-1, with bookies in Vegas offering no more than 16-1.

Here's an example. In 1989 Mike Tyson was a red-hot 1-8 favourite to beat Frank Bruno in their first world heavyweight title bout in Las Vegas. The draw was on offer at 100-1. In 1997, Steve Collins was an equally warm favourite to beat Frederic Seillier in their WBO super-middleweight title clash, yet the draw was as short as 25-1. Even after acknowledging that any fight involving the durable Collins was more likely to end in a draw than one involving the much more explosive Tyson, such a huge discrepancy appears remarkable. But it's perhaps less so when we examine the bizarre scoring system employed in boxing.

In October 1993, the big grudge clash between Chris Eubank and Nigel Benn, the most eagerly awaited bout in Britain for many years, ended in deadlock, hard on the heels of draws in two other high-profile contests – Julio Cesar Chavez v Pernell Whitaker and Eubank v Ray Close. Punters were getting a bit steamed up about it all, and no wonder.

When you remember that athletics judges had a couple of months earlier felt themselves able to split Gail Devers and Merlene Ottey in the final of the 100m, even though both had clocked identical times in a race lasting little longer than ten seconds, it was surely absurd that boxing judges could not split two boxers throwing hundreds of punches over the course of 12 gruelling three-minute rounds.

Hills said at the time that a draw in boxing, once a no-hoper, was becoming almost as common as a stalemate in rugby union, generally a 14-1 chance. Punters were further annoyed when Barry Hearn, promoter of the Benn-Eubank fight, was interviewed on TV immediately after the final bell and predicted a drawn outcome, so perhaps influencing the judges' decision.

But when you examine the sport's scoring system, it's surprising that draws are not more commonplace.

The winner of a round gets ten points and the loser nine or, if he has been knocked down or massively outclassed, eight. But in practice, officials only ever award a 10-8 round when a knockdown has been registered, and will nearly always go 10-9. So a fighter could dominate six rounds, narrowly lose the other six, and listen to the judges call a draw. Such a scoring system means any bout that goes the distance has a far greater chance of being drawn than perhaps the true nature of the fight suggested.

It's a far from perfect system, which leaves little room for manoeuvre - but ring aficionados will argue that the scoring in tennis is not much different. Pete Sampras could thrash Tim Henman 6-0 6-0 in the first two sets and then lose the next three 7-6 7-6 7-5. He'll have lost the match, despite winning 29 games to Henman's 21.

The controversy over the result of the Lennox Lewis v Evander Holyfield world heavyweight title fight in Madison Square Garden in March 1999 staggered me. Yes, it looked as though Lewis had done enough to get the verdict, but he certainly was not the clear-cut winner newspaper reports in Britain and New York later suggested. It wasn't the three judges in New York that night who deserved censure - it was the sport's absurd point-scoring rules that have thrown up so many other unexpected verdicts.

Bookies traditionally have the draw 'running for them' in big fights. In a snooker or tennis match, with no possibility of a draw, bookies will go something like 1-2 the favourite, 6-4 the underdog. But they will offer the same sort of prices in boxing, even though the draw has become a very real contender.

In Vegas they have a rock-solid reason to fear the draw, or 'push' as it is known there. Sports books in Vegas casinos must refund all win bets, while still paying out to those punters who back the draw.

I should explain here why casinos in Vegas and Atlantic City have usurped Madison Square Garden as the home of world title fights, although the Lennox Lewis v Evander Holyfield contest at the

Garden in March 1999 perhaps heralded a fightback by the famous New York venue.

Vegas odds-maker Art Manteris summed up the attraction of big fights superbly in his book *Superbookie*.

"Boxing is conducive to high-stakes gambling," Manteris wrote. "Whatever excitement and anticipation a person feels while waiting for the roll of the dice is the same feeling he or she gets while waiting for a knock-out punch. It's the unknown that creates the thrill. That's why Las Vegas loves boxing and vice-versa.

"People bet on fights. But more important, people wager in the casino pits on the nights of major fights. Those who love the anticipation and electricity in the air prior to a big fight are often the same people who love high-stakes gambling. Sugar Ray Leonard v Marvin Hagler is very emotional. It creates excitement, so does gambling, and there is a correlation between the two.

"I am convinced that the casino drop (the money wagered) on the night of a big fight can be traced directly to the excitement of that fight. Example: on the night in 1987 that a wobbly Thomas Hearns knocked down Juan Domingo Roldan for the WBC middleweight title and Bobby Czyz was stopped by Prince Charles Williams for the IBF light-heavyweight championship, the audience left ringside feeling terrific, and the casino at the Las Vegas Hilton won approximately $7 million. That's excitement.

"That's also why Las Vegas casinos are willing to take a loss on a fight promotion, sometimes even a big loss. They bank on more than covering expenses with casino profits."

And he went on: "Interestingly the sports bettor usually treats a big fight as just another event on which he may or may not wager. On the night the Las Vegas Hilton Casino won $7 million, for example, (other casinos) handled only about $500,000 on the fight in the sports book. The big players, though – the baccarat players and dice throwers and Hollywood celebrities – go nuts over big fights. They like to see and be seen, and Las Vegas offers the ideal setting."

Bert Randolph Sugar sums it up more succinctly. The reason big-time boxing has now made its home in Vegas, he says, "is the same one that Willie Sutton gave when asked why he robbed banks: 'Because that's where the money is.'"

And Bob Halloran, former president of sports at the Mirage Hotel in Vegas, was even more to the point: "If the casinos ever get out of boxing the purse money will be cut by 80 per cent or more. About 60 per cent of the people who attend casino fights are fight fans. The other 40 per cent are customers or gamblers who need to have a reason to justify their trip. When we get ticket requests from celebrities we know we've got a winner. You can't put a number on the potential value of a big fight to a casino. Basically, we use boxing as a marketing tool to improve business."

We've all seen the old Hollywood movies of the fifties when boxing was portrayed as unmistakably seedy – pugs taking a dive, palookas winning against all the odds – so some of us can be forgiven for thinking that the game is not entirely straight. Think again.

At the lower levels there have almost certainly been results that would make even the most trusting eyes blink in disbelief, but at the pinnacle of the game boxing is 100 per cent straight. Bookies price up only the high-profile fights, contests in which the two fighters will almost certainly benefit more through winning than they ever could through bribery, so when you do your dough at boxing, at least take comfort in the fact that you've done it honestly. Well, at least as long as you ignore rumours of promoter-influenced decisions.

Of course it wasn't always that way. In 1900, boxing was outlawed in Chicago following a fixed fight between Joe Gans and Terry McGovern. This contest was suspect from the very first moment it was announced. Word was that Gans had been paid by big-time gamblers to go down early. When he was knocked out in the second, there was chaos. Referee George Siler said next day: "I do not wish to accuse any fighter of faking, but if Gans was trying last night, I don't know much about the game."

Probably the biggest boxing sting in Britain occurred in April 1992 when bookmakers were rocked by a £500,000 gamble on Lennox Lewis before his European and Commonwealth heavyweight title clash with Derek Williams at London's Royal Albert Hall. It wasn't an outright Lewis victory that punters plunged on – he was as short as 1-9 in places – but a rapid-fire victory inside the first three rounds in a fight screened live on the then fledgling Sky TV.

Two days before the fight Lewis was 40-1 with Corals to win in the first-round, 40-1 for a second round win, and 33-1 to stop Williams in the third. By the time the first bell sounded each of those rounds had been cut to single figures, with the third round as short as 7-2 with Hills. Lewis won in the third.

The scale of the gamble sent shockwaves through the industry, amid rumours that the BBC were investigating an alleged coup following an anonymous tip-off.

But bookies, normally the first to cry foul at any hint of skulduggery, laughed off suggestions of a pre-arranged result.

Hills spokesman Graham Sharpe, so often the industry's voice of reason, said: "When you have two heavyweights and one fighter is considered a certainty, then it doesn't take much imagination to predict an early finish. I think a bandwagon effect caused punters to lump on an early victory. Somebody sees the big prices, gets on, tells his friends, they then get on and word gets around. Suddenly everybody wants a slice and we've got a massive gamble on our hands – they jump on the bandwagon.

"I'm pretty sure there was nothing untoward in the fight, although what was unusual is that punters continued to get on regardless of what price we went. I would also say it was unusual that a fight not on network TV should attract such interest. Although Lewis was a big contender for a world title, he was still a division two fighter as far as public awareness was concerned, so it was surprising there was so much interest in him."

Boxing is such a well-established sport, with rules written almost in tablets of stone, that you'd imagine that nothing in the sport could ever catch bookmakers on the hop. But they were well and truly caught out when Chris Eubank's fight with Dan Sherry in March 1991 ended in bizarre circumstances. The 12-round contest for the WBO middleweight title finished prematurely in the tenth round after Eubank landed a butt on Sherry, who was cut so badly that he was unable to continue. Eubank was docked two points by each of the judges but was still given the verdict on points, even though the contest had finished early.

That immediately raised the possibility – as welcome to the layers as daylight to Dracula - that bookies would have to pay out twice: once to punters who backed a points decision, and again to punters who backed a Eubank tenth-round victory. And those bookies who offered prices for a victory 'inside the distance' faced a three-way pay-out – as welcome as a bed of garlic served on a crucifix-shaped plate in blazing sunlight to the good Count.

Hills immediately announced they would pay out twice. "There's no way around it," a spokesman said. But other firms waited on an official ruling by the Green Seal Service, the much-maligned arbitration service run by the *Sporting Life*.

Punters who had always suspected that Green Seal had more than a foot in the camp of bookmakers, whose advertisements helped keep the *Sporting Life* going until May 1998, were given what they saw as confirmation when the arbitration service ruled that bets on a Eubank points victory were winners but bets on a tenth-round stoppage were losers.

Even now, many years on, that decision beggars belief, so thank goodness the demise of the *Life* also heralded the demise of Green Seal, which to my knowledge never won a single punter's seal of approval, green or otherwise. Just imagine the reaction of those poor punters who in good faith had backed Eubank at around the 16-1 mark to win in round ten. Would you like to have been the betting shop manager telling some hairy-arsed hod-carrier that his bet was a loser?

I lost faith in boxing betting in 1992 when what I considered to be one of the shrewdest bets I'd ever placed came unstuck through a mixture of bull-headedness, brashness and bravado by a man named Bowe.

I backed Riddick Bowe early that year at 8-1 to be undisputed world heavyweight champion by the last day of December 1992. I'd cleverly mapped out leading contender Bowe's schedule and reasoned that he was almost certain to get a crack at champion Evander Holyfield late in the year. All he had to do was win that –

and I calculated he'd be no bigger than 6-4 – and riches were mine.

Everything went gloriously to plan. Bowe did indeed beat Holyfield and had no more fights arranged for the rest of the year. All I had to do was sit and wait for 31 December and a big fat cheque would be winging its way towards me. Oh happy days. Oh happy, happy days.

Even when it became apparent that Bowe had to sign an agreement to fight Lennox Lewis the following year or be stripped of the WBC portion of the crown, I wasn't really worried. True, Bowe wasn't showing any willingness to agree to the deal, but he wasn't due to be stripped of the WBC belt until January 1993, by which time the readies would have already been trousered.

But then the big, fat, boneheaded lummox – and I'll call him that to his face next time I see him – came up with a stupid publicity stunt which saved a certain bookie a small fortune. On 14 December, just 17 days short of pay-out day, Bowe dumped his WBC belt into a London dustbin to register his contempt for their command that he must agree to fight Lewis.

People remember where they were when Kennedy was shot. I remember more vividly where I was when Bonehead's belt hit the bin. I was in the office. And I began to weep.

When the tears dried, I figured I had only two options. Either convince bookies that morally they were obliged to pay me my winnings since Bowe's terrible actions were only prompted by a misguided publicity stunt; or, failing that, persuade them to refund my stakes. Option one was a 33-1 chance, option two altogether more likely.

At the beginning of that year, bookies had included eight names in their list of boxers to become undisputed heavyweight champion by December 31. But significantly there was no price available for there to be 'no undisputed champ'. As the eventual winner ('no undisputed champion') was not quoted, surely all bets should have been made void. If punters couldn't possibly win, it surely wasn't right that they could lose. But those hard-hearted bookies were having none of it. They said that if any punter had requested odds for no undisputed champion, they would readily have quoted it.

A spokesman for independent chain AR Dennis, later to be swallowed up by Ladbrokes, drew an interesting parallel. "It's like the betting for the Christmas No.1," he said. "People might back, say, a Cliff Richard record and then suddenly the week before Christmas a top performer like Freddie Mercury dies and Queen's *Bohemian Rhapsody* is rush released and goes straight to the top. That's just tough luck for the Cliff punters."

At first glance the bookies would seem to have had a case, but the facts bear closer inspection. The bookies said they would have quoted a price if asked, yet they also admitted in an unguarded moment that when they first framed their odds, they'd overlooked the possibility of there being no undisputed heavyweight champion.

The Corals betting was: 13-8 Evander Holyfield, 7-4 Bowe, 3-1 Michael Moorer, 4-1 Lennox Lewis, 7-1 Razor Ruddock, 9-1 George Foreman, 10-1 Frank Bruno, and 14-1 Larry Holmes.

The AR Dennis betting was: 1-2 Holyfield, 4-1 Bowe (cut from an early 8-1, presumably after a lumpy bet from myself and *Racing Post* colleagues), 7-1 Lewis, 10-1 Moorer, 12-1 Foreman, 25-1 Ray Mercer, 33-1 Ruddock, and 40-1 Holmes.

The Corals book therefore yielded a percentage of a whopping 158 and the Dennis book 125.

Such is the tempestuous nature of world heavyweight boxing politics that the likelihood of no undisputed champion must always have been fairly high. Indeed at the beginning of that year, when I asked Hills to frame a similar market, they declined for exactly those reasons. So we weren't talking about a 20-1 long-shot here. We were talking around the 2-1 mark, or 3-1 at the very most. If you added a 3-1 runner to the Corals book the percentage soared to a totally unacceptable 180 per cent, and to 150 with Dennis.

What it all boiled down to was that bookies penalised punters for overlooking something they themselves had missed. Corals and Dennis failed to recognise the possibility of there being no undisputed champion. Punters missed it too, but it was only the punters who were made to pay.

Boxing in my eyes is not a sport that offers serious punters any golden opportunity of riches. So much depends on inside information – how seriously a fighter has trained for a bout, whether he's carrying any niggling injuries, whether his wife has walked out on him, that kind of thing.

Too many fights are mis-matches, and even those with true betting potential are so hard to call because one single lucky punch can transform a fight. For instance Oliver McCall is not in the same league as heavyweight rival Lennox Lewis, yet he defied the odds in their first meeting in September 1994 with a right-hander in the second round that knocked Lewis senseless.

American boxing guru Bert Randolph Sugar, a keen student of styles, argues persuasively that for any re-match punters should always bet on the same result as the first fight. Yet there have been too many reversals of fortune for that advice to be followed blindly.

Sugar also maintains that in boxing more than any other sport, money on the favourite tends to come in early, shortening the odds. Therefore, he says, if you intend to lump on the jolly, do so before the weight of public opinion forces down the price. Conversely, if you're dabbling on the underdog, wait in most cases until the very last moment when odds are longest.

None of this advice is going to make you rich. Indeed I do not think it's possible to make serious money from betting on boxing unless you have the confidence of men on the inside – the promoters, the trainers, the fighters themselves. By all means bet on boxing to give yourself an added interest in a live TV fight, but never kid yourself you're going to knock out the bookies. They are always likely to get the verdict.

# chapter 11

## cricket

I was at Bank tube station on the London underground and the news bulletin flashing on the Reuters billboard stunned me. "Call for two-year ban after Shane Warne and Mark Waugh admit taking bookmaker's money," it said.

Christ, I thought. It was bad enough when they closed our accounts for winning money from them, now those bastard bookies want to ban us, too.

The Warne-Waugh revelations in early 1999, coming hard on the heels of the match-fixing allegations that have rocked the sport in Pakistan, were further proof that betting on cricket has become big, big business, as this chapter will confirm.

The call for the lengthy ban on the two Australian Test cricketers went unheeded. Indeed Warne and Waugh emerged from the darkest days of their lives relatively unscathed - and that to me is the biggest scandal in sport, particularly as the careers of Pakistani counterparts Salim Malik and Wasim Akram were almost ended in similar circumstances.

If you're not familiar with the story, let me briefly recap. Warne and Waugh, who had, along with Test colleague Tim May, accused Malik of twice offering them huge sums of money to fix matches in 1994, admitted they had taken money from a Delhi bookmaker for information on weather and pitch conditions for a one-day clash between Australia and Sri Lanka in that same year. Waugh accepted £2,400, Warne trousered £2,000. The Australian Cricket Board learned of the payments soon after they were made and in Sydney in February 1995 fined the players £4,000 and £3,200 respectively, yet foolishly they kept the news hush-hush for almost four years. Given such a murky background you'd have thought the ACB might have mentioned the payments when their two Test stars gave evidence against Malik at the match-fixing inquiry in Pakistan in late 1998 but, no, they clearly didn't deem them relevant.

The double standards were disgusting and rightly condemned but in concentrating their vitriol on the ACB, observers allowed Warne and Waugh to get off lightly. The accounts given by the two players of their meeting with the Indian bookmaker, known only as John, ask us to accept naivety of breathtaking dimensions. When the news first broke in late December 1998, Warne and Waugh suggested they'd met this shadowy figure only briefly, yet in statements at an inquiry in January 1999 the two admitted speaking to him on several occasions.

'John' first met Waugh during the Singer Cup in Sri Lanka in September 1994. According to Waugh's statement in Melbourne to the Pakistani judicial inquiry into betting corruption in international cricket, John told him that he was involved in bookmaking and offered him A$6,000 to provide information on weather and pitch conditions. The following day John was introduced to Warne, who was losing on the roulette wheel at a Colombo casino.

They met again the following day in the team hotel. Warne recalled: "He said: 'It was an honour to meet you last night. I'm a bookmaker from India. I bet on the cricket. I've won lots of money on Australia. They are winning all the time. You have won plenty of Tests for Australia. I saw you lose some money at the casino last night. Here's a token of my appreciation. You're my favourite player.' He then handed me an envelope. I looked and saw that there was money in it."

According to Warne, he refused the money twice before accepting it after John had insisted that he would be offended if he did not. "He said: 'Good luck, see you later.' I went to the casino later that day. I put the money on the table and they gave me chips to the value of A$3,000." Warne said

John became a strange creature, an Indian given to Australian idioms. When he telephoned Warne for information on what the player described as the last of three occasions – all during

England's 1994-95 tour of Australia – he introduced himself by saying "G'day". He rang off by saying "No worries". According to Warne, the information he supplied to John could hardly have been more obvious.

Before a one-day international against England in Sydney, he responded to the question: "Do you think you will win?" by saying: "Bloody hope we will." Before the Melbourne Test he said that it might rain, and before Perth that it was hot but that the pitch should hold together. Waugh insisted under cross-examination from Ali Sibtain Fazli, lawyer for the Pakistan Cricket Board, that John's approach had not seemed suspicious.

"I judged him to be a fair man," he said. "Bookmaking is not illegal in Australia. I have no idea whether he was involved in match-fixing. There was no mention of match-fixing. I didn't know that giving information on weather and pitch conditions to a bookmaker was wrong."

"Did it not strike you that there was no need for John to pay you money for this information that was readily available elsewhere?" Fazli asked.

"Not really," Waugh replied.

Waugh and Warne are grown men who, as international sportsmen, have seen more of the world than most of us. They are no innocents abroad. Are we to believe that when they jumped so willingly into bed with this Indian bookmaker the thought never occurred to them that further down the line this benefactor might want more from them than mere information on the weather?

A sugar daddy may give a teenage blonde money for clothes and holidays when they first meet but the blonde, however naïve, will know that sooner or later she will be expected to deliver more than a goodnight kiss.

Given that the bookie payments to Warne and Waugh came just a month before Malik allegedly offered them A$200,000 (£80,000) to fix matches during Australia's tour of Sri Lanka and Pakistan in 1994, we are surely right to suspect a clear link. If Malik did indeed ask them to fix a match, was he given the confidence to make such a brazen approach by the apparent willingness of Waugh and

Warne to pocket an Indian bookmaker's money?

Australian Test skipper Mark Taylor said when the scandal broke in late 1998: "I don't know if there is a link but there certainly could be. Shane and Mark became easy targets because they like to have a bet. They were approached for an easy dollar."

One other point largely overlooked in the press coverage of the affair: by taking the bookie shilling, the two Australians left themselves wide open to blackmail, along the lines of, "Throw this match or we'll tell the world you're on our pay-roll."

Cricket writer Simon Wilde, in an admirable piece for the *Sunday Times* in December 1998, wrote: "Uneasy questions remain – A$11,000 for weather and pitch information to two players in the same side, from a bookmaker who was in Colombo himself at the time, can only have been a down payment for future assistance.

"Was it forthcoming, even if not to the extent the bookmaker desired? Speed (Malcolm Speed, chief executive of the ACB) said last week that the two Australians were in contact with the bookmaker for 'between one and two months', yet Australia were in Sri Lanka only for a matter of days in 1994 before moving to Pakistan for the series in which Malik allegedly made his approaches. Did Warne and Waugh give tips in Pakistan as well?

"There is also the mystery as to why an unidentified Australian journalist tipped off the ACB about the link between players and bookmakers – leading to Waugh and Warne being secretly fined a total of A$18,000 in February 1995 – yet did not write the story. Conspiracy theorists suggest the Malik bribery story, which had lain untold since October 1994, was offered in return for his silence, but the fines story was hard to prove. The ACB kept all reference to the fines out of their minutes."

It's worth bearing in mind here that both Waugh and Warne are hardened gamblers who are more aware than most of the do's and don'ts of the betting jungle, and who, we therefore should imagine, would have been conscious of how dangerous the territory was the moment they agreed to their Faustian pact with the Indian bookmaker.

Warne, as we've seen, was first approached in the middle of a session at the roulette table; Waugh is a racehorse owner in Australia and lists punting as one of his chief interests.

In a lifestyle interview in the *Racing Post* in February 1996, Waugh was asked which sports he likes to bet on. This was his answer. "I'd love to bet on cricket but I'm not allowed to! I like soccer, rugby league and golf."

I asked the journalist who interviewed Waugh why the exclamation mark appeared at the end of his first sentence about betting on cricket. He told me it was to denote a tongue-in-cheek response. Furthermore, Waugh admitted that he once threw away his wicket in a match just because he wanted to watch a race in which a horse he had backed was running.

"I was playing for (Sydney club side) Bankstown and we were winning easily," he said. "I knew we would win the game for sure. It was coming up for race time for the (1992) Cox Plate and I had backed my favourite horse, Super Impose. So I hit one in the air. It is the only time I have ever done that but I have no regrets. We won the game, Super Impose won the race and I had a good win."

In his *Sunday Times* article, Wilde observed: "Some claim bribery and match-fixing are global problems, but as yet there is little evidence implicating anybody in England, South Africa or the West Indies. There *is* a problem in Asia and Australia. Gambling is king in these parts, and the one-day game is its dangerous consort, nowhere more so than in Australia. Refusing to acknowledge these facts is the lie Australia has been living these past few years.

"Australia is reckoned to be the biggest nation of gamblers in the world and its leading sportsmen are most exposed to betting's corrosive effects. Betting is rife in sports clubs, many of which owe their existence to funds raised by Pokies (fruit machines). Most leading hotels possess amusement arcades attached to casinos, and punters rub shoulders with sporting stars at horse, trotting or greyhound meetings."

I write all this to make clear just how betting-savvy Waugh and Warne are. Surely it takes a huge suspension of disbelief to accept that such worldly men could fail to spot the dangers of a bookmaker bearing brown envelopes.

Days after the Waugh-Warne scandal broke, Adam Hollioake, the former England one-day captain, claimed that he had been asked by a bookmaker to provide information during the 1997 Champions' Cup tournament in Sharjah. Hollioake received phone calls on successive days in his hotel room in Sharjah in the lead-up to England's opening game against India. He said the second caller had offered to make him rich – "If you help me I will make you a millionaire."

Hollioake added: He wanted me to give him inside information on the team, what we would do if we won the toss, and said that in return for fixing matches by using certain bowlers at certain times he would make me wealthy." Hollioake said that after telling the caller that he wasn't interested, he put the phone down and reported the incident to team manager David Graveney, who had already issued warnings to his squad to be wary of such approaches during the one-day tournament.

Given the Hollioake story and the vast sums hinted at, we should perhaps wonder why players of the wealth of Warne and Waugh should be tempted by the very modest sums mentioned earlier. Reportedly the two were paid a total of only A$11,000 (little more than £4,400) which is peanuts when we consider their dealings with the bookmaker lasted almost two months.

Warne, quite apart from his earnings from cricket, had a £500,000-a-year sponsorship deal with sportswear firm Nike. Why should his pulse quicken then at the thought of pocketing a mere £2,000 for an inescapably sinister deal with a foreign bookie?

There is not a shred of evidence to suggest that Waugh or Warne have ever thrown a match, or even considered fixing a result. But what deepest cynics will argue is that since the arrival of spread betting on cricket in the early 1990s, a player need fix only his own performance to deliver a result to a bookie.

Spread firms will bet on the number of runs a player scores, the number of wickets he takes, even the catches he makes. It's conceivable that a cricketer could deliberately turn in a below-par performance, for a suitable reward of course, and believe he has done nothing wrong so long as his team still manages to win.

I am not suggesting for a minute that Warne and Waugh are guilty of such a sin; merely that some may be prepared to believe the two Test stars are more capable of that than the act of breathtaking naivety we have been asked to accept.

Harsh though I may have been on Waugh and Warne, I would argue that their 'crime' is easier to forgive than the stunt pulled by fellow Aussies Dennis Lillee and Rodney Marsh in 1981, when they backed England at 500-1 to pull off a miracle against their own side in a Test match at Headingley. What Lillee and Marsh did was tantamount to treason, yet their actions were passed off as little more than a minor misdemeanour with a roll of the eyes, a resigned smile, and a shrug that said, "Well, Aussie boys will be boys."

The failure of cricket authorities to act against Lillee and Marsh perhaps gave future generations of Aussie cricketers the green light to proceed without caution. Where, in that unsavoury Headingley affair, were the words of condemnation for Lillee and Marsh? Where were the calls for a ban? Where were the apologies? Waugh and Warne would have read everything about this little legend and detected only mild amusement instead of outrage.

I've read many accounts of that Headingley miracle and none is as illuminating as the one told by Ron Pollard, the former voice of Ladbrokes, in his book *Odds And Sods*.

Pollard, with the help of England Test legend Godfrey Evans, was the man in charge of Ladbrokes' cricket betting operation at the time of that Headingley Test.

"We had our good days and our bad ones," he wrote, "but the worst two we ever spent were during that Headingley Test match in 1981. Once more the Ashes were being contested: Australia won the first Test at Trent Bridge and the match at Lord's was drawn. This one was marked by Ian Botham getting a 'pair' and immediately renouncing the captaincy with which he had been honoured amid considerable controversy.

"The third Test was mid-July at Leeds and Mike Brearley, restored as captain, spent two days fretting, while Australia spent most of them compiling 401 before declaring. The irrepressible

Botham had guaranteed his skipper five wickets 'if you keep me on'. Brearley kept him on – for 40 overs! – and Both actually delivered six. Nevertheless, the Aussies seemed in a strong enough position and it looked positively rosy for them on the Saturday evening as England, bowled out for 174, were invited to follow on. They then lost Graham Gooch for a duck, the Essex man thus having the rare misfortune to be out twice in the same day in a Test match.

"Having been home for the Sunday, I drove back up to Yorkshire on the Monday morning feeling that it really was a waste of my time. The Aussies were heading for an overwhelming victory – everyone was agreed on that in all the newspapers. The Leeds public was not renowned for turning out in huge numbers on a Monday in such circumstances. Add those two points together and it was clear that I would not be doing much business and might be better employed in London.

"England began the day 222 behind and their position – and my depression – steadily worsened; 2 for 18, 3 for 37, 4 for 41. Before tea any vestige of hope appeared to vanish with the departure of Geoff Boycott. Bob Taylor came and went and Graham Dilley joined Botham with the score at 135 for 7.

"Godfrey agreed with my reasoning; we should book out of our hotel room and head for home. England would have lost before we were halfway down the M1. If there was anyone left on the ground foolish enough to want a bet, he could have 500-1 on an England victory. I could just as easily have said 5,000-1 but, thank God, I did not do so because two of those so-called 'mug' punters had a bet on England at 500-1 and won £10,000 between them.

"Those two 'mugs' were fast bowler Dennis Lillee and wicket-keeper Rod Marsh. Like so many Aussies, they were real gambling men; neither could resist what they saw as a bargain.

"They sent the team coach-driver over to place their bet and when news of their big win inevitably leaked out of the dressing-room there was a huge row, with allegations of cheating and throwing the match. The lads made it crystal clear that they had done their damnedest to win, wanted to win and had a bet only because the odds, in a two-horse race, seemed too good to miss. That apart, it has to be said that it was also a good insurance for them. The players were due a bonus if they won the match; if by any chance they lost, Lillee and Marsh would still be financial winners.

"Godders and I were in blissful ignorance of all this as we steamed down the M1 towards Newport Pagnell, where I was to drop him off. We tuned into *Test Match Special* on Radio 3 to find unexpected England resistance: Botham and Dilley were hitting out. It could not last. Could it? Godfrey and I exchanged glances once or twice; we did not need to say anything.

"At this point it was still only a question of asking ourselves whether England could make the Aussies bat again, which had seemed most unlikely as we set off on our journey south. Yet in 80 frenetic, momentous minutes, Dilley (smashing 56) and Botham put on 117 runs to push England ahead. In homes and offices all over the country, TV sets were being switched on with everyone (and I was among them) asking breathlessly: 'What's the score? We can't really do it, can we?'

"The buccaneering Botham, intent upon expunging all memory of his dreadful experience as captain, was proposing that he could, that England could, with the greatest Test innings he would ever play and was, perhaps, ever played. Between tea and the close he scored 106 runs, his century coming off 87 balls. Fast bowler Chris Old, on his own Yorkshire strip, stayed out there with the hero of the hour while another 67 runs were added.

"Last man in was Bob Willis, who would claim his own fanfare on a climactic final day yet to come. No batsman, Bob, but a dogged fighter who was to see Botham through to the close, enabling England to fight that one last dramatic day.

"I had dropped Godfrey off at his Newport Pagnell home. 'Well, master ...' he said. His words tailed off but there was nothing much else he could say.

"When I reached my home I rang him. England, at 351 for 9, would go into the last day – the day Godfrey and I had cancelled – 125 runs ahead. I was fractionally more conversational than he had been. 'Bloody hell, Godders. If we have this one wrong we will take some stick,' I said to him.

"I slept uneasily, I must admit. I *knew* that I had not made a mistake; if England's nine, ten, jack could score so freely, surely Australia would get whatever target they were set comfortably enough. And that target was modest indeed when play did resume the next morning. Willis was out quickly and Australia needed only 130 to win. It should have been a doddle, but now Willis tore into them with his finest performance for his country.

"The easy target for Australia became an Everest and Bob Willis took eight wickets for 43 runs. Australia finished 18 runs short. England's was the first victory by a team following on this century and it so demoralised Australia that they lost the next two Tests and with them the Ashes.

"I also lost a lot of money (£21,000 on the game) and for a while a little self-respect, I suppose. Everyone thought we were idiots – or almost everyone. My most gratifying moment of that whole affair came with a phone call from a Yorkshireman who knows his cricket, Len Cowburn, the chairman of William Hill. He rang Peter George, then managing director of Ladbroke Racing, to say: 'Don't blame Ron for those odds, Peter. I would have thought 5,000-1 would have been nearer the mark.' Little did either of them know that those were the odds I might very easily have offered on that fateful fourth day!

"That telephone call made me feel a little better, but in fact it mattered not. When the news of two players betting against their own team came out, another million pounds' worth of publicity echoed around the world. Much of it was desperately unfair on the two players. Lillee and Marsh were nothing if not patriots; not for a single moment would they have considered trying to lose any match, let alone one against the Poms. It was simply that, to a gambling Aussie, the odds were so good that they could not be missed."

Pollard tells a good story but I must pick him up on a couple of points. First, when news leaked out that Lillee and Marsh had backed against their own team, there was indeed an initial outcry, but this soon subsided and the matter was then largely treated as something to smile about. Second, Pollard is at pains to point out that Lillee and Marsh backed England only because the odds of 500-1 were too good to resist. Yet in the same account he admits that his first thought was to offer 5,000-1, a figure also suggested by Hills chief Len Cowburn as a more realistic assessment of England's chances of victory.

If Lillee and Marsh were to pull a similar stunt today in the wake of the long-running match-fixing saga in Pakistan and the more recent Waugh-Warne revelations, they would be turfed out of cricket in double-quick time. That they escaped censure for arguably the worst crime a professional sportsman can commit is a terrible indictment of Australian cricket chiefs. The Waugh-Warne scandal is the harvest reaped by that shocking failure to take action, perhaps the most shameful dereliction of duty in sporting history.

Waugh and Warne were not the first Australian cricketers to be linked with a betting scandal. Former Aussie skipper Allan Border admitted in February 1995 that he was offered a £500,000 bribe to gift England a 1993 Test win and help land a massive gambling sting.

England were already 3-0 down before the fifth Test at Edgbaston when Border was approached, with Australia needing 120 to win. The Aussies went on to win and take a 4-0 lead in the six-Test series. A Sydney newspaper claimed the offer was made to Border on behalf of a Pakistani betting syndicate.

The report quoted an unnamed former Australian Test player saying: "The Pakistani said he could get 7-1 about England winning the Test match and the money was there in cash. AB (Border) just told the Pakistani to get lost and don't come back."

A day after the report surfaced, former Pakistan Test star Mushtaq Mohammed admitted it was he who could have triggered the scandal, but denied he had tried to bribe Border and laughed off the incident as a joke.

"I just happened to mention it was a similar position to the 1981 Headingley Test, and if someone offered him a lot of money to lose, what would he do," said Mohammed. "It was just a hypothetical conversation. Nothing was offered by me on anyone's behalf. It was just a joke. I categorically deny having made an offer. I have no links with people in Pakistan who gamble. It's been blown out of all proportion and I'm not happy about it at all. I jokingly passed a remark and said 'What happened? Did somebody offer you money? What are you going to do?' He said 'I have never messed with my cricket.' I said 'Fine, that's good enough for me. I'm glad we've played our cricket at a time when it was clean and proper.'

"Now a lot is being said in the paper that Allan Border is upset about what I said to him 18 months ago. It's a farce. If he was that upset, why didn't he come out with it then and there?"

The Border claim came just days after another Australian Test ace, Dean Jones, revealed he had been offered £30,000 by an Indian bookie to disclose inside information about his side on the 1992 tour of Sri Lanka.

At the same time, an investigation by myself and colleagues at the *Racing Post* revealed that payments had been withheld on recent matches involving Pakistan. Illegal bookies in India refused to pay out on Pakistan's 324-run thrashing by South Africa amid rumours of a betting syndicate's operation in Dubai.

The triangular tournament in South Africa involving Pakistan, Sri Lanka and South Africa at the end of 1994 also triggered a huge betting interest. South Africa, after winning their first three qualifiers, faced Sri Lanka, who had lost their first three, at Bloemfontein in December. South Africa were quoted locally at 1-3, a price which "looked generous" to an independent observer I spoke to. He said the Bloemfontein ground authorities received several phone calls from a man purporting to be from Dubai and anxious to know how his £1 million on South Africa was faring. They lost by 35 runs.

A Bombay bookmaker, who refused to be named, later marked the *Racing Post*'s card on the betting background to that series in South Africa.

"The problem was the first one-day international in Cape Town," he said. "A lot of money was bet on Pakistan before the game by a Dubai syndicate. After South Africa scored 215, they were about 5-2 to win, but the Dubai people suddenly wanted to bet heavily on them, and against Pakistan. The Bombay bookmakers were warned about the impending flood of money against Pakistan, so they did not pick up their telephones for the next couple of hours, by which time Pakistan had slumped from 102 for two (11-10 then) to 133 for seven. From a position of reaching 116 in 28 overs with eight wickets in hand, Pakistan lost by 37 runs with 7.1 overs left.

"The problem was that some bets in that match, and the next one at Wanderers where Pakistan again fielded after winning the toss, this time losing by 157 runs with 7.3 overs to spare, were related to matches in the World Series in Australia. So when the Dubai punters refused to pay on the Cape Town game, the bookmakers voided all bets."

In early 1995, former Northamptonshire and Pakistan fast bowler Sarfraz Nawaz claimed a 1992 Trent Bridge one-day international between England and Pakistan was thrown by the tourists. England plundered 363 runs off 55 overs and then skittled Pakistan for 165.

Allan Lamb, who played for England in that match, recalls: "They only had four bowlers. We just thought we'd stuffed them out of sight. But now you don't know." And he went on: "I didn't realise how big the betting was in Bombay until the World Cup there in 1987. It was quite amazing. People were betting on everything."

With so many rumours flying around about the skulduggery of the Pakistan team, it was perhaps no surprise when three players - former Lancashire star Wasim Akram, Salim Malik and Ijaz Ahmed - were accused of match-fixing in 1997, after Pakistan were beaten 3-2 in the Sharjah Cup. The three have since been at the centre of a long-running investigation that was due to reach its conclusions after the 1999 cricket World Cup.

Akram was stripped of his country's captaincy but has waged a vigorous campaign to clear his name, and early in 1999 once again led his nation into the momentous Test clash with bitter rivals India in Madras.

In his autobiography, published late in 1998, Akram described movingly the impact of the allegations on himself and his family – death threats were commonplace – and painted a vivid picture of the importance of cricket betting in his society.

"It's now such a feverish, obsessive activity that if you lose a cricket match you are blamed for also losing fortunes for people and ruining their lives. I know of gamblers in Pakistan who have lost their businesses as a result of this epidemic, yet they can't kick the habit. Many who place bets on cricket just don't understand the subtleties of the game.

"Cricket is on the television almost every day in Pakistan – not just internationals but veterans' and women's tournaments – so there is always scope to make a fortune. And to lose one. The press fan the flames with rumours and ill-researched statements that a certain player is sure to do well in the upcoming match, and many uneducated, naïve readers lay down money on such information.

"One-day cricket is now so popular in Pakistan that vast crowds watch it on television or pack the grounds. Many of those watchers don't realise that fortunes fluctuate so wildly and so quickly in one-day games because of their very nature; pressure can get to players and they do rash things that seem corrupt to gamblers, who are simply obsessed with winning a bet rather than enjoying the twists and turns of a cricket match.

"So I got sucked into this frenetic gambling atmosphere because I committed the cardinal sin of losing a couple of one-day matches as Pakistan captain. It all blew up in December 1997 when four international teams played in the Sharjah Trophy.

"Under my leadership, Pakistan were well fancied and vast sums of money were placed on us, as individuals and as a successful team. Yet we played poorly, losing to England and the West Indies, although we were pleased to beat our arch-rivals India. I didn't captain the side as well as I would have liked. Our batting order wasn't right in the England game, and in retrospect I should have sent in Azhar Mahmood ahead of me at number eight. I scratched around for 19 balls to make only four, and we lost by eight runs when we really ought to have won.

"Against West Indies, I dropped two simple catches, bowled poorly, and was involved in run-outs that were my fault. Fair enough – I had a bad series in a tournament in which I usually do very well. That's cricket, it happens. So we lost, despite trying our best. End of story? Not a bit of it.

"When we got back to Pakistan the temperature had really risen. Former Test players had put their names to newspaper articles, saying that the reason we had lost in Sharjah was because we had taken bribes to throw the games. I was right in the firing line, as captain and all-rounder who had performed below-par in the tournament.

"Some papers reported as a matter of fact that I had made a lot of money out of losing those two games, and that one of my brothers is a bookmaker, so he had the inside track. It didn't seem to matter that neither of my brothers has ever been a bookmaker. The fact that some former players had castigated me in the press gave these amazing allegations credibility.

"It was all sadly reminiscent of 1996, when Pakistan lost in the World Cup quarter-final against India in Bangalore. I had to withdraw through a painful rib injury and when we lost, the rumours started that I had taken a bribe to stand down, and defeat for us also made me a small fortune. That had really hurt, and the subsequent events when my house was stoned and my family threatened only added to my misery. I really don't know how these people can imagine that I could influence the result of a match in which I wasn't even playing.

"I have never attempted to throw a match, and have never even considered such a thing for a second. I also have no knowledge of any Pakistan player taking money to influence events on the field. That is a slur that just won't go away in Pakistan cricket, and it claimed Salim Malik when he was sacked as captain."

Akram explained the background to the expulsion of Malik as captain. Malik won the toss in two one-day matches, in Cape Town and Johannesburg, in the triangular one-day tournament in South Africa in 1995. But even though local wisdom demanded that the team winning the toss batted first (because later in the day the ball tended to boomerang about), Malik opted to field first. His players openly questioned the decisions, especially after Pakistan lost by a thumping 157 runs in Johannesburg after being bowled out for just 109. Team spirit evaporated, said Akram, in the build-up to a Test match in Johannesburg soon afterwards.

"During one particular bitter team meeting in Johannesburg, things came to a head. Players were squabbling openly in the room and nobody was listening to the captain. Someone then shouted 'What's all this about the toss and bets?' – a clear reference to Salim's two costly decisions in the recent one-day matches. We all looked at each other and wild accusations started to fly around. Our manager Intikhab Alam realised he had to pull things together, otherwise the fall-out would be spectacular and very public. Inty produced the Koran and suggested we all swear on it that no-one had been involved with betting in any of our matches. To a Muslim, the Koran is hugely important, and everyone in that room took the oath."

Yet still the scandal refused to die down, with the Waugh-Warne allegations about Malik offering them money adding further fuel.

Akram summed up: "When you get a surprising result the gamblers who have lost out blame the players and allege there's been a fix. The press shows its gullibility by printing such allegations, and some start to believe in them, even though there's never any concrete proof.

"Cricket is an obsession to many in Pakistan. We are a young country, and success in world cricket can sometimes be over-emphasised by some who also stake large sums of money on Pakistan victories. Betting is part of the sporting culture on the Indian sub-continent, as much as a few beers are for sports fans in Britain, Australia or South Africa. You'll never stamp out betting on cricket matches in India or Pakistan.

"It would be shocking and sickening to me if I knew any of my team-mates had been involved (in bribery). In a team game like cricket, I would have thought you had to bribe all 11 players because if you concentrate on just three or four, the others will still be trying their best and a defeat won't be certain. It's not like other sports that are individual contests. If all 11 are then bought up, the chances are that somebody else will find out because it would be hard to keep it a secret among so many."

It's notable that in all this talk of skulduggery, English cricket has been largely untainted. Indeed the only whiff of scandal came in November 1994 when a Sunday newspaper claimed that Lancashire and Essex had struck a deal to alter the course of their County Championship and Sunday League matches at Old Trafford in August 1991. But even then there was no hint that betting was involved.

According to the newspaper, Essex needed to win the three-day match to stake a claim for the County Championship, while Lancashire, who stood no chance in the Championship, were in a good position in the Sunday league and needed to put a winning streak together. Essex player Don Topley alleged that after two days of the county match against Lancashire, his side were promised an easy declaration on the Monday if Essex were prepared to lay down in the one-day game on Sunday.

Lancashire won the Sunday game and Essex wrapped up the Championship match the next day with an eight-wicket win on their way to winning the title. Lancashire eventually finished second in the Sunday League behind Nottinghamshire. Although the allegations rocked cricket, an investigation persuaded the Test and County Cricket Board to take no action.

Former Kent batsman Graham Cowdrey was acknowledged as one of the keenest punters in cricket. Cowdrey, who retired in 1998, is now a dealer for spread betting firm City Index and for several years in the 1990s penned a cricket betting column for the *Racing Post*. He is adamant that, in England at least, the sport is clean.

"In my 15 years of playing first class cricket in England, I never came across any instances of bribery or throwing matches," he said. "For six years I wrote on cricket betting for the *Racing Post*. But I never once said anything about games I was involved in and I certainly never advised anyone to bet heavily on Kent."

The long-running Pakistan inquiry, and the Waugh-Warne scandal, prompted a significant change in January 1999 in the policing of the sport. Formerly, individual Test-playing nations were allowed to deal with such problems in-house, a situation which allowed the Australian Cricket Board to keep a lid on the fines they imposed on Warne and Waugh in February 1995. But now the International Cricket Conference has been armed with the power to tackle corruption.

At its annual meeting in Christchurch, New Zealand, in January 1999, the ICC set up the Code Of Conduct Commission which has the authority in any of the nine Test-playing countries to investigate betting, bribery and match-fixing claims, and the muscle to impose heavy penalties, including life bans.

In late February 1999 a two-month independent inquiry cleared Australian cricket of any involvement in match-fixing or bribery but, quite significantly in my opinion, the man heading the inquiry, lawyer Rob O'Regan, said Waugh and Warne should have been suspended for their misdemeanours. "I do not think it is possible to explain their conduct away as the result of merely naivety or stupidity," he said damningly.

While it would seem from all of this that serious betting on cricket has been around only for the last ten or so years, the sport in fact had its gambling aficionados as long ago as the 18th Century. In his fascinating book *Double Century*, Tony Lewis, the TV cricket commentator, wrote: "Cricket (in the late 1700s) was very much a betting game. England, indeed, suffered from gambling fever. Men bet on political events, or any future happenings. 'For a few pounds, challengers galloped against the clock, gulped down pints of gin, or ate live cats,' writes Roy Porter in *English Society In The Eighteenth Century*. 'A common wager was to take out insurance policies on other people's lives. When George II led his troops against the French in 1743 you could get four to one against his being killed.' Cards were described as 'the opium of the polite'. Gaming was the lifeblood of London clubs like Almack's, White's and Boodle's.

"In 1751, when the Earl Of Sandwich was still arranging some (cricket) matches at Newmarket between Old Etonians and England, a contemporary report said that 'near £20,000 is depending' on bets associated with these games. For the gambler, cricket's special piquancy was the second innings, where there was always a chance to recover a stake which looked lost."

The Laws of Cricket, Lewis states, were framed in 1774 largely because of gambling. Modifications were made to deter players from acts of gamesmanship, like charging headlong towards an opponent about to make a catch, or using a bat as wide as the wicket. "With money riding high on cricket it was only to be expected that those who put up the money for the 'great' matches should frame the rules and regulations; they had the most to lose. This explains why the aristocrats who had drafted the 1774 code not only emphasised the gentlemanly qualities of fair play, but included regulations for the aspect of the game they had done most to encourage – gambling."

Lewis goes on: "Sorting out the gambling was a priority, but almost impossible. Players were especially open to bribery when there was big money riding on the result. As Thomas Lord's ground became the centre for 'great' matches, the semi-professionals came to London for the summer. Those who could afford it put up at the Green Man and Still in Oxford Street, a jolly tavern but infested with 'legs'. 'Legs' were bookmakers' runners. They offered shady deals in dark corners and some players could not resist.

"The 'legs' would prey particularly on those who had been on a losing side but who were still tucking into the good beef and best of wine at the Green Man. Everyone knew the playing fees. It was five guineas for a win and three for a loss if the player lived in London; it was six guineas for a win, four for a loss for someone who had to travel to London and take accommodation there. Inevitably there was many a young cricketer up from the country, struggling to keep his money in his pockets in the big city. The 'legs' would be at him with ready cash. Even in winter, when the cricketer had gone home, a knock on the door could mean a 'leg' down from London trying to fix a contest for the next season.

"There is no shortage of examples of how cricket gambling was all the gossip. After a low-scoring match in 1793, in which Hornchurch scored 54 and 67, MCC 56 and 68, a revealing notice was published: 'The above game is remarked for the small number of runs on each side, which is fewer than was ever known for four innings together. The usual betting on a good eleven is that they do or do not get 110.

"There were bets on individual innings, even on one stroke. In 1748 a London magistrate had ruled over a disputed wager at a cricket match that, 'It is a manly game, and not bad in itself, but it is the ill-use that is made of it by betting above £10 that is bad and against the law, which ought to be constructed largely to prevent the great mischief of excessive gambling.'"

One historian argued that cricket offered the aristocracy a less threatening alternative to duelling. "Cricket contests with betting for high stakes was replacing duelling in the minds of gentlemen: maximum excitement, minimum of danger. A bloodless joust. The pain was in the money lost," Christopher Brookes noted in his *English Cricket*.

In Britain today, betting on cricket, while not yet at the same kind of fever pitch as in India and Pakistan, is nonetheless almost a way of life. To football supporters, August is a golden month, offering as it does the chance to dream of untold riches by backing at the very start of the season the winners of the four English divisions in the same accumulator bet.

Cricket's equivalent is April when bookmakers aggressively advertise their ante-post prices for the four domestic competitions – the County Championship, Sunday League, Benson & Hedges Cup, and NatWest Trophy, although the B&H was scrapped in 1998. They are the competitions that keep the interest of the cricket punters alive through the summer months, with Test matches the icing on the cake. The Cricket World Cup in England in May and June of 1999 promises to see betting interest go through the roof.

Considering the prestige the County Championship enjoys, its weekly slate of matches has consistently failed to capture the imagination of punters. Sussex v Gloucestershire at a windswept Hove over four days in early May is not the most pulse-quickening of prospects, and the frequency of the draw further discourages punters.

It was not until the late 1990s that bookmakers even bothered to quote odds for County Championship matches, perhaps prompted by the sporadic live TV coverage on Sky Sports, and few punters of my acquaintance are tempted. Bookies will bet 'without the draw' (which of course means that bets are void if the match is drawn) but even that has failed to increase turnover. The fact that layers require minimum trebles hardly helps.

I'm confident even the most ardent cricket fan will be bewildered at the acres of press coverage devoted to the County Championship, which has all the box-office clout of a Beirut bingo session. I put it all down to a giant slice of public-school propaganda. Able, by being born to privilege, to commandeer influential positions in TV, radio and newspapers, the cricket-playing public-school brigade is perfectly placed to brainwash the rest of us.

Its insistence that cricket is part of the fabric of society is allowed to go unquestioned. The bombardment of coverage in newspapers has a drip-drip effect. Page upon page in the broadsheets of turgid County Championship reports persuade us that, hey, these games really are important. Pretty soon we begin to question our own judgement. As confidence tricks go, it's a gem; a masterpiece of manipulation.

Bookmakers Hills place betting on the County Championship a rock-bottom fifth of five in their list of domestic contests in terms of turnover. Test matches are clear leaders, followed by one-day internationals, the latter stages of the domestic cup competitions, and then the Sunday League. Hills began betting on County Championship matches in 1998 and only reluctantly decided to continue in 1999.

Sunday League one-day matches, for which team news is at best sketchy, on the surface offer punters a fair chance to make money but bookies have their bases covered, with most leading firms demanding minimum trebles. Singles are accepted only on those matches shown live on TV.

For years I suspected that the only sensible strategy for making a profit on Sunday League matches was to oppose the favourite. A bowler hitting a purple patch, even if only briefly, is capable of turning a match on its head so it seems ludicrous to accept short prices in these one-day matches. But I'm afraid that despite intensive research, I have been unable to come to any conclusion.

In 1997, a policy of backing the outsider blindly would have resulted in a loss of 35 per cent of stake-money. And that's before tax, with singles available on every game, which of course they aren't. The story was much brighter in 1998 with a profit of around 25 per cent, again before tax and on the understanding singles are available. I should point out here that any match which failed to throw up a clear favourite was left out of calculations. If you do intend to follow an oppose-the-favourite strategy, results over 1997 and 1998 suggested that the most fruitful period is late July-early August. If I had to hazard a guess why this might be so, perhaps it's because by that stage even teams in respectable League placings realise that their prospects of silverware lie in other competitions and begin to take their foot off the gas.

It is no surprise that Test matches are the greatest money-spinners in cricket for bookmakers. Even I, a cricket-hater, will concede that the thought of England taking on the West Indies or Australia on a sunny summer's day at Lord's holds a certain appeal.

There are two things I've learned from observing Test-match betting over the last decade or so. First, the draw is generally under-priced, meaning there must be value in backing a definite result. Second, if an England team has shown useful form heading into a Test series, punters are loathe to desert them, even if it becomes horribly apparent once the series has begun that they are nowhere near so good as promised.

Let me justify those observations. In the late 1990s, sports betting has become a global industry. Money wagered by British punters on a Test match involving England may be only a fraction of the amount staked by high-rolling foreign punters, particularly in India and Pakistan where, as we've already seen, cricket betting is practically a religion. All the major firms in Britain offer betting facilities, mostly tax-free, to these high-staking clients, to whom a

£100,000 bet is normal. Cricket punters in the sub-continent are a rare breed – they traditionally lump on the draw in Test matches. Several bookmakers have told me this, and the only explanation they can give for such an unusual betting strategy is the desperation of India and Pakistan not to lose to each other over the course of history. Indeed 33 of the 44 Tests between the countries up to the end of 1998 were drawn. Statistics like that are bound to influence a punter.

Knowing that they will take vast amounts on the draw from these foreign high-rollers, British bookies will offer only around 6-4, when a study of recent Test statistics says the draw should be around the 9-4 mark. What these punters have not taken into account are the rule changes implemented in Test cricket over the last few years. Nowadays a minimum of 90 overs must be bowled in day, increasing the chance of a positive result. And further, play lost to the weather is nowhere near as significant as it once was, as so much extra time can nowadays be allotted to make up for lost hours.

In January 1997, England were in Zimbabwe for three one-day internationals. The home side were available at 7-4 for the first game, even though England had lost 11 of their previous 18 one-day games. Zimbabwe won by two wickets, yet were still available at 13-8 for the second one-day clash, which they won on a faster scoring rate.

For the third clash, with England's morale at an all-time low, clued-up punters were expecting Zimbabwe to start no longer than evens, with 5-6 each of two the logical call. Yet somehow the layers saw fit to make England the 8-15 favourites, with Zimbabwe, quite incredibly, available at 11-8. It was no surprise to see Zimbabwe roll over a shell-shocked England by 131 runs.

David Brown, odds-compiler for Hills, explained at the time: "If we had looked purely at the formbook and ignored the effects of patriotism and the expectation of what punters would do, then there's little doubt we would have gone shorter about Zimbabwe. But all the way through the series punters took the view that England could not play as badly as in their preceding game."

That's an important point to remember. Odds-compilers may have their own view on a match but their odds must also reflect the likely strategy of punters, with patriotism a significant factor.

In the course of researching this chapter, I interviewed several professional gamblers who insisted that they make a huge profit every year from betting on cricket. Cleverly I managed to prise dozens of 'foolproof' strategies from them, many of which are not worth a balloon. What follows are arguably the best.

In one-day matches always phone the ground to find out which team has won the toss. Very often there is no clear advantage but at least a dozen times a season the team given the choice of batting or fielding first will automatically improve its chance of winning, on the basis that the skipper will know better than anyone the vagaries of the pitch. If you like the chances of the underdog already, don't think twice about backing them once you learn they've won the toss.

Do not get carried away by a particularly good start for a batting team as, in top-class cricket, bowlers are far more important than batsman and can change the course of a game within minutes. That's quite an original argument but its logic is inescapable.

A team reaching 80-0 will look in a very strong position and those bookies who bet in running – and certainly spread-betting operators – are likely to get a little carried away, making the batting team very short-priced favourites to go on and clinch victory. But picture what could happen in the next 20 minutes.

The best the batting side can hope for is, say, 125-0, but it could just as easily be 96-5. For example on 29 January 1999 Sri Lanka, chasing England's total of 227 in a one-day international in Perth, Australia, reached 65-1 and looked good things to wrap up victory. Four deliveries later the Sri Lankans were 67-4 and pretty much dead and buried. The pro-punter who slipped me this advice told me that, in the late 1990s, he won fortunes by waiting for England to make a good start with the bat in Test or one-day matches and then backing the opposition at inflated odds.

In domestic cricket try to identify the competitions teams have prioritised. There is simply too much cricket in Britain for counties to be able to give 100 per cent every game. A bit like football in which Manchester United frequently treat the League Cup with ill-disguised contempt. A county with little chance in the County Championship may, even if only subconsciously, take their foot off the gas in the four-day game but pull out all the stops against the same opposition in the Sunday League if a chance of silverware beckons.

Always keep a close eye on the weather, particularly in Test or one-day matches overseas. If you find out from a friend over there that it's chucking it down at six o'clock in the morning local time (11am British time) in Kingston, Jamaica, chances are that the Test match due to start later that day at Sabina Park will be affected, delayed perhaps, therefore increasing the prospects of the draw.

Believe me bookies are intensely nervous about the weather when it comes to pricing up cricket. Some opt to pay for information from the local met office but have been put away so often in the past (I found out on a trip to Australia in early 1999 just how wide of the target official weather forecasts can be; the unbelievably hopeless Aussie met-men made their British counterparts appear positively faultless) that it's becoming more common for national newspaper journalists covering a tour overseas to figure on a bookmaker's pay-roll. That's fine as far as it goes, but can you imagine the response of a hard-drinking cricket hack woken up a six o'clock in the morning after a riotous night in Montego Bay just to be asked if it's raining outside?

Top batsman betting on rare occasions can throw up a golden bet, but only for the punter with his ear to the ground. For instance, in one-day internationals the 15-over rule at the start of games may sometimes tempt sides into throwing in a 'pinch-hitter' as opening batsman rather than one of the specialist openers. The 'pinch-hitter' may lack the technique to carve out a career as opener, but is well capable of slogging for a limited number of overs while the fielding positions are so benign.

Punters with privileged contacts may just hear before the bookies of such 'pinch-hitting' intentions. An example occurred in the early 1990s when Philip DeFreitas, who normally batted way down the order, strode onto the pitch as opening batsman for England in a one-day match. DeFreitas' elevation came as a complete shock and bookmakers frantically had to slash his odds to be top England batsman from 50-1 to around the 6-1 mark.

Don't forget the advice given in an earlier chapter about top-batsman betting when a side is chasing only a moderate total. In such circumstances it's clear that the openers of the side batting second have an even better chance of top-scoring, yet bookies are very often slow to shave their odds.

Be alert enough to take advantage of any bookmaker incompetence. Bookies like to cultivate the impression that they are 100 per cent clued-up, that very little happens in the sporting world without them knowing about it. That is crap. Manpower limitations mean that they cannot possibly hope to keep tabs on everything, no matter how diligent they are.

In 1993, bookies at the start of the season in April gave Sussex a quote of 50-1 for the NatWest Trophy. But the first round proper of that competition was not staged until June, by which time Sussex had shown that they were a far better team than those pre-season quotes implied. Many of the larger firms, with enough staff to keep a watchful eye on form, progressively shaved Sussex's odds but one or two of the smaller bookmakers, figuring that most punters would not bother placing a NatWest Trophy bet until perhaps a day before the first round started, had taken their eye off the ball.

A week before the competition began, one firm was still quoting Sussex at 50-1 when 14-1 were nearer the true odds. A monster pay-out was avoided only when Warwickshire narrowly pipped Sussex in the NatWest final.

It was Warwickshire, incidentally, at the centre of one of the biggest betting rows in cricket history. In 1994, Warwickshire, having just signed master batsman Brian Lara, were heavily backed pre-season in all manner of doubles, trebles, and four-timers for the four domestic competitions. A Warwickshire Grand Slam, the equivalent of a single golfer winning the US Masters, US Open, Open and USPGA Championship in the same season, suddenly became a nightmare prospect, but the bookies didn't worry too much because they believed it just wasn't possible for a single county to achieve such domination in the highly-competitive world of first-class cricket.

The pre-season odds with Ladbrokes were 25-1 for the County Championship, 14-1 for the Sunday League, 14-1 for the Benson and Hedges, and 10-1 for the NatWest Trophy, making the multiplied odds for the four-timer a staggering 64,349-1.

A cluster of unexploded bombs – small-stake bets on a Warwickshire four-timer – lay dormant in betting shops the length and breadth of Britain. But then Lara and his men picked up the Benson and Hedges Cup for the first leg of the Grand Slam and bookies began seriously to worry. Warwickshire were already going great guns in both the County Championship and the Sunday League, with the NatWest Trophy also a very real possibility. Horrifyingly, the Grand Slam was most definitely ON.

It was then bookies, recognising the scale of their liabilities, moved the goalposts. "Ahem," said Ladbrokes one Monday morning. "We know you punters are expecting 64,349-1 for a Warwickshire four-timer but that's only because you missed our special ante-post odds at the beginning of the season. Warwickshire were in fact only 10,000-1."

Hills gave Ladbrokes a hand in shifting the goalposts. "Sorry," they said. "These are related bets. If Warwickshire win one competition, the odds about them winning a second must be reduced, in the same way a horse's Derby odds will shorten if it first wins the Guineas." And before anyone could argue, Hills pointed to a formula they say they introduced in 1989, which allowed them to pay full odds on one competition – but only half on the others. Even Hills punters who placed Warwickshire merely in doubles suffered the same fate – full odds for one trophy, half for the other.

While I could see a certain logic in the bookmaker argument, they were definitely trying to pull a fast one. The Hills formula would be fine – but only if it works both ways.

If we accept that it's fair for Warwickshire's NatWest Trophy odds to shorten if they win the B&H Cup, shouldn't we also expect them to lengthen if they go out in the first-round? After all, you can be damned sure a colt's Derby price will drift if he's beaten out of sight in the Guineas. Similarly, if Hills really do believe Warwickshire's Sunday League prospects are markedly improved by victory in the County Championship, does it not follow that the Sunday League prospects of rival counties are less rosy? But do we see all of them pushed out in the betting? Do we hell.

And anyway, who really believes that the competitions are in any way connected, that it is right to lump them under the 'related bets' heading? Sure, it's easy to see that a double of, say, Liverpool to win 1-0 and Michael Owen to score the first goal is a related bet because Liverpool's chances of winning 1-0 automatically increase as soon as Owen scores, but in the Warwickshire case could we not argue that lengthy runs in the two one-day cup competitions actually *hamper* a county's chances in the two Leagues, what with added fixtures, increased pressure and a greater risk of injuries? No-one in their right mind would argue that a League Cup triumph improves a side's prospects in the FA Cup. Quite the reverse, I'd say.

Hills insisted at the time: "The chance of Warwickshire winning one cricket competition must reflect on their chances of winning another. Let's assume they win the Championship – the most rigorous test of a team. Automatically they must have had a better chance of winning the Sunday League and the other competitions. Team strength becomes the related contingency and has to be reflected in pricing up the various eventualities."

Yet at the start of a football season punters are able to back, say, Manchester United in a treble to win the Premiership, the FA Cup and the Champions League without having to accept reduced odds.

The stance of the big bookies got up the noses even of other, smaller layers. Cheltenham independent bookmaker Steve Hearle pointed out: "The history of cricket will reveal that winning one competition does not increase the chances of that team winning others – almost the reverse in fact. A better investment is to find four different sides to win one each – so why the reduction apart from denying the punter his rights? I'm now worried about my Loch Ness Monster wagers with the big bookmakers. Unless it has

'Monster' in big bold letters engraved on its side I am sure there will be a 20-1 limit."

As it turned out the bookies were spared a monster pay-out when Warwickshire, with three trophies safely in the bag, were pipped by Worcestershire in the final of the NatWest Trophy in September 1994. Worcestershire's triumphant skipper Tim Curtis joked: "I am now waiting for Ladbrokes to pay us a back-hander for ending the Grand Slam and saving them some money." But the whole incident did little for the image of bookmakers who, it seemed to most, were happy to accept what must have appeared at first as mug bets, only to cry foul when such mug bets looked like copping.

Bookmakers had disgraced themselves four years earlier when the second Test between West Indies and England in Guyana in March 1990 was abandoned without a ball being bowled. In the run-up to that Test match, with weather bulletins gloomy, punters had lumped heavily on the draw at all rates down from 5-2 to 4-6.

Guyana's Bourda Stadium was notorious for rain-affected drawn matches so such heavy support came as no surprise. Comments in newspapers and on TV suggested that the match, although abandoned, would go down in the record books as a draw. Rule 21.5 of cricket's bible *Wisden* seemed to imply the same. But that wasn't good enough for bookmakers. "All bets are void," they decreed, with only Hills playing fair (actually more than fair) by paying out on the draw and voiding all other bets.

David Brown, of Hills, said: "I can see no difference between one ball being bowled and no balls being bowled. Nowhere in the rules of Test cricket does it say an abandonment can be anything other than a draw." It appeared bookies did not have a leg to stand on but, no doubt after calculating their massive liabilities, they repeated, mantra-like, that "all bets are void," and punters who'd lumped on the draw could, well, lump it.

Their defiant stance looked likely to spark the mother of all sports betting disputes until they were rescued by a statement from the Test and County Cricket Board. It appeared that Law 21.5 referred only to games which had actually started. Test matches which never even begin, such as Manchester in 1890 and 1938, and

Melbourne in 1970-71, are scrapped from the record books. "The record books don't include matches which never start, such as the one in Guyana, so a five-match series becomes a four-match series," said a TCCB spokesman.

The bookies were saved.

What made it a bitterer pill to swallow for punters was the bizarre decision by England and West Indies officials to scrap the final two days of the Bourda Test and instead slot in two hastily-arranged one-day matches. The first – surprise, surprise - was rained off but the second went ahead on the Bourda Test wicket. Had that weird decision not been reached, the final day of the Test would have gone ahead, and a draw would have been a formality.

Cricket has an uncanny knack of wrong-footing bookies. In February 1997, England bowled bookies an unplayable googly when they produced a tie in the third one-day international in New Zealand. The result caught the industry on the hop as there were no odds quoted for such a scenario and existing bookmaker rules failed to make clear how layers should react. Between them Britain's bookies managed to come up with THREE different ways of settling bets.

Hills were forced to do a U-turn after realising that their major rivals were about to steal a march in the punter-friendly stakes. Ladbrokes and Coral voided all bets on England, the favourites at around 1-2, but said they would pay out on a dead-heat to punters who backed New Zealand at 6-4 or 7-4. Hills, sticking to rules used in Sunday League matches, initially said they would settle all bets on a dead-heat, which was bad news for England punters who in effect had backed a loser – A £100 bet at 1-2 returns just £75. But Hills later changed their tune and fell into line with Ladbrokes and Coral.

Tote bookmakers applied dead-heat rules for bets on either side, just as they do for Sunday League one-day matches. But other firms like Stanley Racing, Surrey Racing and Stan James voided all bets, again just as they do for the Sunday League.

In 1996, betting on the cricket World Cup in India and Pakistan was thrown into turmoil when the ICC ruled that any runs scored and wickets taken in abandoned matches would be counted in end-of-tournament statistics – even if the abandoned game was played at a later date. Dealers at spread-betting firms who'd framed markets around things like the number of runs scored by Brian Lara were seen hurling themselves into the Thames.

And no-one - not bookies, not punters, no-one – can understand the controversial method used to determine run rates in one-day matches cut short by rain. I've never been a fan of cricket. One reason is that it bores me rigid but another is that I refuse to become a devotee of a sport which needs rules framed by nuclear scientists merely to determine who has won a match.

It was clear for a long time that something had to be done to ensure fairness in rain-shortened games. Ensuring merely that each side faced the same number of overs was not enough as it generally gave the team batting second a clear advantage. In instances where the second innings was drastically reduced by weather the target was simply scaled down in proportion to the number of overs available, but this too proved intrinsically unfair.

So up stepped statistician Frank Duckworth and colleague Tony Lewis, a lecturer in computer studies and mathematics, with a solution adopted in 1997 by the England and Wales Cricket Board for all domestic competitions. I leave you with the start of Duckworth's explanation of how it works.

"If we start by taking the case of no wicket lost (w=0), as at the start of an innings, then the average runs Z obtainable with u overs to go may be represented by an exponential curve reaching an asympotic value Zo, corresponding to the average score with no overs limit but with limited-over rules and regulations. Thus: $Z(u) = Zo (1 - exp - bu)$."

So now you know.

# chapter 12

## the oval-shaped game

You will read in this chapter wondrous tales of betting coups on American Football, rugby union and rugby league. The perpetrators will insist it is possible to make small fortunes by betting on such sports.

It is not.

The odds are stacked massively against the punter by bookmakers who have all bases covered. Show me a man who says he makes vast profits from such bets and more often than not I will show you a liar.

Betting on all three sports is dominated by the handicap, with bookmakers awarding the underdog a theoretical start in order to even up a match. So Atlanta Falcons are given a 7.5pt 'start' against Denver Broncos in the Super Bowl, London Irish will get perhaps a four-point start at Northampton in rugby union's Allied Dunbar Premiership, while London Broncos might enjoy a thumping 12-point start at mighty Wigan in the Super League. The aim is to make each match a toss-of-the-coin job, thereby ensuring two-way betting action.

If I was to get evens about the toss of the coin for the duration of a season, I would expect neither to make money nor lose money. Even-money is the correct price for a simple toss so, long-term, I will finish level. But in American Football, rugby union and rugby league, even-money is a mere pipedream. For these 'toss-of-a-coin' matches I will be offered only 5-6, or at best 10-11, each of two. That is a passport to poverty.

But that's not all. In rugby union and league, I can be further hit by the draw. Spin a coin and there are only two possible results –

heads or tails. But in both codes of rugby, bets can be scuppered by the dreaded draw, which is generally around the 14-1 mark. I could back London Irish at 5-6 with a four-point start but my bet will go down if opponents Northampton beat them by any margin above three points. In American Football, handicaps come in half-points, ruling out the possibility of a draw.

All this should make any right-thinking punter run a mile before contemplating a bet on rugby, but there is even worse news to come. Almost all bookmakers demand minimum trebles on the weekly slate of domestic rugby. Singles are accepted only on games covered live on TV. So in a nutshell this is what rugby punters are expected to swallow every week:

First, accept a toss of the coin with odds of just 5-6

Next, accept that on every 15th toss (hence odds of 14-1 the draw), the coin will end up rolling down a drain, making all bets losers.

Then accept that it's not possible to bet on just one toss: you have to call correctly three times to be paid out.

It's a diabolical liberty. A correct call of a coin thrice running is a 7-1 chance, but with rugby you get no more than 5-1 (5-6 three times), with the chance of the draw beating you in each match.

American Football betting is marginally more acceptable because not only is the draw not a factor, but some firms will allow unrestricted singles. For instance, for the 1998-99 season, Hills and Stan James accepted singles on every contest right up to the Super Bowl on January 31.

Of course there is a reason for such 'generosity', quite apart from the desire to lure customers away from rival firms and the fact that Hills, with so many USA-based clients, realise that they have to offer terms at least as good as in Las Vegas (which means unrestricted singles and no tax). Bookies know that their handicaps on American Football are nearly always spot on as they are based closely on the Vegas line.

In Las Vegas, odds-makers know everything there is to know about American Football. It's a massive betting medium over there and they cannot afford to be even a smidgeon out. A quarterback sneezes in training on a Tuesday and the Vegas men hear it. His colleague gets VD and they'll know just when he contracted it. On the rare occasions the line is a tiny bit shaky, the Vegas odds-makers will have their card marked by the early money wagered by punters whose knowledge, wisdom and contacts they trust implicitly. By the time British bookies publish their handicaps, the Vegas line is rock-solid.

On a weekly basis you might strike lucky on American Football, ruby league and rugby union but long term you are fighting a losing battle.

## American Football

Perhaps the biggest joke sport in a country of joke sports, American Football has somehow managed to win the hearts and minds of a small band of loyal supporters in Britain. These are the guys who bore you in work every Monday morning about the "humdinger" of a match they watched the night before on Sky. They wear Washington Redskins or Miami Dolphins jerseys, are invariably bald or fat (often both), generally bearded, and almost certainly virgins. But they bet, as that is the only way you can possibly stomach hour upon hour of American Football, and bookmakers fall over themselves to keep them sweet.

Look at the amount of bookmaker advertising in the *Racing Post* devoted to American Football. The sport accounts for probably less than half a per cent of general sports betting turnover, yet you'd think from the volume of advertising that it runs football - proper football - a close second. This is because bookies know a good thing when they see one.

Yes, the turnover on American Football is small but, because of the reasons I outlined earlier, it is pretty much risk-free. Whatever the spend on advertising, bookmakers know they will recoup it, and lots more, from the loyal band of bearded virgins.

There's a character called Dunbar in Joseph Heller's famous novel *Catch 22*, who is petrified that life is passing him by too quickly. He takes up hobbies he hates so that time will seem to pass so much more slowly. Dunbar comes to mind whenever I have the bad luck to watch an American Football contest on TV. The game lasts about three hours but feels like three weeks. There is no stretch of action that lasts longer than seven seconds but so much energy do the players expend in those madcap bursts of activity that they must rest for the next two minutes. No wonder fat Yanks love it – just think of all those opportunities to open another six-pack and shovel another burger down the throat.

For large parts of a game it is impossible to tell where the ball is. Truck-sized figures lurch about all over the field, thudding into one another, but the ball could be in another state for all they know. It would be an interesting exercise to confiscate it and see how long it takes players to notice.

Despite its all-too-obvious shortcomings, American Football is the single most popular gambling activity in the States. Yet it was not always thus. Baseball was the national pastime for the first four decades of the 20th Century. But then, in Minneapolis, Minnesota, in the late 1930s, something happened that changed the course of betting history.

Bill Hecht invented the points spread.

Let Bert Randolph Sugar, writing in *The Caesars Palace Book Of Sports Betting*, take up the story.

"As a win-lose proposition, football is highly predictable. Even dominant baseball teams lose about four games out of every ten but their football counterparts seem to roll on, week after week, making the odds-making business a dicey one. Before the point spread, bookies had a dilemma. If they set the odds at a level sufficient to attract a lot of business, they were liable to go broke; if they set them high enough to balance the books, they drove away customers. It was a two-edged sword because picking winners was simply too easy. Football was not a betting sport because betting it was not a sporting proposition.

"The point spread works like a golfer's handicap, allowing duffers to compete with scratch players. Where once there had been a sure thing, now there was room for a difference of opinion, which is the essence of gambling. It is the garlic in the salad, the one ingredient without which there is no dish. It is the great leveller, the device that brings true parity to the NFL. Unlike former NFL Commissioner Bert Bell's famous – if somewhat dubious – claim of parity: 'On any given Sunday, any team in the NFL can beat any other team,' the spread makes it happen, allowing pussycats to play powerhouses straight up. Because of it, sports betting was on the brink of a revolution."

Hecht initially quoted double-numbered point spreads - for instance "Yale is 13-15 over Harvard" – which worked on the same principle as spread betting today. Those who fancied Yale had to give (or lay) 15 points, while Harvard supporters received 13 points. But so many contests landed right in the middle – in this case a 14-point win for Yale – that punters became thoroughly pissed off.

Sugar writes: "Sometime around 1935, Bill Hecht resolved the difficulty by quoting a single number. To eliminate the possibility of a push (a tie), he added a half-point as in 'Yale −13½ over Harvard.' He offered 9-10 odds up to 14 points and 5-6 above it. He still quoted an odds line on the outcome, but with such outlandish prices as 1/20-15/1 there were few takers. Occasionally someone would take a flier on a longshot underdog, but few were foolish enough to lay 1-20 on the favourite in hopes of stealing a few easy bucks at the risk of losing the ranch.

"Although Hecht might have owned the original copyright, there was still room for improvement. The evolution of the point spread as we know it was finally completed in 1941 by Ed Curd of Lexington, Kentucky. Known in gambling legend as Frank Costello's bookmaker, Curd eliminated the outcome line and set the odds on the spread at 10-11, guaranteeing the bookmaker a ten per cent commission, or 'vigorish', on every bet booked."

The introduction of the point spread helped the sport make massive strides in popularity, but it took the events of 1958 to catapult it into super-stardom. A dramatic finish saw New York Giants grimly hang on to a 19-17 lead against Detroit to close the gap on Eastern Conference leaders Cleveland Browns with just one game of the season to go. That final game? Giants v Browns in the Yankee Stadium. The Giants won 13-10 to force a play-off for the division championship, and the following week clinched the play-off 10-0, again in the Yankee Stadium, to book a showdown with Western Division champions Baltimore Colts for the League title.

All this would normally have passed without too much comment in New York, which had always been a rock-solid baseball town, boasting the Yankees, the Giants, and the Brooklyn Dodgers. But a year earlier both the Giants and Dodgers had upped sticks and moved to pastures greener in California. Millions of baseball fans, deserted by their one-time idols and more willing to slice off their testicles than support the Yankees, instead latched on to the football Giants, whose run of success was admirably filling the void left by the absconding baseball stars.

"Overnight they became the idols of a fandom starved for heroes," Sugar writes. "Lines formed nightly outside PJ Clark's, the legendary Third Avenue bar known to be the players' favourite haunt. A glimpse of Frank Gifford or Charlie Conerly sent spinsters swooning; after an evening signing autographs, Kyle Rote had to seek shelter for fear that writer's cramp might threaten his ability to catch passes.

"None of this of course was lost on the broadcasting and advertising types of Madison Avenue. They too spent their drinking time on Third Avenue. Fans themselves, they were quickly swept up in the hysteria that surrounded the Giants. And it showed. CBS, the network fortunate enough to be carrying the Giants-Colts championship game, ballyhooed it from morning till night; had there been commercial time available, it would have been snapped up in a moment. The game was already being billed as a clash of the titans.

"And that it was. Late in the fourth quarter, Steve Myra kicked a field goal for the Colts and regulation time ended in a 17-17 tie, thereby forcing football's first 'sudden-death' game. The Giants won the toss and elected to receive, but the Colts' stonewall defence forced them to punt. Under the steady hand of Johnny Unitas, the Colts worked the ball smartly down the field and full-back Alan Ameche dove over from the five to win, 23-17. The Giants had lost their first game in four weeks, but in so doing they had played their way into sports history.

"Pro-football would never be the same again. Not just New York had watched 'The Greatest Game Ever Played,' the entire nation had. Pro-football mania swept the land. After 39 years it had finally arrived. Never again would it take a back seat to baseball."

It's been estimated that for Monday night live TV games in the States, up to 30 per cent of the viewing audience have a betting interest. I'd hazard that over the course of a season, 0.000 per cent show a profit. To buck odds of 5-6, a punter must win 54.55 per cent of his bets merely to break even – and that's before tax. If he also pays nine per cent tax he faces a practically impossible task. And then very likely he has to satisfy a minimum-trebles requirement.

Still think American Football is a good betting medium?

Perhaps the one thing in the punter's favour is the relative scarcity of matches. American Football may enjoy immense TV exposure but there aren't too many betting opportunities each year. With 30 teams playing 16 games, there are only 240 contests during a regular season. That should, in theory, give the punter plenty of time to keep abreast of all the latest news and views. Pity then the poor horseracing punter who by comparison does not have time to fart.

If you're looking for a fistful of statistics here, you'll be sadly disappointed. American Football supporters live and breathe stats but from a punting viewpoint almost all are pointless – records against the spread, number of yards carried, total points on the road; crap, crap and more crap, although I acknowledge that in the spread betting jungle such information has import.

I remember all the nonsense spouted when Ian Rush was in his heyday as Liverpool striker. "Liverpool never lose when Rush scores," we were forever told. But Rush generally scored *because* Liverpool were the superior team already and created numerous chances for him. And the fact that Rush scored automatically meant the odds about Liverpool losing increased markedly. Remember that games make stats, stats don't make games.

Although I have so far been harsh on the merits of American Football as a betting medium, I must confess that the sport does throw up one or two golden opportunities in the various NFL divisional betting. Bookies update their betting on the divisions - NFC Central, NFC West etc – after each slate of weekend fixtures and with no Vegas guide to go on, very often they make mistakes.

One season a mate on the opening day backed Chicago at 9-4 and Minnesota at 5-2 to win the NFC Central. A week later he backed Detroit at 12-1 in the same competition. Before matches kicked off on the third weekend, he took Green Bay at 20-1 and Tampa at 25-1, again for the NFC Central, thereby covering all angles. Inside three weeks he had managed to complete a punter's book of 76 per cent and, with shrewd staking, had guaranteed himself a fat profit no matter what the eventual outcome. At about the same time I checked out the odds for the market leaders in each of the divisions.

**Washington**, odds-on in places for NFC East, could be backed at 13-8.

**Chicago** ranged from 4-6 to evens for NFC Central.

**San Francisco** were generally 1-3 for NFC West but could be backed in a place at a much more acceptable 4-7.

It was a similar story in the three AFC sections:

**Buffalo**, a prohibitive 2-7 in places, were 1-2 elsewhere for AFC east.

**Houston**, the 4-7 AFC Central favourites, were on offer at evens with one intrepid firm.

**LA Raiders**, as short as 10-11 for AFC West, stood out at 7-4 with two other layers.

I point all this out merely to show that value bets can be found in the most unlikely of places. Here were six odds-on favourites, four of which were available at evens or better.

Midway through the 1998-99 campaign, Hills introduced under-over betting for every weekend match. In this the punter tries to predict whether or not the total score will exceed the odds-makers' number. For instance, in the Super Bowl on 31 January 1999 between Denver and Atlanta, the Hills quote was 53-54, 10-11 the pair. Denver won 34-19 to reward, but only just, those punters who'd taken 53 points or less.

This market can be seriously affected by the weather - the worse the weather, the lower the score – and it's here punters just might be able to grab an edge. Increasing use of the Internet and all its many NFL websites (www.nfl.com is the best) puts us in an ideal position. Weather bulletins are updated regularly and very often hard-pressed odds-compilers, quite possibly reduced to a skeleton staff on a Sunday with a dozen events to keep tabs on, won't have the time to monitor the NFL pages in the way a punter can. Indeed I have it on very good authority that the small handful of American Football punters who manage not to show a loss owe their good fortune only to studious examination in the hours leading up to kick-off time of the NFL Internet pages.

The crowning moment of the American Football season of course is the Super Bowl, or the HyperBole as someone very clever once described it. It's the day everyone in America, and thousands in Britain, goes betting mad. I once read a fascinating book called *SuperBookie: Inside Las Vegas Sports Gambling* by a Vegas odds-maker called Art Manteris. His memorable account of the action on the 1991 Super Bowl between New York Giants and Buffalo Bills deserves a wider audience.

"The Buffalo Bills had been my team all year," he wrote. "I thought they would win the AFC and have a shot in the Super Bowl to beat the 49ers, the team I expected to win the NFC. All season long I had been shading future-book (ante-post) odds to keep the public from wagering on Buffalo. Therefore we were in a tremendous future-book position if the Bills won the Super Bowl against the Giants. Buffalo didn't even have to cover the point spread for us to make a killing. All they had to do was beat the Giants, who had been heavily backed (behind San Francisco) in future-book wagering.

"Before proceeding with my horror story, this about the Super Bowl odds.

"We opened the game at Bills –6 about one minute after the Giants upset the 49ers on Sunday afternoon, January 20. Oddsmaker Michael (Roxy) Roxborough had released the opening number at –5, and some sports books opened it at –4½, –5, or –5½, but we opened at –6 and took a tremendous amount of early money on the Giants getting six points, especially on Sunday night. All the sharp handicappers wanted the points, and we must have taken $200,000 to $300,000 on the Giants that first evening.

"Yet I didn't budge. I knew the public would bet Buffalo and they did. By late Monday and early Tuesday the number had climbed to 6½ and in some places to 7. It put us in an absolutely ideal situation, holding all the money on the Giants at +6. If the game falls exactly on that number we beat almost everybody because by now everybody is betting the Bills at –7 and even –7½. Indeed, if Thurman Thomas breaks that big run for a TD on the Bills' last drive, the game falls on 6 and everybody in the country who opens at –5 is screaming. It would have been a disastrous middle for most bookies.

"Except at the SuperBook. We would have made a killing because I felt I had been at my absolute best as a bookmaker, positioning us against middle risk. I had considered all options and had gotten best value for the house.

"Best value, though, doesn't always win.

"Let me tell you how Scott Norwood's missed 47-yard field goal moved millions of dollars and almost destroyed my digestive system.

- The Giants won the game, straight up (20-19), cashing all future-book wagers on New York. We needed Buffalo.
- The Giants won all money-line wagers, with many bettors having New York at +200 (2-1) to win the game.
- The game total (39) went under 41½, 41, and 40½, the most often-wagered total-points numbers. Had the field goal been successful, the game would have gone over 42.
- The half-time total was 20 points, and we had one casino high-roller who wagered almost six figures on the 'under' which came in at 17.

"Indeed at the SuperBook almost everything was riding on Norwood's final field-goal attempt and the miss swung at least $700,000. If he makes it we win more than half a million dollars for the day. The miss made us small losers for the entire Super Bowl. Oh, what it could have been. We had gone into the day with a best-case scenario (Buffalo wins and covers) to win more than $1 million and a worst-case scenario of losing peanuts. In fact, there were six potential wagering outcomes in the game, and we were in great shape on five of them.

- Bills cover and over.
- Bills cover and under.
- Giants cover and over but lose the game.
- Giants cover and under but lose the game.
- Giants and over with the Giants winning straight up.
- Giants and under with the Giants winning straight up.

"Only the last possibility could have kept us from making a Super Bowl killing, and it happened. I was devastated. It's one thing to lose. It's something else to lose on the last play of the game. It was like my entire world caved in and it was the closest I've ever come to throwing in the towel."

I make no secret of my aversion to American Football and it follows that I am not the world's leading authority on its betting secrets. But I have carried out enough research and conducted enough interviews in the course of writing this chapter to be sufficiently qualified to put forward a few obvious tips.

**1.** Always back singles. The odds are difficult enough to overcome; in trebles they are practically insurmountable. I realise that at odds of 5-6 or 10-11, this is hardly a pulse-quickening prospect for the smaller punter, but it's the only way if not to make money at least to avoid losing too much.

**2.** Don't bet the underdog when the spread is two touchdowns or more.

**3.** Favour the home team when both sides have nothing to play for.

**4.** Pester bookies every Monday for their updated divisional odds. Howlers can be frequent.

**5.** Invest in the Internet. American Football is one of the hardest of all sports in which to find an edge and the Internet at least offers the glimmer of a chance.

## Rugby League

I asked four punters who bet regularly on rugby league and claim to make hefty profits to recount their most enjoyable coup. All pinpointed the World Club Championship in the summer of 1997, when clubs sides from Australia took on English teams in a clash of the hemispheres. An Australian bookmaker was first out of the traps with his odds and framed handicaps which paid, as many rugby fans immediately recognised, the English teams undue respect.

One or two firms in Britain, perhaps unsure of the strength of the Australian challenge and perhaps believing that the Aussie bookie knew his onions, based their own sums on his line. They were quickly made to pay. For instance, Halifax were given only a 28-point start against the mighty Brisbane Broncos, who to the delight of clued-up rugby punters proceeded to run up a cricket score against their shell-shocked Pommie opponents. Several other matches followed the same pattern. It became quite clear from the first batch of matches that there was a huge gulf in class between the Australians and the Brits, and so for the second slate of games the hard-hit bookies took no chances.

This time they asked the Broncos and their fellow Aussie sides to concede huge starts to their puny Pommie rivals. But they went too far. Rugby punters, the same ones who had cleaned up by backing the Aussies to cover the spread in the first games, this time recognised that the task facing Broncos and co was Herculean. This time they took the Brits with the points and, once again, pocketed huge winnings.

An interesting tale. More pertinent, though, is the fact that all four sources picked the same coup as their most memorable, hinting perhaps that in reality there are few chances for the rugby league punter to get his nose in front.

One of the four admitted that to stay ahead of the game he has to take advantage of unorthodox (illegal) bookies who will offer him unrestricted singles, tax-free. Without such an option, he came close to admitting, there's no prospect of beating the bookies.

But perhaps we are being a trifle harsh on the sport's merits as a betting medium. The bookmaker position is only as solid as his handicap mark, and who's to say that on occasions the handicap mark is not way out of line? There are few sound rugby league judges in a bookmaking industry whose heartland is the non rugby league-playing south of England. Many firms rely upon a 'tissue' – a mark offered by a rugby league 'expert' as a guide to what the handicap should be – but this tissue could be hopelessly inaccurate.

Furthermore, the major firms issue their rugby league coupons on a Wednesday, leaving themselves vulnerable to late-breaking team news. Rather than alter their handicaps in the face of significant injury bulletins, bookies will instead revise their prices. So where Wigan are 5-6 to concede successfully a 12-point start to Leeds, they will shorten to perhaps 4-6, with the handicap mark remaining at −12, if news breaks that Leeds are without star man Iestyn Harris. Some punters may argue that while at 5-6 they were a good bet, at 4-6 Wigan no longer represent value. But others will insist that, as they considered Wigan good things to cover the spread against a full-strength Leeds side, the chances of them doing so against a severely weakened line-up are even greater and therefore stakes should be increased to offset the reduction in odds.

There's also the very real possibility that as rugby league is not the most widely-covered sport in the British press, particularly away from its northern heartland, and that, even in the north, information about lower-division teams is at best sketchy, the punter with good contacts and prepared to do his homework can find himself a position of strength. Bookies of course recognise this, which is why they will never relax their minimum-trebles ruling apart from live TV matches.

Few rugby punters are in a more privileged position than Jackie Edwards, father of rugby league legend Shaun Edwards, and himself a former pro star for Warrington. Edwards Snr never considers backing trebles – it's singles or nothing for him. And he insists that it's essential before placing a bet to have reliable information about injuries and suspensions.

"By waiting until the last moment you may very well miss the price, but it's the only logical strategy," he said. "For instance in a live Sky match on a Friday night a few seasons back, I really fancied Warrington to overcome a four-point start for Leeds. I waited for the team news to be given on Sky at about 7.20pm and learned that Leeds were without three of their seven first-choice backs. When I rang to place my bet on Warrington, I found that the odds had shortened from 5-6 to 8-11. But as far as I was concerned Warrington were now absolute certainties."

Edwards says one of his greatest rugby bets was on the famous Bath v Wigan clash-of-the-codes challenge match at Twickenham in 1996. This was the rugby union showdown and Bath were asked to concede around 22 points. "That equated to around 1-8 for Bath to win the match but some firms were offering them at 4-9 – an absolute steal."

Rugby League is a tough, gruelling game which is why there are few midweek fixtures. It's asking a lot of players to compete in a tough fixture on a Wednesday night and then another one a few days later. Punters should always consider opposing sides who face such daunting back-to-back fixtures. The same argument does not apply in soccer, which is perhaps not so physically demanding.

On rare occasions there will be a huge difference of opinion on rival coupons about a certain match, let's say for argument's sake Sheffield v Warrington. Bookie A may give Warrington an eight-point start, Bookie B deciding on the other hand that Sheffield merit a two-point start. This gives a ten-point 'middle' and offers punters a huge chance to cash in. It's a game scheduled for live TV coverage, so singles are accepted. We stake £120 on Warrington +8 and another £120 on Sheffield +2, both at odds of 5-6. Our outlay, including tax at nine per cent, is 261.20 and our minimum return, since one of the bets has to win, is £220. But there is such a huge middle that it's possible both bets will cop - for example, if Sheffield win the match by anything up to seven points or Warrington win by a one-point margin, or even if the match finishes all-square. Our return then for the same £261.20 outlay is £440.

Of course very often the match with the largest handicap discrepancy is not a contest on which single bets are allowed, setting punters the task of finding two other selections to satisfy the dreadful minimum-trebles requirement. The common mistake made by punters here is to place two separate trebles – for example Warrington +8 with two other selections, and Sheffield +2 with the same two selections. This, though, does not give any margin for error, and I have a more sensible strategy.

Find *three* more selections and make the Sheffield-Warrington game your banker in these two bets:

**Bet A:**
Three trebles – perm any two of three with banker Sheffield +2.

**Bet B:**
Three trebles – perm any two of three with banker Warrington +8.

One of your bankers, as I've already explained, *must* win, so you need only two of the other three selections to cop for a winning treble. Better still, all three of the other selections could win for three lovely winning trebles. And there's always a real chance of the dream scenario: The Sheffield-Warrington game finishing in the ten-point middle, and the other three selections also obliging for SIX winning trebles. Happy, happy days.

Incidentally, I don't think it's possible to illustrate the destructive effect of tax better than by using this same Sheffield-Warrington example.

You stake £100 on Sheffield +2 at 5-6, and another £100 on Warrington +8 in tax-free single bets. Your outlay is £200, your minimum return is £183.33 (a loss of £16.67), and your maximum £366.66 (a profit of £166.66). You are in effect risking £16.67 to win £166.66 and therefore getting 10-1 that the game finishes in that ten-point middle. A reasonable bet in anybody's language.

But the moment tax is included, your odds are dramatically reduced. Your outlay on the above two bets would now be £218 for the same minimum return of £183.33, a loss of £34.67, and the same maximum return of £366.66, a profit of £148.66. Now you are risking £34.67 to win £148.66, giving you far less tasty odds of little more than 4-1. Even more horrifying, if Sheffield and Warrington in the above example were each available at 10-11 instead of 5-6, your pre-tax odds of hitting the magic 'middle' are 20-1. After tax they are around 6-1.

Do not take this awful news as an excuse not to pay tax on your bets. If you can find an illegal bookie, all well and good. But if, like most of us, you are forced to bet legally, then make sure you always pay tax on your bets. It is a mathematical fact that this benefits the punter, as I will explain in a later chapter.

Maurice Lindsay, managing director of the Super League and former chairman of all-conquering Wigan, has a background steeped in bookmaking. In the 1970s, as head of Lindsay Bookmakers, he produced his own rugby league handicap coupon and although he has not bet on the sport since he joined Wigan's board in 1979, he admits that punting friends of his do benefit on occasions from his inside knowledge. Lindsay, who in December 1998 paid out more than £200,000 to acquire betting pitches at four major racecourses - Cheltenham, York, Doncaster and Haydock – believes it is still possible for informed punters to defy the odds stacked against them on rugby league.

"In the early days of rugby league betting, in the 1970s, the major firms took a caning," recalls Lindsay. "Rugby league punters know their sport and they were able to spot immediately when a bookmaker had made a mistake with his handicap mark. Since then the likes of William Hill have radically improved their rugby operation, but there are still ways the punter can cash in. The key is to leave your bet as late as possible, when you have heard reliable team and injury news."

Lindsay, who will begin his racecourse betting operation in late 1999 when he is expected to quit the Super League, went close to being offered the chairmanship of the Tote in succession to Lord

Wyatt in 1997. He is the architect of the switch to summer rugby and the man who steered the domestic game into the arms of media mogul Rupert Murdoch in 1995, brokering an £87 million TV deal that now forms the backbone of the sport. His actions split rugby, with winter diehards in particular loathing the switch to summer fixtures, but Lindsay argued that so many clubs were in terrible financial trouble that he had no option.

He said he never bets on rugby "because it would be improper" for a man in his position, but recalls when he was at Central Park tipping off his friends whenever Wigan were due to make an important signing. "I think quite a few cashed in on our Challenge Cup odds before the bookmakers got wise and began making us odds-on every season," he said.

I can reveal here, though, one planned Wigan sting that went horribly wrong. Wigan were cast-iron certainties to beat Sheffield in the final of the Challenge Cup at Wembley in April 1998. A Sheffield victory was just not an option, as outright odds of 14-1 implied. So certain were Wigan of coasting to victory that several of the players staked substantial sums on one team-mate in particular to score the last try at odds of 40-1. All they had to do, the logic went, was set him up for a try in the closing minutes, by which time Wigan would be miles clear and Sheffield would already have thrown in the towel. But in an upset that rivalled Buster Douglas's defeat of Mike Tyson, Sheffield miraculously won the Challenge Cup by a 17-8 margin.

Bookmaker Ron Wadey compiled the odds for the Rugby League Action coupon for ten years before retiring at the end of 1998. He said that he would take ten opinions from trusted aides – regular spectators – before finalising a handicap mark, and believes that on some occasions rival odds-compilers were not prepared to show similar diligence. "If I was prepared to wait, sometimes, weeks, for just one bet, then I could definitely make the game pay," he said. And his advice to would-be rugby punters? "The best time to bet is towards the end of the season when many teams have little to play for. Several teams opt to blood youngsters, and bookmakers do not always take that kind of information into account."

# Rugby Union

Harlequins ace Chris Sheasby spelled out in robust terms one Saturday early in the 1998-99 season just why betting on sport has become THE growth industry of the 1990s.

England star Sheasby was interviewed on Sky Sports minutes before the start of the mouthwatering showdown between Harlequins and unbeaten Saracens in the Allied Dunbar Premiership match at The Stoop.

Told that Harlequins, despite home advantage, had been made 15-point underdogs by bookmakers, Sheasby, no stranger to betting, became indignant.

"Bookmakers never make a mistake on racing," he said, "and they're hard to beat on football, too. But in rugby union they are so vulnerable, it's untrue. It's absolutely crazy to make Saracens the 15-point favourites. If any side is going to win by 15 points, it's us."

Even allowing for natural bias, Sheasby's words should have sparked the armchair punter into action. And his confidence was justified because Quins turned in the performance of the season to win 41-28.

I'm not sure that many would share Sheasby's bullishness about the merits of rugby union as a betting medium, and I'm afraid that despite repeated requests for an interview, Sheasby was unwilling to elaborate further. But the man recognised by most rugby punters as the betting brains of the sport was happy to list the pros and cons.

Former England star Stuart Barnes, a hard-core punter, is now the linchpin of Sky's excellent rugby union coverage. His frequent discussions about odds in the build-up to live matches have made the Sky broadcasts unmissable for thousands of punters. Barnes admits to betting frequently on rugby union, but concedes that it's very difficult to make a profit. "I don't think punters who try to find a winning treble on the handicaps each weekend have much of a chance," he said. "The bookies have so much in their favour." But Barnes did reveal his betting secrets.

"To me the key is not how good a team is in attack, but how solid the defence is. You need to look for back-row forwards who are good at killing the ball. Look for instance at the Five Nations clash between Wales and Ireland (in February 1999) at Wembley. If you went through the teams man for man, you could perhaps understand why Wales were the favourites and why Ireland were given a five-point start on handicap. But what I considered far more significant was that Ireland had the edge in four of the five forward positions. To my mind that more than outweighed Wales' strength in other departments and it was no surprise to see Ireland winning 29-23. Yes, I know Ireland's record against Wales was poor but I take no notice whatsoever of history or statistics. Each game must be judged on its own merits, not on what went on ten years ago.

"All punters should recognise the key positions in a rugby union match. Team A may lose two wingers and an outside-centre for a particular match while Team B might lose their regular fly-half. To the uninitiated, Team A would be worth opposing because they have lost three regular players, while Team B are missing only one. But any shrewd punter will tell you that the loss of the fly-half will have more of an impact on Team B's performance than the absence of the other three."

Barnes says there are five key positions in rugby union: Loose-head prop, middle line-out jumper (to guarantee good set-piece possession), open-side flanker (with a very high destructive capacity), scrum-half, and fly-half. To illustrate his point, he says that betting on England without Neil Back is like backing Arsenal without key midfield duo Patrick Vieira and Emmanuel Petit.

The former England man believes that in matches which feature a very strong favourite, it pays in the long run to back the underdogs with a massive start on handicap. "Very often the favourites could be leading in the closing minutes by something like 21 points, comfortably covering the 18-point handicap they were asked to concede. But there's nothing to stop them taking their foot off the gas, maybe making changes, and allowing the opposition to steal a try late on. That's why I always think it's dangerous to back teams, however strong, to defy large handicaps."

Barnes also maintains that weather conditions are hugely significant in rugby union, and gives a graphic illustration. On the

British Lions tour of South Africa in the summer of 1997, he watched in glorious sunshine a two-hour training session by Border players, who were due to take on the Lions a day later. Bookies in Britain knew nothing about Border and, after watching them at first-hand, Barnes was convinced that the Lions would murder them, certainly by more than the 22-point margin bookmakers in Britain had guessed. "They looked diabolical," Barnes recalls.

But overnight the heavens opened, the pitch cut up terribly, Lions played an appalling tactical game (according to Barnes), and the final result was 18-14 for Lions. "I'm not saying how much I lost just in case the wife gets to hear about it, but I dropped a seriously heavy amount," said Barnes.

It was further, conclusive proof that even the most sensible reading of a game can be made to look silly if conditions deteriorate. Just as a plodding stayer becomes a real threat against the classiest of runners in a Grand National on heavy Aintree going, so even the most limited of rugby sides can go close to causing an upset against far superior opponents on mudbath pitches.

Though domestic club rugby runs throughout the winter and enjoys considerable TV coverage, from a betting point of view it hardly amounts to a hill of beans compared to the Five Nations Championship fixtures in the early months of each year. Indeed, bookmakers Hills told me that their turnover for a Friday night rugby league match live on Sky is generally four times greater than the turnover for a Saturday afternoon Allied Dunbar Premiership contest, again live on Sky. It was only in 1993 that Hills and Ladbrokes began betting on the weekly rugby union programme, and the following year the two firms announced that they would accept singles on matches covered live by a new satellite channel, Sky Sports 2.

But it's the Five Nations Championship – and of course the World Cup, staged in Britain in 1999 – which is the betting flagship of the sport.

"Five Nations weekends are very, very big business," confirmed Hills spokesman David Brown. "It is the first major domestic sporting event of the year and traditionally commands a high profile in the media and also with the betting public. The intense press coverage raises the whole profile of the event, which further assists betting turnover." It helps too that, for the Five Nations, bookies see fit to offer 10-11 each of two rather than the more regular 5-6, and of course singles are accepted in all ten internationals.

Instinct would tell you that for the Five Nations, first try-scorer and winning-margin betting would prove popular with the smaller punters not turned on by 10-11 handicap odds, but Brown says first try-scorer accounts for less than one per cent of Five Nations turnover, and winning margins (England to win by between 11 and 15 points for instance) no more than six per cent. Smaller punters prefer, said Brown, to have a handicap double on the two matches played each Five Nations weekend. Curiously, such punters generally bet the two favourites to cover the spread or the two outsiders to win with the points, rarely a mixture.

I asked bookmakers why they don't take a lead from American Football betting and introduce half-point handicaps that rule out the possibility of the punter-shattering tie. These were the responses:

**Hills:** "Traditionally sports such as rugby and football are priced with the option of a draw, whereas American Football is not. We see no evidence of a need for a change. Far from being 'punter-shattering' the reverse is often the case, with many punters enjoying taking a chance on the tied result at the rewarding odds (generally 14-1) on offer. If both matches on a Five Nations weekend were tied we would expect to take a caning."

**Ladbrokes:** "Plenty of fans back the draw at long odds. Quoting the tie adds to the skill and judgement of the rugby fan when he chooses a handicap bet."

**Coral:** "The games are different in that a tie is more likely in American Football. By dropping the half-point in rugby it allows us to bet to more generous odds, such as 10-11 instead of the 5-6 more common for the average NFL game."

**Tote:** "On Five Nations matches punters get a choice that they don't get from American Football. We have betting on each match, with and without a handicap. In both events we expect to take money on all three outcomes. Most punters will not just back one of the matches to draw but will double up on both. Both matches being drawn would be our worst possible result."

Well if that's the case, boys, I'd have thought your very first move would be to introduce the half-point handicap to rule out any possibility of the nightmare scenario. Are we to believe here that you really do have the interest of punters at heart?

In the early 1990s, bookies regularly got away with one of their greatest con-tricks on the Five Nations. Odds for each of the five competing nations were freely offered, but there was something missing. Now, erm, what was it? Oh yes, they'd forgotten to quote the favourite. It's true. The strongest likelihood in those years, when the tournament was wide open, was for no team to do the Slam –

Surrey Racing went just 4-7 about such a possibility in 1991 - but none of the leading bookies ever featured it in their lists. It was like a racecourse bookmaker refusing to price up and lay the odds-on favourite in a six-runner contest and at the same time insisting that if that favourite obliged, all bets were losers.

Prize for the weakest attempt to justify the evil tactic went to Hills, whose spokesman said at the time: "It's a question of betting on the positive and not the negative. We often quote prices about things like teams to do the League and FA Cup double, but we don't give a price for no team to do the double. If a punter doesn't fancy any side to complete the Grand Slam, then there's no pressure on him to have a bet."

Happily, bookies nowadays play ball and punters can easily back 'No Grand Slam', odds for which have drifted out over the last few years to around 13-8 in the face of English and French domination.

Considering the betting bombshells that have rocked football and cricket in the 1990s, it's a little surprising that rugby has been largely untainted. The nearest thing to raised eyebrows came in March 1995 when England players were publicly banned from betting on their Grand Slam decider with Scotland at Twickenham. The ban followed England prop Victor Ubogu's attempts to put £100 on himself at 18-1 to score the first try in the earlier Five

Nations match with Wales in Cardiff. "Keep your cash in your pockets; there'll be no gambling," England manager Jack Rowell warned his players. But the move angered the England men, particularly Ubogu who insisted after the Cardiff game that he had not even managed to get his bet on.

"It is outrageous to suggest that I, or any of the other players, would refuse to give a scoring pass just because it might wreck a bet," he stormed. "It's very insulting. The great hallmark of this England side is collective teamwork rather than individual glory. But it's a bit rich to stop us from betting a few quid when gate receipts for a game from which we won't earn a single penny are going to top £1 million."

There is no suggestion that the 1995 Rugby World Cup in South Africa suffered any betting skulduggery but there are one or two people in the game who wonder about some of the results and the incidents behind them. This tale may be of interest to punters who believe that in any global showdown, whatever the sport, home nations always have a massive advantage and should invariably be backed.

Graham Sharpe in his book *Sporting Skulduggery* wrote: "An incredible row broke out after South Africa defeated New Zealand in extra-time of the final of the 1995 Rugby Union World Cup. The All Blacks coach made an amazing statement to reporters. Laurie Mains revealed that two days before the final the New Zealand squad had dined together at the same place: 'Of our 35-man party that ate at that particular lunch venue, about 27 went down in the space of 12 hours. You can read what you like into that, but I don't think it was coincidence. We certainly have our suspicions.' Ten of the All Blacks in the line-up for the final were affected, said Mains, who added: 'I don't have any doubts that it left many of them pretty flat.'

"Mains' sensational comments were made as South African Rugby Union President Dr Louis Luyt caused great offence at the gala dinner marking the end of the tournament with remarks claiming that South Africa would have won the two previous World Cups had they been permitted to take part. The All Blacks immediately walked out.

"England's Damian Hopley later referred to 'the discovery of bugging devices in the New Zealand hotel', and concluded: 'A far darker picture emerges. It seems the South Africans had to win at all costs.'

"And top French referee Patrick Robin said: 'One has the impression that not everything was very clear during this World Cup and that it was very hard to beat South Africa. In the semi-final against France, I noted four doubtful situations. All four decisions were favourable to South Africa. In the final there were ten contested situations and all those went in favour of South Africa as well. I find there were too many discrepancies.'"

While I am surprised that rugby union has not yet been hit by any sinister betting allegations, perhaps it is only a matter of time. Allied Dunbar Premiership clubs have betting facilities at their grounds, and the presence of the perceptive Stuart Barnes as frontman of so many rugby union programmes on Sky Sports ensures that betting will gain a increasingly high profile in the game.

Indeed, in December 1998, we heard the first of what I'm convinced will be many interesting betting yarns following rugby union games. Leicester's Neil Back, for the third time since the start of the season, scored his club's first try in a game, this time in the 31-18 defeat of Newcastle at Welford Road. Back had been heavily backed before the match at 12-1, but insisted afterwards: "I got nothing on. We're not allowed to do that. A lot of fans pat me on the back these days and I've just found out why. I think they've just broken Ladbrokes again."

Two weeks later Back did it again, with his ninth try of the season in Leicester's 26-0 Boxing Day win over Bedford. "We can run but we can't hide," said a Ladbrokes spokesman. "We continue to trim his odds but people still back him. We are not going to go out of business but his scoring exploits have put a dent in the local area manager's profits." By this stage Back was 7-1 to be first try-scorer. "I think the bookmakers need to wise up a little bit," said Leicester scrum-half Austin Healey.

I must confess here that rugby union has never been my favourite sport. An environment in which skill and artistry is sacrificed at the altar of brute strength can never hope to entice me. But what rankles even more is the blind eye consistently turned to acts of thuggery that, if perpetrated in the street, would earn the offender a prison sentence.

Think back to February 1999 and to Healey's stamping horror against London Irish, and to England star Martin Johnson's relatively unpunished stomp on the neck of Scotland's John Leslie in the Five Nations clash at Twickenham. Think back in particular to the late summer of 1997 and the Brive v Pontypridd Heineken Cup showdown that sparked a mini-war between French and Welsh opponents.

Rugby union, I remarked at the time, was once a hooligan's game played by gentleman but had turned into thugs' game populated in part by psychopaths. To many of us this has come as no surprise. For years the media and the sport's authorities have overlooked outbreaks of horrifying violence on the field. Stamping, raking, gouging, punching – all have become legitimate weapons of the modern-day union man. All too often games owe more to a brawl between nightclub boozers and bouncers than a test of sporting prowess. Yet only rarely do we read of punishments for these violent offenders. All too often with violence in rugby there are no fines, no suspensions, not even raps across already blood-spattered knuckles.

It would be hypocritical here to suggest that such brutality offends our sensibilities. There is something shamefully compelling about watching these dinosaur figures slug it out. But even the most blood-crazed among us would admit that we expect the transgressors later to be reprimanded, to be taught that you cannot rake studs across a man's skull and expect to escape scot-free.

Every schoolboy will tell you that among his peers there is always a handful to whom violence is a way of life. A small proportion may have above-average sporting talent. What an attractive proposition rugby union must seem to such teenagers – top-class sport with a licence to maim. Had rugby union years ago clamped down on acts of thuggery, it would not now be attracting the types whose very presence in the game ensures such thuggery thrives.

The sport's long-time amateur status is no longer a valid excuse. When rugby donned professional clothing it should also have acquired a more responsible attitude. But what made the Pontypridd incident referred to earlier such a watershed is the brawl in a Brive bar-room several hours after the game. This dispelled once and for all the myth that rugby is a physical battle during which bust-ups will inevitably occur but after which rival players carouse long into the night in a spirit of comradeship.

Brive v Pontypridd taught us that rugby players are just as likely as sweaty Sunday League soccer oiks to harbour grudges, to allow grievances to turn septic in what should be the neutral territory of the bar-room. Footballers have only to raise their hands to risk a lengthy ban. But today's rugby union stars by comparison seem to operate under a thugs' charter.

With the betting requirements stacked so high against us, and with the sport apparently happy to accommodate almost weekly bouts of brutality, let's just say you won't catch me a part of the union ...

# chapter 13

## the punters' day of action

Every day, we crouch on all fours, wave our backsides in the air, and let bookmakers roger us senseless. Day after day; week after week; year after painful bloody year.

Every time we place a bet on sport we contribute, whether the bet wins or loses, to the bookmaker 'winter in Barbados' benefit fund.

It's the biggest injustice in the British economy and it's high time it was stopped. The mathematics of it will appal you. If you realised just how much bookies are creaming off sports punters every day of every week, absolutely risk free, you'd never go near a betting shop again. In a way, that's the step I'm asking you to take – but for one day only.

Bookies have so far ignored every call for action, so it's up to punters now to take up arms against them. I call for a betting boycott, a one-day betting strike to ram home to bookmakers that no longer will we tolerate this kind of larceny. In any other business police would be called in, but a blind eye is turned to bookmaker theft.

I've looked through the betting calendar and have earmarked Tuesday 13 July 1999 as the day, finally, that the Punter Strikes Back. I urge you now to boycott betting shops and credit offices for 24 hours that day. It's a crap day anyway – hardly any decent sport to bet on and only two crabby race meetings, at Beverley and Brighton – so even the addicts among us can surely get through it without too much pain.

And if withdrawal symptoms do begin to kick in as the night wears on, then get a card school going in the pub, play penny up the wall, monopoly for real money, Escalado – anything as long as you don't let those bleedin' bookies have a penny of your money.

The action may sound desperate – but then so too is the problem. This boycott WILL work if planned meticulously and with the backing of you punters. I can call on powerful allies, as I'll explain later, but without your support all is lost. The very thought of a punters' strike will have bookmaker chiefs choking on their caviar and toast. They know that, united, we are an unstoppable force. But they know, equally, that it's the nature of punters to look only after number one, which is why well-meaning organisations like NAPP (National Association For The Protection Of Punters) have crumbled. Together we can make this boycott work.

You may ask why we need to take such drastic action. Well, consider this. Every time we place a £10 bet on a football match or a golf tournament, or any sporting contest, bookies automatically pocket anything between 11p and 20p. Pure, risk-free profit. Our selection might win, but that 11p-20p is safe. Nobody can take it away from them. It's an unbelievable scam and here's how it works.

**Bet A** is £10 (plus 90p tax) on Earth Summit to win the Grand National.

**Bet B** is £10 (plus 90p tax) on Liverpool to win the Premiership title.

Consider the 90p tax charged on the Earth Summit bet. In reality only 67.5p is tax raked in by the Government. Slightly more than 10p - let's say 11p to be charitable - goes to the Levy Board, which funds racing, leaving a shortfall of around 11.5p, which bookmakers insist helps offset the cost of 'tax on tax' plus 'non-recoverable VAT'. Not everyone accepts these explanations from bookmakers, but I'll come to that shortly.

Now consider the 90p tax charged on the Liverpool bet. The same 67.5p is deducted by the government in the form of betting tax and, if we are hugely charitable to bookmakers, we'll accept that around 11.5p covers tax on tax and non-recoverable VAT. But on sports bets there is absolutely no levy to pay so the other 11p goes directly into the bookie's pocket, funding those winter holidays in the sun, the wife's new fur coat, and the blonde mistress' boob job. A minimum of 11p for every £10 bet. Some who refuse to accept the bewildering bookmaker figures for VAT and 'tax on tax' argue that it could be anything up to 20p.

If one or two of you are thinking right now that 20p for every £10 sports bet is hardly a hill of beans, let me introduce you to the real world.

Real World: "How do you do. I'm the Real World."

Dickheads: "Nice to meet you. We're the Dickheads."

Introductions over, chew on this: In 1990, sports betting was estimated to have only a five per cent share of the betting market, with racing comfortably leading the way and greyhounds in second. With yearly betting figures of around £6 billion, that meant around £300 million a year, £25 million a month, £6 million a week, or almost £1 million every day was generated by sports betting. And that was before the sports betting explosion of the 1990s.

By early 1999, unofficial sources estimated that sports betting accounted for at least 12 per cent of annual bookmaker turnover (bookmakers like to keep the figures artificially low to disguise the scale of their sports betting scam). If we stick with yearly betting turnover of £6 billion, it means that £720 million is bet, legally, every year on sport. That yields a weekly figure of £14 million, and an incredible £2 million every day.

If bookies are creaming off 20p from every tenner, that's £2 from every £100, £20 from every £1,000, and £20,000 from every £1 million. Just think of it. Every day bookies open their doors safe in the knowledge that before they shut up shop they'll have been given a £40,000 gift from the nation's sports punters.

That's £40,000 seven days a week; £280,000 a week; almost £15 MILLION PER YEAR. Our money. Their risk-free profit.

Some bookies come up with fantastic excuses to justify the existence of this £15 million slush fund. One highly esteemed industry representative in the north of England once told me it was "the price punters must pay for the privilege of having a bet". Oh yes, of course. Imagine a barman charging you £1.90 for a pint (£2.50 in London) and then saying, "By the way, that'll cost you another 5p for the privilege of buying that pint."

Another claimed it was to cover costs like the production of football coupons, ignoring the obvious fact that football coupons would soon be ditched by bookies if they weren't already making obscene profits, as well as bringing new customers into shops.

For a more considered explanation, I approached Ladbrokes' managing director Chris Bell and his William Hill counterpart John Brown, giving them the chance to assuage fears among sports punters that we are being criminally short-changed.

Bell wrote back, saying: "We are delighted to answer queries on the deduction, because as a leading bookmaker on customer information and customer protection we welcome any opportunity to fully explain it. Turning to your specific questions, the deduction on bets is intended to cover all duties and levies for which we are liable.

"Our rules state that: 'A deduction (generally known as TAX) is made to cover the cost of general betting duty and the other statutory taxes and levies.' We pay betting duty at the rate of 6.75 per cent on turnover (not stakes). In other words, if a customer has a bet of £10 plus 'tax', we pay duty on £10.90 rather than £10.00. We also pay a levy on horseracing and greyhound racing bets, which between them account for 91 per cent of our turnover, and once again this is based upon the total stake plus deduction (again, tax on tax). Betting on football (around five per cent of turnover and rising), results in a charge from the football authorities of a fixed amount per shop per year.

"Ladbrokes under-deducts on horse racing bets (71 per cent of turnover) in that we deduct slightly less from customers than we pay in duty and levy, and marginally over-deduct on most sports bets. The principle is that the rate of deduction across all turnover amounts to the total of the various taxes and levies.

"As with most businesses, we pay Value Added Tax on all our costs and Corporation Tax on our profits. We could, according to the letter of our rules, pass these onto our customers, but in practice this does not happen.

"In theory we could charge differential rates of deduction for bets on different sports – on that basis, bets on the Loch Ness Monster would be the cheapest because as far as I know Nessie does not

260 . sports betting and how to make it pay

charge for the use of his/her name! The practicalities of this are that we would end up deducting, say, 9.36 per cent on horseracing bets and various other bizarre fractions on bets on other sports, and the common-sense solution is to charge one rate of deduction for all bets.

"I am sure you appreciate that this is a very complex issue and there is no simple answer. There will be a small number of customers who bet exclusively on sports, and who will remain slightly disgruntled, but our research shows that the majority of customers who bet on sports also bet on horseracing, so they are effectively cross-subsidising themselves."

Before I comment on Bell's refreshingly honest response, here's what Hills MD John Brown had to say.

"Betting Duty and Horserace Levy are a charge on the bookmaker, not the customer, unlike for instance VAT, which is a charge on the customer. Bookmakers, therefore, are free to recover these expenses in any way they choose, save that competition obviously limits their action. For example, instead of betting for 112 per cent on a football match, with a nine per cent deduction, we could bet for, say, 115 per cent and make no charge for betting duty.

"William Hill chooses to standardise its deductions for ease of operation. However, the deduction is no more than a pricing mechanism which, coupled with the in-built percentage on sports betting, gives a competitive operating profit margin."

Now you can see why I prefer to comment on Bell's response!

I think what Brown might be saying, in an extremely round-about way, is that the nine per cent deduction on sports bets, allied to the in-built profit margin in their odds, means that Hills clean up on sport. I apologise, John, if that's not the case!

Bell's comments are much more thought-provoking. He says that Ladbrokes, and by implication all bookmakers, "under-deduct" on horseracing bets and therefore, to make up the shortfall, "marginally over-deduct on most sports bets."

Pull the other one, Chris.

To swallow that Ladbrokes make a loss, however minuscule, on every bet placed on horseracing is like accepting, given that horseracing is their core product accounting for 71 per cent of turnover, that pubs make a loss on every pint of lager and try to make up that loss by charging slightly extra on pints of bitter, even though lager outsells bitter by 6:1. If bookies discovered seven out of every ten bets were costing them money, irrespective of whether the bets win or lose, do you honestly believe their reaction would be "Oh, never mind, we make a slight profit on the other three out of ten bets we take, and with a bit of luck that might even things out"?

Even if what Bells says is correct - and it is not - why should we sports punters swallow it? I am no longer remotely interested in horseracing. It bores me, and it's impossible to make it pay. Too many non-triers, too much market manipulation; skulduggery at every turn. Why then should I pay over the odds for my bet on Pat Rafter to win the US Open merely to subsidise some halfwit who's placed a four-timer on horses beginning with the letter 'T' (for Tithead) on the All-weather at Wolverhampton?

Bell's comments about the Loch Ness Monster imply that bookmakers are forced to cough up to various governing bodies for the privilege on betting on different sports. Bollocks. Football charges a fee - £225 per betting shop per year - but no other sport does. It costs bookies the same to bet on golf's US Masters as on the chances of life on Mars – i.e. sod all.

I should, in the interests of fair play, at least pay lip service to the bookmakers' VAT argument, even though it's incredibly boring to write, and I suspect even more boring to read. This is how Tom Kelly, director general of BOLA (Betting Office Licensees' Association) and fluent in gobbledygook, explained it to a Home Affairs Committee in 1991, before deductions on bets were reduced from ten per cent to nine per cent following a government cut in betting duty.

"People say that other businesses pay the VAT out of their profits. That's simply not true. They build it into their costs to the customer. If I go into a shop to buy a suit priced at £100, it costs me £115 because of the VAT. The retailer puts VAT on to his price.

But in off-course bookmaking the man providing the product for his customer does not control the price. VAT has to go into the deduction after duty and levy because it can't go anywhere else, and the total sum of duty, levy and VAT comes out roughly at ten per cent. There are other businesses like betting which cannot recover their VAT, such as banks and building societies, but they make charges for their services. If you go into a bank for foreign currency, they charge you a fee. The betting shop business is no different."

In a curiously inelegant way Kelly possibly has a point. But because he blusters so much (the example above is the most concise he's ever been); because he talks in a language designed to confuse, he consistently gives the impression that he has something to hide. Surely if the bookmakers' case was so just, we say to ourselves, they'd explain it more clearly. Kelly to my knowledge has never yet uttered or written a sentence that made a morsel of sense to any other human being – I suspect many of the mathematical formulae he uses to get his point across have detonated nuclear devices in some far-off Pacific atoll – and while he is chief defender of the bookmakers' tax-on-tax and VAT arguments, we will always believe that figures are being massaged.

What is not in dispute is that we sports punters are being ripped off something rotten. So what are we going to do about it? Those bookies have our money – a cool £15 million every year – and we want it back.

The only solution, dear readers, is to down our punting tools. Make 13 July 1999 our day of action. Let's show these bastards we mean business.

SIS and the Racing Channel will beam pictures from the racetracks that day, no matter how many requests we make of them to pull the plug, because they are there to serve bookmakers. The *Racing Post* will publish racecards, too, because otherwise circulation would plummet. But there's nothing to stop racing editors of national and provincial newspapers lending their considerable weight to our campaign. All we want is for them not to publish racecards on July 13 (July 12 for evening newspapers which print the following day's cards). It's not too much to ask, is it?

I'm sure their sports editors, many frustrated daily by the amount of valuable editorial space gobbled up by lists of runners and riders at tuppence-ha'penny race meetings, would be ecstatic at being granted such freedom. Remember that one or two of the broadsheets already drop minor racecards on particularly busy days, so it's hardly a giant step to do away with them all for just one day. And if all national newspapers agreed to a blanket racecard ban, there'd be no question of losing readers to rival rags.

I have spoken to racing editors on three mass-selling British daily tabloids (I kept the list select because I did not want news of the campaign to leak out before publication of this book) and all three have given the betting boycott their tacit support. They say it's hard to imagine every daily newspaper agreeing to drop racing – and greyhound - coverage on the big day, but have promised to publicise the campaign once given the green light. And once the ball's rolling, who knows where and when it will stop?

Some may scoff at the idea of horseracing diehards sacrificing their day in a betting shop merely to help out their sports betting brethren but ultimately this day of action is in their interests too. If bookies see that punters nationwide can indeed be roused, can indeed be persuaded to join this most worthy crusade, they will no longer be so quick to treat their clients with contempt, to shave odds continually, to knock back bets. All of us will benefit.

Make no mistake, the threat of this campaign will send shivers down the spines of bookmakers. Initially they will laugh it off, but then their accountants will number-crunch and discover that if yearly turnover is £6 billion, daily turnover averages out at something like £16 million. Tuesdays aren't great betting days, especially one with two trappy race meetings and no other sport, so we can guess that somewhere between £10-£12m of bookmaker turnover will be lost on our day of action.

As well as the support of some of our best-selling daily newspapers, we also have the backing of top names in the worlds of sport and entertainment.

West Ham manager Harry Redknapp, a regular punter who

writes a weekly football tipping column in the *Racing Post*, has pledged his support.

"I bet on several sports," said Redknapp, "and while I knew that I was paying over the odds with nine per cent deductions, I never realised bookies were profiting by such vast amounts. It's time they played fair with the punter, and if they consistently refuse to, then what alternative does the punter have other than to withdraw his custom? I won't be betting on July 13. I hope I can persuade others to follow suit."

TV heartthrob Nat Parker, who played Rawdon Crawley in the hit BBC drama series of late 1998, *Vanity Fair*, and replaced John Hannah in the popular ITV series *McCallum*, also believes a one-day strike is merited.

Parker, a subscriber to The Winning Line tipping service and a regular punter, said: "It is an absolute scandal that the bookmakers take so much money from us and the government turns a blind eye. I've asked bookies several times how they can justify it and each time they mumble something about administrative costs. That's bollocks. I'm glad that at last punters seem ready to do something about it. Tuesday 13 July 1999 seems the perfect day for a strike. I'm just glad England aren't playing cricket that day because there's always money to be made by opposing them."

TV screenwriter Jimmy McGovern, creator of Fitz, the gambling-mad psychologist crime-buster in hit TV series *Cracker*, said: "At last the punter strikes back. Bookies have had it all their own way for too long and I sincerely hope this one-day strike is a success."

McGovern (and in case you are wondering, yes, he's my brother) is no stranger to campaigning for the underdog. He championed the cause of the relatives of the football fans who died at Hillsborough and his docu-drama of that name, screened on TV in 1996, revealed startling new evidence about what really happened on that tragic Saturday afternoon in April 1989.

More recently he has backed the Liverpool dockers in their long-running dispute with bosses and his film about that bitter feud, written with the help of the dockers themselves and *Trainspotting* writer Irvine Welsh, is scheduled to be broadcast on Channel 4 on

18 July 1999, five days after our punters' day of action.

Mark Coton, former chairman of the National Association For The Protection Of Punters, is also anxious for the strike to succeed. "The betting audience is traditionally a passive one and notoriously difficult to rouse," he said. "But by the sound of things this campaign really could work. Certainly it's about time the scandal of the unacceptable deductions on sports bets was brought into the public domain."

Of course there will be scabs, as there are in every strike. Bookies will get around any newspaper racecard ban by printing their own lists of runners and riders, and scabs will pop in the betting shop for their scabby bets. But we can swallow that. No strike can ever be 100 per cent successful; all we want is to hurt the bookies enough to force them into reconsidering their deductions on sports bets. And who knows, if the campaign is successful, there may not even be enough racegoers at Beverley and Brighton to form an on-course market. It would be impossible therefore to return any SPs and all stakes would have to be refunded. Oh, what joy!

On 23 September 1993, *The Sun* refused to publish selections from their tipsters for the day's three meetings at Nottingham, Pontefract and Folkestone in a bid to put pressure on BOLA, the Betting Office Licensees' Association, to change their stance on the famous 'Jo N Jack' affair.

Two punters, Peter Haran and Chris Wellham, won £40,000 on the 33-1 Lingfield winner but BOLA, citing their familiar "irregular betting patterns" excuse, advised bookmakers to withhold payment. Ben Newton, at the time *The Sun*'s racing editor and now features editor at the *Racing Post*, said: "This is part of a national day of protest against BOLA. *The Sun* recommends betting shop punters stay away to force BOLA to withdraw its instruction to withhold payments on Jo N Jack." But Newton, or at least his bosses at Wapping, did not have the bottle to go the whole hog and withhold racecards in a tit-for-tat measure.

"We are printing them for information purposes," he said.

If *The Sun* felt strongly enough to get behind Jo N Jack punters, it should surely recognise the injustices meted out to sports punters every day.

In a bid to gauge the chances of the betting boycott capturing the imagination of punters, I canvassed opinion in betting shops in Liverpool and London.

Paul Dwyer, a 42-year-old Liverpool taxi driver, said: "It's a fantastic idea and I'm all for it. I knew I was paying over the odds with a nine per cent deduction on my weekend football bet but I had no idea bookies were making so much money out of it. Anything that improves the lot of the punter has to be a good thing. And I think I can stomach a day without betting. In fact I wish I could stomach a year without it."

Stephen Myrie, an unemployed 28-year-old of Tooting, South West London, said: "I know that every time I place a football bet, a small portion of it is going directly into the bookmakers' pockets. Every time I think about it, it annoys me, but I've never been able to do anything about it before. I'm all for this one-day strike. It'll cost the bookies plenty of money – and it'll probably save me money, too."

Just think about that £15 million a year for a moment. Think of what could be done with it. The obvious call would be for a cut in sports betting deductions from nine per cent to eight per cent, but I believe there are other options that sports punters might deem more desirable.

Calls during the 1990s for the appointment of a betting ombudsman have fallen on deaf ears, even though there is a crying need for a truly independent arbitration service. The Tattersalls Committee deals only with horseracing disputes; and the Independent Betting Arbitration Service (IBAS), set up on 2 November 1998 as a successor to the Green Seal Service, will always be treated with suspicion by punters who never took to Green Seal, and who will not easily trust an organisation backed by MGN, the publishers of the *Racing Post,* which derives a large part of its income from bookmaker advertising.

Surely part of this risk-free £15 million could finance an ombudsman's office. Is that too much to ask?

Alternatively, with a £15 million per annum slush fund, bookies could nominate one day a year as the sports punters' benefit day. For every sports bet placed on that day, bookies will add £1 to the stake. So a £10 bet becomes an £11 one, and so on.

More imaginatively, each-way terms could be made much more punter-friendly on the BIG sports events of the year. So for outright championship bets on Wimbledon, punters could be offered each-way terms of one-third the odds down to fourth place, in other words a pay-out on the two losing semi-finalists. And for golf's Open Championship, bookies could advertise each-way terms of one-quarter the odds right down to sixth spot. After all, there are almost 150 runners in the field, so selecting one of the first six is no mean feat.

These are not pie-in-the-sky ideas. After years of paying through the nose for our sports bets, they should not be looked upon as bookmaker hand-outs. They are our bloody right.

So mark that date in your diary. Tuesday 13 July 1999. The day the punter strikes back. It's a battle that will take some winning. But we have strong allies on our side. We have desire on our side. Above all we have right on our side.

Power to the punter ...

# chapter 14

## the trouble with Ladbrokes

For punters still worried about the ethics of trying to hoodwink bookies, either by after-timing or by the more legitimate methods outlined elsewhere in this book, let me give you the name of Philip Tilson.

Tilson was the poor guy who in 1993 thought he'd won more than £100,000 from Ladbrokes but ended up with precisely nothing after Ladbrokes, following a long-running and highly acrimonious dispute, were tipped off that Tilson was only 17 years old and therefore not able legally to place a bet.

Though Ladbrokes, in paying Tilson a big fat zilch, were adhering to the strict letter of the law, their attitude stank to high heaven. A company of their size surely should have been prepared to offer the teenager an ex-gratia payment as a consolation for his rank bad luck. Instead, in what many saw as a show of stomach-churning vindictiveness, they rubbed his young nose in the dirt as punishment for having the nerve to take his case to arbitration.

The background to the dispute I'll come to shortly. Of more pressing concern here is how Ladbrokes were allowed to get away with playing the under-age card to trump Tilson's otherwise powerful hand. Their strategy should have opened up an enormous can of worms in the betting industry but the trade press, with fat advertising revenue from Ladbrokes to consider, turned a blind eye.

Ladbrokes, in arguing that as Tilson was under 18 (the minimum legal age to bet) they were within their rights to pay him nothing, begged one obvious question: if under-18s are not allowed to win money from gambling, is it right that they are allowed to lose? I guess that more than 80 per cent of us were under 18 when we placed our first bet. In that case, let's go to Ladbrokes and demand a refund on all our losing bets placed before our 18th birthday. Clearly, in the light of the Tilson judgement, we could not possibly have won.

On 6 February 1999 David Parkinson, a baby-faced 17-year-old, walked into a Ladbrokes shop near the centre of Liverpool and placed a £10 win bet on Scotmail Boy, a 50-1 no-hoper, in the 2.00 race at Catterick. David is frequently asked for proof of age in pubs and clubs in Liverpool when on nights out with mates and looks no more old enough to bet legally than Bart Simpson. But although the shop was relatively quiet and the staff far from under pressure, he was able to place his bet with not a single question asked.

Predictably, Scotmail Boy finished unplaced. Now the drama began. The 17-year-old returned to the Ladbrokes shop 20 minutes later with his passport in his pocket. A budding actor who dreams of TV stardom, he played his next role to perfection. This is an edited (for brevity) recording of the conversation that took place.

**Parkinson:** "Excuse me, mate. I was in here 20 minutes ago and I had a £10 bet that lost. The only thing is, it was my mam's money for the shopping and she's gonna kill me. Can I have it back, please?"

**Male cashier:** "What?"

**Parkinson:** "Well, I'm only 17 and I'm not allowed to bet, so can I have my money back please?"

**Cashier:** "Sorry, we can't do that."

**Parkinson:** "But it was my mam's money for the shopping. She's gonna kill me."

At this, the shop manageress lifted herself out of her seat towards the rear of the shop and approached the counter.

"What's the problem?" she asked, and Parkinson repeated what he had told the cashier.

**Manageress:** "No, you're not on. If your horse had won, there's no way you'd have come back here and said you were only 17. You'd have wanted paying out."

As Parkinson's bottom lip theatrically began to tremble, an interested bystander interjected. "Excuse me, but the lad's got a case. I remember a few years ago when a young guy won a small fortune from Ladbrokes but they wouldn't pay him because someone tipped them off that he was only 17."

**Manageress:** "I don't care. I have to abide by company policy and that policy says that if someone under-age has a bet, he loses his money."

**Bystander:** "What? Even if the bet wins?

**Manageress:** "Yes."

**Bystander:** "So you're saying that if someone has a bet and it wins, but you subsequently find that he is only 17, not only will you not pay him his winnings, but you will also keep his stake money?"

**Manageress:** "That's right. Look, there's a poster on the wall. No-one under 18 is allowed to bet."

**Bystander:** "But how can that be fair? Who gave Ladbrokes the right to confiscate a teenager's money? How can it be fair that you can lose when you can't win?

**Manageress:** "That's our policy."

**Cashier** (looking faintly sympathetic): "If we gave him his money back we'd have dozens of people coming in every day trying the same trick."

**Bystander:** "Surely it's up to you to find out his age before he places the bet if you're going to keep his cash?"

**Manageress** (in a heartwarming show of solidarity with her staff): "Well that's up to the person who took the bet. I didn't take the bet."

**Bystander:** "This can't be fair. How can he lose if he was never able to win? I'd be interested to know what your head office has to say."

The manageress at first ignored this request, but agreed to contact head office when the bystander continued to argue on the 17-year-old's behalf. At no stage did either the manageress or cashier ask Parkinson for proof of his age. The telephone conversation with head office (the shop's area head office in St Helens, Merseyside, rather than company HQ in London) was inaudible, but the manageress returned to the counter moments later to tell Parkinson that head office had backed up what she said and had instructed her to tell him that unless he left the shop, she would call the police.

Parkinson perhaps should have stood his ground. It would have been interesting to witness how the police treated Ladbrokes' heavy-handed approach. A Merseyside police spokesman later told me that they would not have got involved since a bet is not a legally enforceable debt, and added that Ladbrokes would have been stepping into dangerous territory had they tried to withhold stake money if Parkinson's horse had won.

Certain that the shop manageress, and her immediate superiors, were in the wrong, I contacted the Ladbrokes HQ in London. Their response makes interesting reading, but before I document it, I should first recount the sad and sorry tale of young punter Tilson, another 17-year-old who felt the full force of the heavyweight Ladbrokes' muscle.

Tilson, who worked at his parents' pub in Mansfield, placed a £1 Tricast with Ladbrokes on the day of the 1993 Derby at Epsom. He also had a 50p Tricast combination bet on the same horses, taking his stake to £4. The Tricast, naming the first three horses in the correct order, is normally available only for handicaps, but had been in operation for the previous three runnings of the Derby. There was no reason for punters to think it would not be available for a fourth.

Clearly not fancying the odds-on favourite Tenby, Tilson's selections for the Derby 1-2-3 were Commander In Chief (SP 15-2) to win from Blue Judge (150-1) and Blues Traveller (also 150-1). That was exactly how the race finished and Tilson, jumping for joy, returned to Ladbrokes expecting to be paid £116,400, the Tricast dividend declared by William Hill, the only firm, it later emerged, to offer such a bet on the Derby.

"I had planned to pay off my mum's mortgage and overdraft, then buy myself a second-hand BMW," he said.

Ladbrokes had bad news for him. They did not operate a Tricast on the Derby and said that his bet had been accepted in error. Instead they offered him £728, the amount he would have received from a bet on the straight forecast (the first two home in the correct order).

Ladbrokes' derisory offer completely ignored the existence of their own highly-publicised SP Trio bet, which asked punters to select the 1-2-3 in any order, and which would have paid Tilson almost £68,000.

I should draw a distinction here between a 50p combination Tricast, like the one Tilson staked, and a Ladbrokes Trio.

A 50p Tricast combination is a bet costing £3, where a punter tries to forecast the first, second and third in any order.

A 50p Ladbrokes Trio is a bet costing £3, where a punter tries to forecast the first, second and third in any order.

Got that? Absolutely no difference between the two, and yet Ladbrokes initially offered to pay £728, pointing as justification to antiquated rules that had not been updated to take into account the existence of the newly-formed SP Trio. As one betting expert said at the time. "Surely it is reasonable to assume that a customer who asks for a non-existent Tricast would prefer an SP Trio rather than a forecast."

Their offer sparked public outrage, with even top-selling tabloid newspaper *The Sun* leaping to Tilson's defence. In a strongly-worded editorial, *The Sun* urged punters to boycott Ladbrokes shops and instead bet with Hills - a PR disaster for Ladbrokes.

An industry-wide Tricast was not available on the 1993 Derby because of the presence of an odds-on favourite (Tenby) and the potential liabilities if that favourite finished out of the frame. Frank Dixon of the Betting Office Licensees Association (BOLA) said at the time: "The Derby is not a standard Tricast race, which is normally confined to handicaps. We took a look at the race this year and because the favourite was odds-on decided not to offer the bet. We have to think of the effect it would have on both large and small bookmakers if the favourite finished out of the frame."

Tilson took his case to the now-defunct Green Seal arbitration service, attached to the also-now-defunct *Sporting Life*, and widely regarded with suspicion by punters baffled by what they perceived as a string of bookmaker-friendly verdicts. Green Seal found that Ladbrokes had acted properly but questioned why their rules had not been updated to take into account the recent introduction of the SP Trios, and privately suggested that they might consider a higher payment.

The public outcry, greatly embarrassing to Ladbrokes, forced the company to back down. But instead of offering Tilson the £116,400 he claimed he was due, or even the near £68,000 the Trio would have netted him, they dangled a cheque for £33,870, a figure which on the face of it appears to have been plucked out of thin air but which had a certain grotesque logic.

Ladbrokes argued that if the third horse, Blues Traveller, had finished unplaced, under their rules Tilson would have been paid out on a forecast of first and second. In effect, they said, he was getting two bets for the price of one. So they split the bet between the forecast and the trio, arriving at a pay-out of almost £34,000.

Berjis Daver, at the time the Ladbrokes MD, said rather pompously: "I do wish punters would come to us first with any complaints." This ignored the fact that Tilson had indeed gone to Ladbrokes, only to be met by hostility.

Tilson, disturbed that he was to be paid less than £34,000 when he expected more than £100,000, rejected Ladbrokes' offer and opted to take the case to Tattersalls' Committee, the ultimate arbiter in horserace betting disputes.

At the time, Ladbrokes said they would keep their £33,870 offer open whatever the outcome at Tattersalls. A spokesman said: "The settlement stands. It is an *ex gratia* payment arrived at when independent arbitration found we had applied our rules correctly."

At this point Tilson still had a powerful hand. A guaranteed £33,870, with the chance of Tattersalls increasing it to £116,400. But then it all went horrifically wrong. The day before the Tattersalls hearing, Ladbrokes were tipped off that Tilson was only 17. It is not known for certain who grassed on him, but Tilson suspected at the time that it was a 16-year-old to whom he had refused to serve beer in his family's pub.

The irony here is that Tilson says he did not even place the bet himself. A semi-regular in his pub, an 18-year-old fairground worker, placed the bet on his behalf, Tilson maintains, although the fairground worker has since been impossible to trace. Ladbrokes, at the Tattersalls hearing, said they had a CCTV recording of Tilson actually placing the bet in question, but this tape was never produced.

On discovering Tilson's age, Ladbrokes immediately asked Tattersalls to rule that there was no case to answer, a move that was confidently expected to succeed. But Tatts rejected the application, with secretary Peter Guard saying: "Historically, Tattersalls rule on the specific issue of a bet, not the legality or otherwise of it, which is a matter for the courts." That was the last bit of good news Tilson received. He had already learned that Ladbrokes had gone back on their word to keep open their offer of an *ex gratia* £33,870 payment. And to complete a double whammy Tattersalls then ruled that Ladbrokes were within their rights to make an initial offer of just £728.

Mark Coton, chairman of the now-defunct National Association For The Protection Of Punters, which had advised Tilson not to go to Tattersalls, reacted angrily. He said he was "deeply shocked" that they decided to stand by the letter of the law "when Ladbrokes had admitted partial liability in offering over £33,000". He criticised the lack of consumer protection for punters and described Tattersalls as a "star chamber, a kangaroo court, and a disgrace to the British tradition of justice".

A distraught Tilson argued after the Tatts verdict that it was up to Ladbrokes to have told him whether a Derby Tricast was available or not, given that one had been in operation in each of the previous three years. "Tattersalls are saying that it was down to me. But the cashier even wrote the prices I asked for on the slip; they knew it was for the Derby. Tattersalls threw out Ladbrokes' request to make the bet void on the grounds of my age but I feel it may still have weighed on their minds."

But if Tilson thought things couldn't get much worse, he was wrong. Ladbrokes, after taking legal advice, refused to abide by the

Tattersalls ruling and paid him just his £4 stake. A company statement claimed Tilson's bet was, because he was only 17, in contravention of the Betting And Gaming Act and that, in returning his stake money, they now considered the matter closed. Significantly, they said that Tilson, a regular in his local Ladbrokes shop, was entitled to a refund of any losing bets that could be identified as his.

*The Sun*, which had agreed to foot Tilson's Tattersalls bill (£400, not counting expenses) in return for an exclusive story, foolishly lost interest the moment his age was confirmed when a far better story - the dangerous precedent Ladbrokes had set - was staring them in the face.

It did not take long for clear-thinking punters to identify the huge can of worms Ladbrokes had opened. In a letter to the *Racing Post*, North London punter Dave McLean wrote: "I note that (Philip) Tilson, a regular in his Ladbrokes shop, is entitled to a refund of any losing bets that can be identified as his. Let's be quite clear on this issue. Ladbrokes have set a precedent and anybody under the age of 18 who can identify losing bets of theirs that were placed with Ladbrokes are entitled to a full refund of those losing stakes. They cannot apply one rule for Tilson and one rule for everybody else."

And another London punter, Paul Dawson, wrote: "I must confess to Ladbrokes that I lost approximately £1,000 in their branches during the period of 1987 to 1989 when I was aged between 15 and 17. Surely Ladbrokes' rules apply equally to winners and losers, so I will be happy to accept their offer of voiding all the bets that I placed while under age and I look forward to receiving the refund of my stakes."

When the Parkinson incident, and the behaviour of their betting-shop manageress, was recounted to Ladbrokes' chiefs, there was an almost audible wince on the other end of the line. It was as though sooner or alter they knew they would have to tackle this thorniest of subjects.

A spokesman told me that Ladbrokes pay serious attention to under-age gambling, with detailed staff briefings and mystery shoppers (whose aim it is to test the vigilance of shop staff) part of their defensive measures. They also pin posters on the walls of every shop warning punters that they must be 18 or over to place a bet. And shop managers must fill in an under-age incident log even if they merely ask a punter his age.

"It's very disappointing when an under-age punter slips through the net because staff are briefed in detail over this," the spokesman said.

But now to the nitty-gritty. What is the Ladbrokes official policy over an incident like Parkinson's

Was the manageress correct to bully him out of the shop?

"We don't want to make a big deal of this problem because once you do you get under-age punters thinking it's a great scam," the spokesman said, probably through gritted teeth.

"The manageress in this instance was wrong, although maybe she had reason to think the punter was trying it on and that it served him right if he lost his money."

"If someone under 18 places a bet he will get his money back, providing that he can prove he's under 18, but a responsible manager will tell him not to return to the shop and that he's informing the police. He is after all seeking to gain a pecuniary advantage dishonestly and is therefore breaking the law."

Read those words again and, after ignoring the irony that a punter must produce a birth certificate to prove he's *under* 18 rather than over it, consider the implications. They give young teenagers, at least those who can reasonably pass as adults, *carte blanche* to place all manner of bets safe in the knowledge that if they lose, they can produce a passport and demand a refund of stakes. Why should any of us, no matter what age, strike a bet in a betting shop when we can get a 17-year-old relative to do it for us, with a very strong chance of reclaiming our cash if the bet goes down?

Bookmakers have for years agonised over ways of attracting younger punters into their shops, fearful that the old horseracing diehards are dying off. Ladbrokes, and by implication every other bookmaker, have unwittingly outlined the perfect strategy, one that is unlikely to please shareholders.

Just to make sure I hadn't misunderstood his words, I asked the Ladbrokes spokesman if Parkinson, given what he (the spokesman) had said, was entitled to a refund of his wasted £10 on Scotmail Boy.

"Yes," he said, "Tell him to contact our customer relations department."

When I caught up with the unfortunate Tilson in February 1999 his bitterness had eased, but he has never since bet with Ladbrokes – "never will" – and said he returned their cheque for his £4 stake money the same day he received it.

"I wanted nothing from them," he said. "It was an insult."

Tilson, a 23-year-old part-time DJ, did not take up Ladbrokes' offer of trying to identify previous losing bets. "It wasn't physically possible," he said. "When you back a loser you throw away the slip immediately, and there's no way I could have gone through thousands and thousands of slips in the Ladbrokes archive to find a few of mine."

When I told him of Liverpool teenager David Parkinson's experience, he said: "That does not surprise me in the slightest. Ladbrokes want it both ways – it's what bookies are all about."

For a young man who could have pocketed a no-questions-asked £33,870 pay-out, Tilson is remarkably blasé about a decision which saw him finish empty-handed.

"You never miss what you've never had," he said. "Yeah, looking back I should have accepted the 33 grand. It certainly would have made my life easier. But I was 17 years old. Imagine what I'd have done with that kind of cash in my pocket. I'd have partied every night and probably ended up killing myself. Many people can't understand why I went to Tattersalls even though I was only 17. But I thought Ladbrokes were being brutally unfair and Tattersalls was the only recourse I had. The £33,870 figure had been reached after negotiations between Ladbrokes and the Green Seal service. It was never imposed on them, and that's why I wanted to take it further."

Although at the time he thought he'd been grassed up by a 16-year-old with an axe to grind, Tilson is now cynical enough to believe that Ladbrokes employed outside help – police contacts – to uncover information about him, hitting the jackpot when his true age was revealed. And his memories of Tattersalls are far from fond. "I was a 17-year-old kid, but I was allowed no legal representation," he said. "What chance did I have?"

It's worth noting here that the Tattersalls Committee in the early 1990s generally comprised 14 members, none of whom was likely to side naturally with an ordinary punter. For instance, in 1994 the Tatts Committee featured two Jockey Club-nominated figures, an Ascot steward, four racehorse owners, and seven bookmakers.

Think of a black man facing a jury of Klu Klux Klan members, or a low-down cattle rustler pleading for mercy with a small-town sheriff and a lynch-crazed posse, and you'll have some idea how Tilson felt.

Tilson bets seldom now, his interest in gambling crushed by what he calls "the disgusting behaviour" of Ladbrokes.

In the aftermath of the case, an article in the *Racing Post* stated: "Philip Tilson was on a loser the day he walked into a betting shop. Just 17, he is under age. No matter the 'justice' of his case. Ladbrokes, as a public company, could not be seen to condone illegal gambling. Their licence would be at risk – their 1970s casino 'disaster' had taught them the consequences. No matter what Tattersalls Committee awarded, Tilson would not have been paid."

It was the first time I'd heard of any such casino 'disaster' and got me wondering just what happened. With Ladbrokes having forked out, in February 1999, £1.2bn for Scottish Hotels group Stakis, adding 22 casinos to their portfolio, it's perhaps an ideal time to recount Ladbrokes' role in the incredible 'car numbers' scheme that cost the company its West End casino licence in 1979-80.

At the time, the British casino industry operated under strict controls imposed by the Gaming Board under the 1968 Gaming Act. This prohibited any form of casino advertising, a marketing strait-jacket that, in the late 1990s, was to be considerably loosened.

Despite these restrictions it was estimated that Ladbrokes, towards the end of the 1970s, took more than 50 per cent of their annual profits – approximately £23 million out of £41.5 million – from casino gambling. Ladbrokes, at this time, were the largest West End casino operators, running the Park Lane Casino, the Ladbroke Club, the Park Tower Club and the Hertford Club, as well as six provincial casinos. These were money machines, with reports that in one six-week period tycoon Adnan Khashoggi lost £7 million at the Ladbroke Club.

Yet despite these massive profits, Ladbrokes wanted an ever bigger slice of the hugely lucrative casino cake. According to evidence given at court hearings into Ladbrokes' fitness to hold a gaming licence, company bosses wanted to set up a marketing department for the casino division, even though marketing was pretty much banned by the Gaming Board.

A Danish-born marketing brain called Andreas Christensen hired a private detective to "isolate and identify" high-rolling gamblers at rival clubs. This detective logged the registration numbers of luxury cars as they dropped off wealthy gamblers outside non-Ladbrokes casinos. The numbers were then passed to a former police inspector who was able to obtain the names and address of registered owners. That was part one of the operation.

Part two depended upon the involvement of seductive women since a high-roller's not a high-roller without a fox on his arm. Approaches were made by attractive Ladbrokes public relations girls to some of these luxury-car owners. Punters honoured in this way were offered free dinner at their choice of Ladbrokes casino restaurants, plus complimentary membership of the casino.

As Martin Tomkinson wrote in his examination of the affair in 1993: "The whole scheme was known as Operation Unit Six and was fraught with elements of both danger and farce.

"People who owned impressive-looking cars but had never been inside a casino in their lives were mysteriously approached by attractive women. Inevitably, it ended in tears. But the consequences for Ladbrokes were out of all proportion to any possible gain that might have accrued to the company."

The existence of Unit Six was revealed in satirical magazine *Private Eye* in 1978, and although Ladbrokes chief Cyril Stein denied all knowledge, company shares dipped alarmingly, and both the police and Gaming Board announced they were to launch inquiries.

An objection to the renewal of Ladbrokes' casino licence was upheld by Westminster magistrates, but Ladbrokes casinos remained open while an appeal was heard at Knightsbridge Crown Court. This lasted four weeks in December 1979, with magistrates hearing from Stein's personal secretary Janet Ballard that she had seen several documents relating to the marketing department scheme.

Ballard said that in a telephone call one afternoon she was told by a man called John Morris, director of Ladup Ltd, a wholly-owned subsidiary company that ran the Ladbrokes' casino division, that police had just been to his office and were planning a return visit. First thing next morning she told her boss, Stein: "He was very abrupt, and said 'I don't care – I've got nothing to hide'." He then came into her office and asked: "Where are the casino files? Let's go through the lot," chucking virtually the whole lot on the floor before instructing Ballard to shred the files.

Magistrates took less than ten minutes to decide that Ladbrokes were not fit to run a casino and all of their West End casinos were shut down that day. Chief magistrate Judge Friend said: "The company's behaviour was absolutely disgraceful."

Marketing has perhaps not been Ladbrokes' strong suit over the years. In 1991 the newly-appointed marketing director Chris Bell, who by the start of 1999 had risen to the lofty heights of managing director, finished a letter to Bill Warren, advertising director of the *Racing Post*, with these words: "As discussed this morning, I expect this situation to be resolved and I would like the name of the person you are firing confirmed by close of business on Friday 4th October 1991 in order that we may be assured that somebody has been dismissed for such outrageous sloppiness. Until an apology has been printed in the paper, which I expect to be on Friday 4th October 1991, and the appropriate person is fired from the *Racing Post*, Ladbrokes will no longer advertise in any way sort or form within the publication."

The arrogance was - still is - breathtaking. The person responsible for such "outrageous sloppiness" could, for all Bell knew, have been married with six kids and struggling to pay the mortgage. That didn't matter. Bell, previously a marketing big wheel at Victoria Wine and with such a deeply impressive track record clearly a budding captain of industry, had new-found muscle and couldn't wait to flex it.

Earlier in the letter, dated 3 October 1991, Bell listed the heinous crimes perpetrated in the *Racing Post* against Ladbrokes. Goodness, no wonder someone's head had to roll. This is how it began: "Following our telephone conversation this morning, I confirm my total dissatisfaction with the way Ladbrokes have been portrayed, both in image and fact by the *Racing Post* over the past few days. Of course this is not the first time that has happened and creates a very difficult situation for the company and myself. To confirm the points we discussed this morning:

"Friday 27th September 1991, p19, under the Betting on Football section – it stated that Ladbrokes pay a ten per cent bonus on weekend football bets. This only applies to credit customers.

"Front page of today's edition – the reference to Marling being 25-1 for the fillies Classic next May, when we all fully understood it was 16-1 by 4.00pm on 2nd October.

"The first try scorer at Twickenham on p13 – the odds attributable to Ladbrokes in this table were not our odds and are therefore terribly misleading.

"Mr Tozer's letter on p13 refers to the ten per cent football bonus mentioned in point (1). If the correct facts had been featured and indeed we had been contacted, this situation would have been avoidable.

"Again on p13, it must be unlucky for some, again in the letters section – the reference to our odds on Chelsea in the Rumbelows Cup is definitely aggressive, and I believe malicious and is totally and utterly unacceptable."

Most readers of the *Racing Post* at this time could have told Bell that whoever was responsible for the 'mistake' about Marling was highly unlikely to have had anything to do with the football information, since the horseracing and sports betting sections at the *Post* were quite clearly separate. And two of his five "unacceptable" errors referred to the same point about the ten per cent bonus on football bets.

What really appears to have got up Bell's bugle that day was the response in the *Racing Post* to a letter from a reader named Colin Butler of Aylesbury, Buckinghamshire, who had written: "I would be grateful if you can find out from Ladbrokes why, just after 9.30 this morning, they would lay Chelsea to win the Rumbelows Cup only at 20-1 when their price in your paper is clearly shown as 33-1. I was told by the telephonist that the price had changed, and when I asked her when the change had taken place, she left me hanging on for a couple of minutes and then told me that the *Racing Post* 'had got it wrong'.

"I would be grateful if you could take up with Ladbrokes on my behalf the precise sequence of events. I am aware that prices can change quickly but to give the customer absolutely no chance at all of getting on at the published price by changing it before the credit offices open is most unsatisfactory."

Mr Butler's point was reasonable. There is nothing that annoys punters more than finding an advertised price has been shortened even before bookmakers open for business.

This is the *Racing Post* response to his letter, published the same day: "Boy, oh boy, did we have some complaints about that one. Anyone with half a brain could see that, at 33-1, Chelsea were value. Ladbrokes claim they realised it at 5.30 the night before it appeared in Sports Betting and changed it to 20-1. Unfortunately they forgot to tell us. The telephonist's explanation that the *Racing Post* had got it wrong seems to be an increasingly used excuse among bookmakers when they're out of line, although on this occasion it's perhaps forgivable. It's a regrettable trend. Can we appeal to punters to let us know immediately if you're ever fed such a line?"

In the face of such horrendous cock-ups and such blatantly anti-Ladbrokes sentiment, it was no wonder Bell the omnipotent demanded the sacking of this incompetent *Racing Post* oik. After all, he was the marketing director of a massive company whose advertising revenue helped pay this oik's wages. Surely he was entitled to demand such a sacking. Well, dear readers, I was that oik and I'm happy to report that Bell's ludicrous demands drew only sniggers from *Post* chiefs who, happily, lived in the real world. My employment continued, as did Ladbrokes' advertising in the *Racing Post*.

What Bell's threats did bring to light was the unacceptable attitude of certain advertisers to newspapers. If a centimetre of knocking copy is printed their immediate reaction is a threat to withdraw advertising and, more often than not, newspapers kow-tow, not wishing to jeopardise revenue. What many newspapers have still to realise is that companies such as Ladbrokes don't advertise merely as a gesture of goodwill to a newspaper. They advertise because it gets results. If they don't advertise, the danger is that clients will take their business elsewhere. The *Racing Post* would do well to remember that when next rejecting copy for fear of upsetting a valued customer.

After all, is it any coincidence that the stunt carried out by Liverpool teenager David Parkinson outlined at the top of this chapter, the account of Ladbrokes' casino disaster, and the behaviour of that same company's managing director when employed as marketing chief, have not once figured in the pages of the *Racing Post*, even though at several editorial meetings in the 1990s such ideas were earnestly suggested?

The Tilson, casino, and Bell stories are included here to illustrate that the big bookmakers, despite enviable reputations, are quite capable of riding roughshod over the ordinary man in the street – a 1998 survey of employers reported that Ladbrokes were the second poorest payers in the UK, after Rentokil - and that punters for their part should have no qualms about using every weapon available to defend themselves.

Maybe after reading this chapter your reservations about the ethics of after-timing will have disappeared. Mine haven't – but only because I never had any in the first place.

# chapter 15

## motor racing

There are few sports that polarise opinion like motor racing. To some it's the yawn of all time, about as gripping as watching traffic zoom around the M25; to others it's what sport is all about, men risking all in the pursuit of speed and glory.

Although I belong firmly in the first camp I concede there must be something special about Formula One racing, given that it draws vast crowds, attracts top-drawer sponsors, and has TV companies falling over themselves to broadcast it.

Indeed it's one of the mysteries of life that while football, by far the most popular sport in Britain, is traditionally ignored when the end-of-year sports personality awards are voted for, grand prix drivers are almost always among the favourites. Nigel Mansell and Damon Hill have each won the coveted BBC gong twice – and there's not a personality between them.

My views on the sport as a betting medium are pretty much the same. It leaves me cold, but there are thousands of punters who on alternate Sundays between March and October will not leave their TV sets as Schumacher, Villeneuve and co roar noisily around some grand prix circuit.

My big beef is that the best drivers automatically get the best cars and therefore automatically win. Bookies know this and automatically make them red-hot favourites. Automatically, the race dies as a realistic betting contest. Of course there are exceptions to this tiresome rule, but only in one of three circumstances.

If Michael Schumacher, the best driver in Formula One, is also driving the best car, he will win unless:

He spins off the track or smashes into another car.

A pit-stop takes longer than anticipated, allowing the driver in second to nip through.

He is under orders to let a team-mate win.

It all makes motor racing in my eyes something of a farce. I swear I've managed to sit through four grand prix races in their entirety and not once, not bloody once, has one car overtaken another. On the three occasions per year it happens, TV commentator Murray Walker, owner of without doubt the most annoying voice on TV, has kittens.

But motor racing was killed off once and for all as a worthwhile betting medium (betting tedium is perhaps a better description) on Sunday 8 March 1998 at the Australian Grand Prix in Melbourne. David Coulthard, half of the all-powerful McLaren team, had been well backed at 5-1 to pip his team-mate and hot favourite Mika Hakkinen.

The Scot looked home and hosed over the closing laps but inexplicably slowed down to let Hakkinen, the No.1 driver at McLaren, take the chequered flag. He later explained that under the terms of a pre-race agreement, whichever McLaren driver was in front at the first bend (in this case Hakkinen) would be allowed to go on and win the race if both McLaren drivers were fighting it out over the closing laps. Note, by the way, that such an agreement implied that Hakkinen and Coulthard knew that barring accidents they'd have the race to themselves because of the dominance of the McLaren engines, reinforcing all our suspicions about this ludicrous sport.

A similar incident occurred in Jerez at the back end of the 1997 season. Williams driver Jacques Villeneuve, already assured of the world title, acknowledged a debt to McLaren for blocking Ferrari's Scumacher by moving aside in the closing stages to allow Hakkinen and Coulthard to take first and second.

Just what kind of message does this send out to punters? Not only is the game not straight, it's not straight with the blessing of the governing body, which turns a blind eye to such blatant examples of race-rigging. Indeed, the day after the Melbourne scandal, McLaren boss Ron Dennis cheerfully admitted that the pact between his two drivers would be in force in the next grand prix in Brazil.

It's all very well bookmakers saying, as Hills did, that punters should be aware of the possibility of such shenanigans in Formula One racing. It's hard enough making the game pay as it is without having to second-guess the underhand tactics of drivers and their bosses.

Coulthard's actions in Melbourne turned thousands of punters off Formula One, and the Scot himself is all too clearly aware of the impact his pre-race agreement had on the betting fraternity. "People were actually sending me their betting slips afterwards," he said. "A lot of them seemed to understand that it wasn't my fault, which I was grateful for. But a lot of them wanted me to send the slips on to Ron with some quite inventive and colourful instructions as to what he should do with them."

The beauty of sport, and indeed sports betting, is its unpredictability. We may have a good idea of how a match or a race will go, but we can never be sure. That's why Norton's Coin can win a Gold Cup at 100-1, why Buster Douglas can knock out Mike Tyson, and why Premiership sides can go out of the FA Cup to non-League opposition. But in motor racing, at least when underhand strategies are not at large, we can be sure not only that the best car will win if the best driver is in the cockpit, but that the best car will win if even a run-of-the-mill driver is behind the wheel.

At random I studied the results of the 1993 Formula One season. Of 16 races that year no fewer than 13 were won by the first or second favourite. To give the sport a fair crack of the whip, I looked at the results from 1994. Again 13 races went to one of the two market leaders. What's more, every grand prix of 1993 threw up an odds-on favourite. That's like going racing every Saturday to be confronted by a red-hot favourite for all six races on the card, every single week. In 1993 and 1994, the big four drivers – Alain Prost, Ayrton Senna, Damon Hill and Schumacher – won 31 of the 32 races contested.

In 1998, Hakkinen won eight of the 16 grands prix, only engine failure or mid-race accidents stopping him from capturing half a dozen more. The other races were won by Schumacher (six), and Coulthard and Hill with one apiece. You do not get outsiders winning a Formula One race – that is one of the rules of the track. Indeed, even when Schumacher won the 1995 Belgian Grand Prix from 16th spot on the grid, it came as no surprise. The heavens had opened at Spa-Francorchamps that afternoon and Schumacher is a stone better than any other driver in wet conditions.

I asked Neil Randon, former motor racing correspondent at the *Racing Post* and now with *Motoring News*, if Michael Schumacher driving a McLaren during the 1998 season would ever have been beaten.

"No," he said.

To give you an example of how dependent upon the car a Formula One driver is, consider this. Jacques Villeneuve was crowned world champion in late 1997. Before the start of the 1998 season Villeneuve's Williams team lost the services of highly-rated designer Adrian Newey. That season Villeneuve was not to win a single race. I've a suspicion that if McLaren paid me a squillion pounds to join their team, I'd win half a dozen races – and I can't even drive.

The more cynical among us would also believe that off-track politics have a huge bearing on the outcome of races. The 1994 season was in danger of becoming a write-off because of the domination of Schumacher, but a two-race suspension for the German offered a chink of light. If only Damon Hill were to win those two races, then we really would see a thrilling battle for the championship. Surprise, surprise, Hill won them both to close the gap on Schumacher to a point.

It was a similar story in 1998, when Hakkinen burst from the traps and threatened to destroy interest in the title race, only suddenly to develop previously unsuspected frailties and allow Schumacher steadily to claw back the deficit, setting up yet another thrilling championship climax. This is a sport, remember, that relies on mega-rich sponsors to fund the massive wages drivers enjoy. If those sponsors begin to suspect that millions of fans are being turned off by one-horse title races, they'll be off in a flash, and where would that leave motor racing then?

Can someone, somewhere, please explain to me the result of the 1998 Hungarian Grand Prix at the Hungaroring circuit, where overtaking is practically impossible?

Hakkinen was the 4-5 favourite, having grabbed the crucial pole position. He had won six of the previous 11 Formula One races that year, with five of those six victories earned from pole position. In every respect he looked a very good thing, particularly as his market rival, 100-30 shot Schumacher, had finished a distant fifth to the Finn on home soil in Germany a fortnight earlier. But in the hours leading up to the Hungarian Grand Prix, Schumacher for no apparent reason came in for a wave of heavy betting support, with that 100-30 quote slashed to 5-2. Schumacher had won three races on the bounce earlier in the season to threaten to make a race of the championship, but Hakkinen's subsequent victories in Austria and Germany looked like sewing up the title. The only chance to keep interest alive was for Schumacher to win in Hungary, but he was only third on the grid, half a second behind Hakkinen and over a track where pole position traditionally ensures victory.

Yet Schumacher won (with Hakkinen sixth), to close the gap in the two-horse race for the title and keep interest alive for the rest of the season.

Incidentally, the two-race Schumacher suspension in 1994 followed a controversial finish to the Belgian Grand Prix, which left bookies in a right muddle. The German, a red-hot favourite, was first past the post but five hours later was stripped of his title and 7-4 chance Hill was placed first. Predictably, both Schumacher AND Hill punters demanded pay-outs. Most of the big firms settled on Schumacher, pointing to recently-established rules which stated "in the event of a disqualification, the podium presentation will count as the 'weigh-in' and this will determine bets". But Tote went it alone in paying out on Hill, with spokesman Tim Pickering dismissing other firms' rules as "a sackload of bull".

Pickering said: "Hill is obviously the winner. If a jockey weighed in after a race and was found to be carrying the incorrect weight he would be disqualified and all bets on his mount would be losers. It's the same with Schumacher. He 'weighed in' with the incorrect gear and was subsequently thrown out. You have to pay out on Hill."

Though Pickering perhaps had a point, it was no surprise to see Tote amend their rules the following season to fall in line with other bookies. His attitude may have been commendable at a time when betting shops were not open on Sundays, but today such an approach would lead to his firm almost certainly paying out twice – first on Schumacher to betting shop punters rushing to pick up their winnings as soon as the race finished, and then on Hill following the amended result.

But although paying out on the podium positions is the common-sense strategy, it does create an anomaly. In the above instance, I could have backed Hill for the Belgian Grand Prix and Schumacher for the world drivers' championship and, through no fault of my own, I'd have lost out both ways. Is it acceptable that unofficial positions count for the race but only the official result affects the championship race?

It's worth pointing out here that in every season bar one during the 1990s, the driver winning the first grand prix of the campaign went on to clinch the world title. The only exception was in 1997 when Jacques Villeneuve crashed out at the first corner in Melbourne but still went on to be crowned Formula One king.

At the start of the 1999 season, in early March, punters were given little chance to make a killing. Schumacher was title favourite at around the even-money mark, with Hakkinen 9-4 and Coulthard 7-2. That yielded a book of 103 per cent on the front three in the betting alone, so in theory bookies had every other driver running for them. That's a stark illustration of how difficult it is to make money on motor racing.

I've made it clear here that 99 per cent of the time motor racing is boringly predictable, but the first race of the 1999 season threw up one of the shocks of the last ten years when Ferrari No.2 driver Eddie Irvine won the Australian Grand Prix in Melbourne.

The sport's devotees would argue that such a result illustrated the capacity of Formula One to raise eyebrows, that it was proof nothing can be taken for granted, not even the dominance of Hakkinen and Schumacher. Yet for punters it was the final nail in the coffin. The unthinkable happened – Hakkinen and Coulthard failed to finish the race, and Schumacher was put out of the running at the start with clutch problems – so those punters who try to make an each-way killing on one of the long-priced outsiders had things for once in their favour. But Irvine was 100 per cent unbackable. He had contested 81 earlier grands prix – and won not a single one. Not only that, in the first practice session for Melbourne, the Irishman trailed in 14th fastest, earning quotes of 33-1.

In short, punters have nothing in their favour in Formula One racing. They can go only on past records at the track, plus times recorded in practice sessions, but that information is freely available to bookmakers, who make sure, with hefty margins in their favour, that they are not going to finish out of pocket too often.

There's a chance in most other sports for punters to steal a march on the old enemy, to take advantage of snippets of information that bookmakers might not have heard. But in the closeted world of Formula One only the closest insiders enjoy that sort of privilege. It's a world of secrecy in which teams have almost to carry out industrial espionage to learn of technological advances made by rival camps. Punters must rely on guesswork alone – and in betting there's no quicker route to the poorhouse.

My advice, then, to punters who want to make a profit from their sports betting is to treat motor racing with caution. In the long-term, losses are inevitable.

I must, though, share with you the thoughts of one punter who insists that he has made a healthy profit over the years on the grand prix circuit, and who started 1999 with a bang by backing Irvine each-way for the Australian Grand Prix at 25-1. These are his betting nuggets.

Make sure you have as many bookmaker accounts as possible as discrepancies are frequent, and move mountains to open an account with Coral, whose grand prix knowledge is sketchy.

Don't place a bet until after the warm-up session on the day of the race. A driver who qualifies higher than expected on the grid and who shows further improvement in the final warm-up session will more often than not give you a good run for your money. To racing teams the hours between final practice and the day-of-the-race warm-up are absolutely crucial. Monitor the news from the warm-up sessions either on the various Internet websites or on Teletext.

Never be afraid to back Michael Schumacher in wet conditions. There isn't an odds-maker in Britain who isn't aware that Schumacher is the bee's-knees in the wet, but it's possible that they are not aware of just how superior he is in such conditions. Lesser-known drivers who excel in the rain are Jean Alesi and Rubens Barrichello, both of whom should be considered at long odds when the rain is pouring down. If it's raining for the Monaco Grand Prix, generally held in mid-May, do not miss Alesi.

Make a note of the Arrows team for the Hungarian Grand Prix. The Hungaroring is not a power circuit and its tight twists and turns suit the Arrows engine.

Such is the dominance of McLaren and Ferrari that drivers from other camps can generally be backed only each-way. But if you're looking to oppose the favourites, do so at the beginning of the season when teams are striving for reliability and upsets are more likely. For instance, the McLaren team had not completed a full race-distance practice session before the season-opening Australian Grand Prix in 1999, so could not possibly be backed at cramped odds.

The important thing to remember about betting on sport, be it motor racing, golf, football or whatever, is that value is king. Always has been, always will be. The halfwits who don't accept this wisdom are destined to be life's losers in the long run. They'll win their petty battles from time to time, ignoring your insistence that a 7-4 underdog in a tennis match has a real chance of upsetting the odds and then smugly counting their paltry winnings when the 2-5 favourite wins a third-set tie-break, but ultimately they are doomed.

Winners are not everything – it's the price of those winners that counts. If you keep on getting 7-4 about 11-10 shots, then you will make money in the long run. That is a stone-cold certainty. If however you belong to the school that identifies a likely winner and then wades in regardless of the odds, then give up betting now. Your existence, pretty miserable now I would suspect, will only get worse.

It's difficult to explain the term 'value' in betting. Most simply, if you're offered 6-5 about the toss of a coin, then that is quite obviously a value bet because you know the true odds are even-money. Similarly, any punter who has ever been tempted to take odds like 5-6 or 10-11 about a side winning the toss before a cricket match should be taken out at dawn and shot.

I would always advise punters to frame their own odds beforehand and then compare them with the bookies' prices. This advice often discourages novice punters, but you'll be surprised how quickly you can develop a feel for odds

Another way of looking at it is this: West Ham are 11-4 to win at Derby County, so bookies are saying that if the match was played 15 times, the Hammers would be expected to win only four of them. If you believe the Londoners are capable of exceeding that expectation, then you should be happy to back them at 11-4.

To make betting pay you must have a strategy and 'getting the value' is the best strategy of all. But there are others, and I shall deal briefly with them now.

● **Treat every bet on its merits.** Do not let other considerations like a long losing run cloud your judgement. This is easy to say, I know. There is nothing that drains confidence more quickly than a month-long diet of losers. But it is imperative to lose all other baggage when contemplating a bet. The 6-4 chance you strongly fancy does not know you've backed nothing but losers for the previous four weeks. By the same token, don't go thinking that your 6-4 poke has acquired a cloak of invincibility just because your last seven bets have copped.

Now put yourself in the shoes of a punter who at the start of a tennis tournament backs Greg Rusedski at 14-1 to win the title. Rusedski plays superbly and storms through to the quarter-finals, where he meets Thomas Enqvist, a player of roughly equal ability. You expect the odds to be something like 8-11 Rusedski, evens

Enqvist, or maybe 5-6 each of two. But Ladbrokes, because of heavy Rusedski liabilities, go 4-9 Rusedski and 13-8 Enqvist. What do you do?

Believe it or not there are punters who insist that you should pass up the chance of backing Enqvist at such gift-horse odds. You've already backed Rusedski, they say. How can you oppose him now?

Such an approach is lunacy. Every bet must be treated on its individual merits. If you rate Enqvist an even-money shot but a bookie is willing to offer you 13-8, you get on, regardless of any other bets you've struck on the contest. Come on, where do the lunatics draw the line? If you follow their argument to its logical conclusion, Enqvist could be offered at 11-2 to beat Rusedski and still they wouldn't be tempted.

● **Always, always, always pay tax on your bets.** This is not just a forceful point of view; it's a mathematical necessity. It does not matter if every bet you place for the next 30 years is a loser; you will still be better off paying tax. Betting shop big-mouths the length and breadth of Britain will never accept this but that is because they are as thick as two short planks. Here's an example using, for ease of explanation, ten per cent tax (the logic applies equally well to nine per cent).

Punter A has a £10 no-tax bet on an even-money shot. If it loses he's down a bare tenner; if it wins his return is £20, less ten per cent deductions (£2), in other words a total return of £18.

Punter B has a £9 bet and pays 90p tax on the same even-money shot. If it loses he's down only £9.90, 10p less than the no-tax merchant; if it wins his return is the same £18.

● **Multiple bets – just say no.** Bookies will lay you these bets till the cows come home. They represent their most profitable form of betting. Let's take a yankee (11 bets – six doubles, four trebles and one accumulator) as an example. Have you ever fancied a selection so much that you wanted to back it seven times? No, of course you haven't – such a strategy would be suicidal. But that's what you are doing every time you place a yankee.

If the first of your four selections in a yankee loses, automatically SEVEN of your bets go down. I realise that for small-staking punters such bets offer the only real chance of a life-changing win; after all, a fiver on a single 11-10 poke hardly seems worth bothering about. So if you can't give up this ruinous multiple-bet strategy, at least amend it.

If you fancy three selections and are considering a Patent (seven bets – three singles, three doubles and a treble), ditch one selection and go for the straight double; If you're dabbling with four picks and the dreaded 'Y' word crosses your mind, immediately ditch a selection and settle for three doubles and a treble. This kind of strategy acts like a nicotine patch – slowly weaning you off the health-damaging, wealth-damaging drug.

● **Don't back each-way.** A controversial piece of advice, I know, but something I'm convinced will help you become a more successful punter. Certain contests, for example eight-runner novice hurdles in which the favourite is odds-on, offer favourable each-way conditions but in sport an each-way bet more often than not is a wasted bet.

I know of several small bookies happy to take each-way bets all day long. In their eyes the punter is paying twice for the same bet. Too often an each-way bet is the refuge of the punter who can't make up his mind, the punter who does not fancy his selection strongly enough to win but who thinks it may just squeak a place in the frame. But if you don't think your runner will win, what are you doing backing it in the first place?

In a contest like Wimbledon or the Open Championship, I would far rather back TWO players on the nose than one player each-way, particularly as in golf the each-way terms are only a quarter of the odds. And straight win bets on players or teams who do progress to the later stages often offer opportunities for hedging.

Following this advice is not guaranteed to turn you into a successful punter, but at the very least it will help you lose less. And that, grasshoppers, is a gigantic step in the right direction.

# chapter 16

## golf

It was the most gripping moment in the history of sport. You can forget last-minute winners in World Cup finals, feats of heroism in the heat of Olympic battle, courageous Test centuries against all the odds – when Bernhard Langer stood over a six-foot putt on the 18th green at Kiawah Island, South Carolina, in 1991, time stood still.

All Langer had to do was sink that putt and the Ryder Cup would have stayed European. *All* Langer had to do! As Seve Ballesteros said minutes after Langer's brave attempt rolled agonisingly wide: "No-one in the world should have had to make that putt."

Ballesteros in his endearingly melodramatic way summed up the immense pressure resting on Langer's shoulders that evening. Had it been a putt for the Open or the US Masters, the German's stroke would not have faltered. But this was for team glory, indeed for the good of an entire continent, and his iron nerve for once deserted him.

Try to remember those nail-biting moments towards the close of the ugliest Ryder Cup battle (The War On The Shore) in history. Try to remember the task facing Langer. Try to imagine the pressure he must have been feeling.

Now try to price up that evil six-foot putt. Was Langer an even-money shot to sink it? Odds on maybe? Perhaps even 6-4 against? As he said later, the 18th green had seen an awful lot of traffic that final Sunday and irritating spike marks littered the path between ball and cup. So how would you have bet?

Time, and the comments of people like Ballesteros, have perhaps encouraged us to believe Langer's task was Herculean, but it's a little-known fact that the German was officially heavy odds-on to make that putt, to square the Ryder Cup at 14-14, and so keep it European. Both Hills and Tote, betting in running throughout that nerve-shredding final day, made Langer 4-7 to hole out and 5-4 to miss. That's a fantastic piece of information to arm yourself with whenever a pub argument about Kiawah Island begins to heat up.

You can talk all night about pressure, about spike marks, about the size of a man's heart, but it's all there in black and white in bookmaker records. Langer, who had minutes earlier sunk a great putt on the 17th green, was 4-7 to hole an easier one on the 18th and missed.

That is another fine example of how betting helps the understanding of history. When a schoolboy in Kuala Lumpur reads in the year 2074 that Langer was 4-7 to hole out on that September day in 1991, he'll know instinctively that the German messed up.

Sympathetic historians can dress it up every which way, but Kuala Lumpur Kid will know the truth. Bookmakers talk our language. We rely on them in so many walks of life to cut through the crap on our behalf. We didn't need to plough through the whole of Zippergate to weigh up Bill Clinton's chances of survival; bookmaker odds of, say, 1-2 would have told us all we needed to know.

Similarly, we wouldn't have a clue what way a referendum on Britain joining the European Monetary Union would go, but if bookies offered 1-3 that the euro would be adopted then we'd all have a pretty fair idea that we were soon to become fully-fledged members. We dream every year of a white Christmas, but so long as the layers say it's a 10-1 chance we know we are more than likely to be disappointed.

When we watch golf on TV, the experts do their best to highlight the difficulties a player faces as he stands over his putt. "This one needs to start way right of the hole," they tell us; or, "There's no possibility of sinking this; he'll be happy to leave it within three feet." All very well. We are grateful for their guidance. But what we really need is a figure who can translate this course knowledge into odds.

"I'd make him about a 7-4 shot to sink this," would tell us all we need to know about the difficulty of a putt. Or, when a player's duffed drive finds the trees on a par-four: "He's about an 8-1 chance to make the green with his second shot from there." Instantly we would know that a bogey is pretty much certain.

The coverage on Sky Sports of both the European and US Tours is first class and, in Ewen Murray, Sky have one of the finest broadcasters in sport. But improvements can be made and, given the massive betting interest in golf, the logical next step is to employ a betting expert. I reckon that eventually Sky chiefs will see the light and that's it's an 11-10 chance such a figure is appointed before Ryder Cup 2001; 6-4 it's me.

Throughout the remainder of this chapter you'll find several tips to help make your golf betting pay. The first I'll give you here and now: never, ever back Ernie Els – the man's a bottle merchant supreme.

There's no questioning his ability: his impossibly smooth swing, his length off the tee, and the sharpness of his short game. But under the heading 'nerve', the name of Els is accompanied by a Timeform squiggle. It's a fault Els tries to hide with his famously laid-back manner, but there was clear evidence in the mid-1990s when he was first making it into the big time, and the early weeks of the 1999 season offered further proof.

Let's first go back to 1994, the year Els won his first US Open and the year I first questioned in the pages of the *Racing Post* the big South African's bottle (you would not believe the abusive letters I was to receive after penning such anti-Els words).

Ernie, I wrote at the time, may have been the fastest milkman in the West, but this Ernie would have been a whole lot slower, searching for his bottle. A close examination of the South African's record that season revealed that when God was dishing out heart, Els turned up late.

Els won the US Open and his supporters argued heatedly that chokers do not win Majors. But Els didn't *win* that Open, it was handed to him on a plate by players who on the day choked even more. Okay, his third-round 66 at Oakmont was a terrific effort, but when he was in the perfect position to ram home his advantage in the final round, he slumped to a nervy 73, a last-hole bogey allowing Colin Montgomerie and Loren Roberts, with rounds of 70 apiece, to force him into a play-off.

This was to be the acid test of nerve; three players all bidding over 18 holes for their first Major title. And what did Els do? He began like an 18-handicapper, spraying the ball all over the place and collapsing to four over par after just two holes. Yes, he improved, but only because he couldn't get much worse. He finished the play-off round level with Roberts on 74, and was handed the title when the American bogeyed the second extra hole. Interestingly, neither Roberts nor Montgomerie have since won a Major, reinforcing the theory that choker Els won only because he was in the company of even bigger chokers.

Later that year Els raced seven shots clear at the halfway mark in the Mercedes German Masters and bookies closed their books. It was all over. Fat ladies everywhere began singing. But the choker from Jo'burg, still four strokes clear with seven holes of the last round to play, was caught by Seve Ballesteros and Jose Maria Olazabal after squandering an easy six-footer at the last. His final-round 73 was a full TEN shots worse than his opening round.

But we shouldn't have been too surprised. In the Volvo PGA Championship at Wentworth earlier that year, he'd gone into the final round three shots clear, shook with fear, and allowed Olazabal to pip him.

Now zoom forward to the opening months of 1999. Even before the US Masters in early April, Els had frozen in no fewer than three tournaments to kick his followers in the teeth again and again and again.

Els was 11-2 favourite at the start of the Heineken Classic, one of the first *European* Tour events of the season, despite its Australian venue. Everything went to plan for Els backers as their man opened up a five-shot lead going into the final round. The result was a foregone conclusion, with most bookies closing their books.

After six holes of the final round, Els was still five shots clear. But a triple-bogey seven at the seventh hole allowed all those old doubts to creep back into the Els psyche and the South African, who had posted scores of 65, 66 and 69 earlier in the week, slumped to a final-round 75 and a three-way share of second place with Bernhard Langer and Peter Lonard.

The winner, the man who had stalked Els so successfully, was that giant of the golf course Jarrod Moseley, a pre-tournament 150-1 chance and still 25-1 when he began the final round five adrift. So Ernie was not pegged back by a Tiger Woods, or a Nick Faldo at the height of his intimidating powers. His nerve had crumbled in the face of an assault by a player he'd probably never heard of before.

At the Andersen Consulting World Matchplay in California the following month, Els went down as a first-round banker in most notebooks at a generous 1-2 to beat Paul Azinger. But with victory in his sights Els made a hash of the final two holes to allow his American opponent to steal an astonishing victory and wreck thousands of bets.

But worse was to come. Els, despite a by-now blatant tendency to crumble under pressure, was made favourite for the Doral Ryder Open in Florida at the beginning of March. For much of the final round, Els was kept company at the top of the leaderboard by a string of little-known Americans, and those punters who'd backed him at 10-1 were allowing themselves smug grins. Even when tougher nut Steve Elkington, on the back of a birdie blitz, posted a clubhouse target of 13 under par, there were still reasons to be cheerful. Els was 12 under with two holes to play, the par-four 17th, eminently birdie-able and the par-four 18th, which although much tougher had yielded him a birdie a day earlier.

Els birdied the 17th to go level with Elkington at 13 under, and at the 18th tee needed a birdie to win the tournament or par to force a play-off.

Now the 18th hole at the Blue Monster course at Doral is notoriously difficult, but only because of the drive, with water all the way down the left and bunker after bunker lining the right. Find the fairway with your drive and a par is plain sailing, with birdie a distinct possibility. Els hit a beauty of a tee shot, a drive that just wouldn't quit, and found the middle of the fairway, just 154 yards from the pin. Elkington in the clubhouse must have groaned.

Els, by now a 4-6 shot or shorter, fished out an 8-iron for his approach shot, possibly rehearsing his victory speech. Then calamity. His swing fell to pieces, his approach almost found water, and he was faced with a chip up a slope from a bad lie for his third shot. Elkington now was favourite, but still you'd have put money on Els getting up and down to par the hole and force a play-off.

Then another calamity. He duffed his chip so embarrassingly that it failed to reach the top of the slope and came to rest almost at his feet. He eventually finished with a double-bogey six to slump from what should have been first place to a five-way tie for third, a hideously costly collapse for his followers.

Sky commentator Ewen Murray said it all: "Oh Ernie, what a mess."

When Tiger Woods or David Duval go into the final round of a tournament with a lead of two or three strokes, they win. A similarly large Els lead carries no such guarantees. When you put your money on Els, you back an undoubtedly great player. But what you also do is put your trust in a bottler. And that, ladies and gentlemen, is not the way to make money from betting.

I have a theory why some players choke when in contention, while others keep their nerve admirably. It's all to do with golf education – how players learned the ropes before the decision to go pro.

Els, by all accounts from a comfortable middle-class background, probably did not have to participate in big-money games to pay for his golf education. The opportunity to strengthen his nerve in matches with big-money wagers was never there. But the likes of Lee Trevino and Ray Floyd in the 1960s had to hustle to get by. Before they hit the big time, their sole source of income was cash won from high-rolling gamblers on the golf course. That nerve-jangling education was to stand them in good stead during their years on the full Tour, as I will explain later in this chapter.

I suppose I've been a trifle harsh on Els, winner of the US Open again in 1997, in castigating him for his World Matchplay collapse. After all, he was in good company. Of the 32 first-round matches at Carlsbad, 15 were won by the underdog, some at huge odds (Michael Bradley at 3-1 to beat Mark O'Meara, Azinger at 5-2 to beat Els, Eduardo Romero at 9-4 to dump out Lee Westwood).

Every subsequent round threw up several shock results, and indeed by the third round only three of the world's top 16 players were left in the competition. At the last-eight stage, Tiger Woods flew the flag for golf's elite, but the highest ranked of the other seven quarter-finalists was Jeff Maggert at 24.

The semi-final line-up had the box-office appeal of a Bulgarian slasher movie – Maggert (80-1 pre-tournament), Steve Pate (125-1), Andrew Magee (125-1), and John Huston (50-1). As Woods approached the 16th green trailing Maggert in their quarter-final, a fan yelled: "Come on Tiger, don't make us watch basketball on Sunday." One wag described Maggert, the eventual winner, as "duller than a used range ball".

It's a shame the Matchplay ended so tamely because the format was a breath of fresh air amid the weekly grind of strokeplay contests. The pattern of shock results in the tournament must be noted by punters. Over four rounds of strokeplay, class has time to tell, but over a mere 18 holes the potential for shocks is massive, particularly in matchplay, where strategy and nerve are all-important.

David Duval, at the time the world No.2, neatly explained why the favourites had such a poor time in the tournament. Duval said after his second-round defeat by Bill Glasson: "On paper there may be a huge difference between the world No.1 and the world No.24, but over a course of a season the difference is only a putt here or a putt there. There's very little to choose between us all."

It's hard to convince betting novices that golf can offer punters a real chance to beat the bookies. All they see are fields of 150 or more and impossible-to-predict results like Maggert's World Matchplay triumph. But golf more than most other sports is a game in which form can be relied upon.

Yes there will be 150-1 skinners, yes there will be occasions when a player lands first prize after a succession of missed cuts, but more often than not the silverware will be captured by players who in previous weeks had hinted that they were approaching something like their best form, by players who had proven they could act on the track, by players who to the shrewd punter were winners waiting to happen.

At the *Racing Post* in the early 1990s, I ran an in-house golf-tipping competition in which contestants nominated three selections in the weekly European and US Tour events, with a theoretical £1 each-way going on all six selections.

In May 1993, five of the 12 contestants plumped for Jim McGovern (no relation!) for the Shell Houston Open. This was such a poorly contested tournament that Dan Forsman was rated 18-1 fourth-favourite by one firm, so McGovern, who had eyecatching form at the Woodlands track and who had performed creditably in his two previous tournaments, had obvious claims, as five of us recognised. His odds? An incredible 80-1.

He won.

Just think about that for a moment. Of 12 tipsters faced with a 150-runner field, five opted for a man quoted at 80-1. That just doesn't happen in any other sport. In horseracing, odds of 80-1 is bookmaker shorthand for 'no chance'.

Two years earlier, I had enjoyed my greatest-ever success in sports betting when Ian Baker-Finch landed the British Open at Royal Birkdale at 50-1. The depth of my confidence in Baker-Finch's chances that year shocked an industry which up to then had dealt in 'might wins' and 'could wins'.

"Ian Baker-Finch, the man who led them all a merry dance for two rounds at St Andrews in 1994, will shock the big guns of European golf by winning the 120th Open, starting at Royal Birkdale tomorrow," I wrote in the *Racing Post*. "He's 50-1 and that's a silly price for a man ranked 25th in the world and who blazed a loud-and-clear Open warning by reaching a play-off in the New England Classic in the States on Sunday."

The big Aussie's record that season leading up to the Open had been mightily impressive. From 18 events he had notched ten top-20 slots, including seventh in the US Masters. He should never have been allowed to start at 50-1.

While it's true that in the late 1990s odds-makers began to do their golf homework much more diligently, opportunities to cash in do crop up regularly. From time to time I have acted as golf consultant to the Winning Line, Britain's most respected horseracing and sports tipping service.

In March 1999, I recommended two golfers for the Portuguese Open. The first was Wayne Riley at 33-1, the second a man who had been in sparkling form all season on the European Tour, who had finished fourth in the Qatar Masters on his previous outing, and who in the 1998 Portuguese Open at the same course had taken a share of 16th spot, just seven shots off the lead.

Riley was in third place going into the final round but faded badly. The other selection, available at 80-1, was John Bickerton, who tied with Van Phillips for first place before losing in a play-off.

On paper trying to pick a winner from a 150-runner golf tournament looks a daunting task but it's frequently easy to reach a shortlist of perhaps half a dozen runners by singling out those players running into form and those with a previous track record.

I always treat early-season tournaments with caution, and events played on a new course should also carry warning signs. I would suggest that solid course form is perhaps slightly more significant than hot current form. There are players with a row of duck eggs next to their name who can suddenly improve by a stone over a familiar track.

For instance Scott Simpson can safely be ignored in most tournaments but something about the Buick Invitational at Torrey Pines in his native San Diego brings out the best in him. Between 1997 and 1999, Simpson's form figures there were 16-1-7. Similarly Jose Maria Olazabal had suffered a wretched 1999 going into the US Masters in April, but he's a course specialist at Augusta so we should not have been too surprised when he stormed to victory.

The *Racing Post* does all the hard work for golf punters with its weekly pricewise tables. Form figures for the previous six weeks are included, together with results of the tournament for the past four or five years. The *Post* has introduced many punter-friendly services over the years but those golf pricewise tables are right up there with the very best. Absolutely invaluable. And author Keith Elliott provides a further useful guide with his annual *Golf Form*

*Book*, although this makes life easier for bookies, too. Monitor, too, the golf websites on the Internet, notably pgatour.com, europeantour.com, and golfweb.com. The information on these sites is world class.

There's nothing more sickening for diligent golf punters than to see a player with no worthwhile course record and with no current form appear from nowhere to scoop first prize. It happens probably a dozen times a season and more often than not is a skinner for bookies. But appeals to these bookies to quote a 'field' price in golf tournaments, like they do in Las Vegas, have fallen largely on deaf ears.

Vegas bookies will quote odds for the top 40 or so players in a tournament, and then lump the rest together in a special 'field' price at odds of around 8-1 to 10-1. So if a complete outsider, say like 500-1 shot Johnny Miller at Pebble Beach in 1994, takes first prize, those punters who backed 'the field' will be on a winner.

One or two British bookies have played ball in the past but the larger firms don't want to know. They say that because they update their golf odds after each round, punters have plenty of opportunity to back these long-shots.

Each-way betting is another bone of contention. Faced with such large fields, punters should surely be entitled to place terms of a quarter the odds the first five, or even six. Not so. All the leading firms offer terms of a quarter the odds the first four. If you want a pay-out for fifth place, you must accept a fifth of the odds.

I'm sure if one of the leading firms followed the example of their smaller rivals and offered a quarter of the odds for the first five, the increased business attracted would more than make up for any short-term cut in profit. Not that I'm a big fan of each-way betting in the first place, as I explain in the previous chapter. Generally it's the last refuge of the faint-hearted.

Some punters insist that it pays to wait until after the halfway cut in a tournament before placing a bet. That way, they say, you can be pretty sure that, barring disasters, your selection will be there or thereabouts on the final day. That's probably true, but the odds will reflect that, too.

A player you perhaps fancied pre-tournament at 66-1 may be only around the 7-2 mark come the start of the third round when he's one shot off the lead. And by the third-round stage any advantage you gained by diligent homework will have been lost.

Bookies will have studied the opening two rounds and will have monitored which players are at home on the course. It's clear by this stage that all the players on the leaderboard act on the track and are, by virtue of being on that leaderboard, in pretty good form, so any bet you now place relies an awful lot on guesswork.

I'm prepared for my bets struck pre-tournament to flop because that's the price I pay for backing 50-1 shots. But when I'm taking 11-4 at the halfway stage, losers become substantially harder to swallow. And further, even those at the very top of the leaderboard are not safe from the assault of an unconsidered player who, under no pressure, shoots something like a birdie-strewn 64 in the third round to upset the most studious calculations.

Some punters swear by 'last-round' statistics, the record of players in the final round of tournaments, which are available on good Internet websites. But these can be highly misleading. As Keith Elliott pointed out in his *Golf Form Book 1999*, the key weakness of such stats is that they do not take into account weather conditions or leaderboard positions. It's far easier to shoot a 66 from way down the field with no pressure on than it is from bang in the firing line. And a 75 in high winds is as good as a 67 in calm conditions.

To illustrate the absurdity of these statistics, towards the end of the 1998 US Tour season the leader in the final-round stats was none other than Chip Beck, whose idea of a good tournament is merely making the cut. Beck had played in only one final round all season, shooting a 68, so his average for the season was 68, putting him top. Absolutely crazy.

I must, though, put in a good word for 'betting in running' over the final round, a service pioneered by the excellent Oxfordshire-based firm Stan James. This gives punters an ideal opportunity to hedge, but also offers quick-thinking gamblers the chance to strike. Bookies are human, remember. Their odds-compilers, watching the same TV coverage as you, must react within seconds to every shot played over the closing holes. They make mistakes, sometimes huge ones, and it's up to us to make them pay.

Another good point from Elliott's book worth repeating here is the damage done to a player's swing by performing in high winds. A pro golfer's swing is finely tuned from hour upon hour, day upon day at the practice range or in the heat of tournament. It's as automatic to them as washing hands after using the toilet is to us. But a couple of rounds in gale-force winds throws them out of kilter. It takes time for the feel to return, and players are often worth opposing if they line up a week after playing in such gusty conditions.

One of my golden rules for golf betting when I first started gambling on the sport in the late 1980s was never put money on a man who the previous week had won a tournament.

My thinking was that on the back of a tournament triumph, a player is content to rest on his laurels, to think, if only subconsciously, that he's done all the hard work and now he's entitled to take his foot off the gas and enjoy himself. If that view had any merits at the time, it certainly does not now.

We are now in an age in which golfers are as dedicated and as competitive as any other professional sportsman. They may allow themselves the odd glass of wine after a victory to savour, but the taste of that victory leaves them wanting more. Immediately. In the late 1990s there were numerous examples of back-to-back victories and I'm afraid that my one-time golden rule has lost all of its glitter. Indeed a player who wins a tournament one week should be definitely on your shortlist for the next because quite clearly he's in tip-top form.

Golf throws up numerous opportunities to bet, quite apart from the outright betting on a tournament. Bookies will lump together two players with roughly equal chances of winning a tournament and quote each at 10-11 in a straight 72-hole match.

The beauty of this kind of betting is that your selection can miss the halfway cut and still land you a pay-out as long as he finishes ahead of his opponent. This is a beautiful way to bet, in my opinion by far the most punter-friendly. For a start it gives us an interest over the four days of the tournament, providing of course the players involved survive the cut.

Unbelievers might argue that golf match betting offers poor value in that we are faced with two players of roughly equal ability in a straight match, yet are getting less than even-money. But it's important to understand that odds-compilers, nearly always under pressure, often take short cuts when devising their prices.

They will not necessarily use care to pair two players in a straight head-to-head. Instead they will cast their eye over their outright odds, pluck out two players from, say, the 50-1 bracket, and lump them together at 10-11 each of two.

A rival odds-compiler, on the other hand, may rate Player A a 25-1 chance to win first prize and Player B, his match-betting opponent with the earlier bookie, a 66-1 no-hoper. So 10-11 about Player A begins to look something of a steal.

Let me give you an example. Michael Bradley, a Florida-born and -based player, went into the 1999 Doral Ryder Open in the Sunshine State with cast-iron credentials. In three previous years, he had a 1-18-2 to his credit at Doral's Blue Monster course, and his form leading into the 1999 running, although not scintillating, was nonetheless more solid than shaky.

Mark Calcavecchia, on the other hand, had finished out with the washing in three previous Doral Opens and his form leading into the 1999 running was abysmal. Coral took the hint and went 28-1 Bradley, 50-1 Calcavecchia in their outright betting, but Ladbrokes had them both on the 40-1 mark. Ladbrokes blundered further by making them 10-11 each in a straight match bet. Any fool could see Bradley was a good thing and he duly finished five shots ahead of Calc.

If you needed any further evidence that bookies feel highly vulnerable on golf match-betting then consider this: Coral scrapped it in the early 1990s and Hills pulled out in 1998 until protests from clients saw them re-introduce match betting but only for the larger tournaments. In January 1998, Ladbrokes decided to change their match-betting odds from the long-standing 10-11 each of two (with the tie 14-1) to 5-6 each, with the tie 16-1. This was only weeks after Ladbrokes' proposed take-over of Coral and confirmed punters' worst fears that with less competition the giant bookmakers would be free to shave odds willy-nilly.

Trying to justify their move, Ladbrokes said it was to play fair to punters who like to back the tie in match-betting. As excuses go this took the biscuit. There are only three punters on the planet who back the tie in golf match betting and they all live in the loony bin at the bottom of our road. Still at the *Racing Post* at the time, I launched a campaign to force Ladbrokes into a U-turn which, to their credit, they agreed to just a week later.

One or two firms have moved to 9-10 each of two but Ladbrokes have maintained 10-11. The incident underlined the need for punters to remain vigilant. If you see odds cut so blatantly, and for no reason other than to increase bookmaker profit margins, then take your business elsewhere.

Another popular form of punting in golf is three-ball betting, where we are asked to pick a winner from a group of three players in the first-round of a tournament. In other words, the only thing that counts is what happens over those first 18 holes. I have to say this is one of the most difficult betting mediums in sport. Any player, no matter how far down the world rankings, is capable of carding a good score over 18 holes, although it should be pointed out here that Britain's most successful sports punter was a 26-year-old from Oxford, who in March 1995 picked up an astonishing £814,257 for an incredible ten-timer on the first-round three-balls in the Doral Ryder Open.

My strategy for three-ball betting has changed over the years. Initially I decided that since the true odds of each player over a mere 18 holes should be 2-1 (or 7-4 once we take into account bookie profit margin), on no account could I back a player below the 7-4 mark. It was a noble viewpoint but deeply flawed. Time and again I earmarked players who looked good things but could not be backed because they hovered below 7-4. Invariably they won.

Now I've changed tack. I very rarely bet in three-balls but will make a move when the following criteria is satisfied: First, one of the three players must be easy to rule out because of woeful form; second, of the two remaining players, one must have a far superior course record. If I can then get 11-8 or upwards about my selection, then I will be tempted to step in. Note that in 72-hole matches your bet is a loser if your player cards the same score as his head-to-head opponents (bookies bet with the tie). If, however, two players finish level in a three-ball, dead-heat rules apply.

Remember that after the halfway cut, the remaining players go out, in leaderboard order, in two-balls for the third and fourth rounds. Two-balls offer more punter-friendly betting opportunities.

Golf is frequently and quite rightly looked upon as the last bastion of true sportsmanship. I'm afraid, though, that the same cannot be said of golf punters who, as I learned over several years at the *Racing Post*, are the first to whinge if things don't go their way.

You wouldn't believe some of the calls we received at the *Post* sports desk. You could guarantee that if one of the two golf tournaments over the weekend saw a group of players tied for one of the minor placings, punters who backed players finishing seventh or eighth would be on the blower to complain that their bookies had cheated them out of a pay-out.

Their insane logic reasoned that if, say, Bernhard Langer won a tournament, with a group of four tied for second spot, the next player home should be classed as third. "Langer won," they would say. "Woods, Duval, Montgomerie and Els were second, so my man Greg Norman must be third." I kid you not. These punters swore blind that Norman was third, even though five players finished above him.

In late-January 1998, the Pebble Beach Pro-Am, one of the early-season events on the US Tour, was badly disrupted by heavy rain. Organisers first reduced it from 72 holes to 54 holes, but when the heavens opened on the final Sunday, they decided to postpone the final 18 holes until a later date – first March and then, when that date was not acceptable, mid-August.

Declaring a result after just 36 holes was not an option because Pebble Beach is an unusual tournament in that THREE separate courses of varying difficulty are used for the first three rounds.

Declaring a result after 36 holes would not have been fair on the players who had not had the opportunity of playing on the easiest of the three courses.

So what were bookies to do?

They could not declare the tournament void for betting purposes because plenty of punters had backed Tom Watson, hotly recommended at 40-1 in the *Racing Post*, who was the leader after 36 holes. They couldn't pay out on the 36-hole result because punters who'd backed players on the fringes of the leaderboard and therefore still in with a shout of first place would quite rightly have gone berserk. And they couldn't give punters the chance to cancel their bets because everyone who backed Watson and the players just behind him would have let their bets ride, while all others would have demanded a refund.

Their only option was to retain all bets and pay out after the final round was completed in August. But this wasn't good enough for punters. Somewhat predictably, the *Racing Post* sports desk was besieged by callers blasting bookies for refusing to void all bets. "How dare they keep our money for seven months, fattening their bank balance with the interest," was the common complaint.

Significantly, though, none of the callers had backed Watson (joint-leader on 10 under par), Tim Herron (10 under), Phil Mickelson (9 under), or Tom Lehman (also 9 under). All were on players no longer in the running. One caller did say that his mate had backed Watson at 40-1 and added that even he wanted his stake-money refunded rather than wait until August for a possible pay-out. Yeah, and I'm the Pope.

By the way, Mickelson eventually picked up first prize in August, with Watson finishing out of the frame.

The nastier side of punters' nature had been highlighted some months earlier after the finish of the 1997 Ryder Cup at Valderrama in Spain. The betting uproar sparked by Colin Montgomerie's controversial decision to concede a 12-foot putt in one of the final singles matches on the Sunday revealed an ugly truth about punters. Many think the world revolves solely around them.

Monty, under orders from European captain Seve Ballesteros,

conceded a very missable putt to American opponent Scott Hoch once he was guaranteed the half-point Europe needed to win the Cup. His generosity meant Hoch and Monty halved their match, and had massive implications on outright Cup betting.

First, instead of what looked a near-certain 15-13 win for Europe, the margin was 14½ to 13½.

Second, the half-point gained rather luckily by Hoch made him the top American scorer with 2½, narrowly ahead of half a dozen better-backed team-mates. And third, and almost certainly more damaging for punters, the concession of the putt meant Monty, the day's banker singles bet, failed to oblige.

Punters spluttered with indignation that Monty could be so inconsiderate to their needs. They likened him to the jockey not riding out for second place once his winning chance had gone. But they were talking through their pockets. Quite rightly, the last thing on the minds of Montgomerie and Ballesteros in the closing moments of Valderrama were the wishes of punters. Their one and only job was to ensure that Europe won the Ryder Cup; once that mission was accomplished, they were 100 per cent right to uphold the sporting nature of the contest and concede the putt to Hoch.

It is no secret that the Ryder Cup is played in such a fair-minded spirit – that is one of the reasons for its spectacular success – so punters who then criticise such sportsmanship are merely trying to excuse their own short-sightedness.

It should be noted here that although Monty's actions robbed some punters of a pay-out, it handed others an unexpected windfall. A 14½ to 13½ scoreline was the favourite European winning margin in ante-post lists so we can reasonably expect it to have been well backed. And Hoch, although a 20-1 chance to top-score for the Americans, had won on his most recent outing so was clearly in great form. To believe, as many punters appeared to, that Montgomerie and Ballesteros should have put their (the punters') needs ahead of Ryder Cup tradition betrays an arrogance of quite staggering proportions.

What Montgomerie did was no different to the behaviour some years back of John Francome, who had the jockeys' title at his mercy but quit riding once he drew level with injured rival Peter Scudamore, who had been well clear until sidelined. The two therefore shared the championship.

BBC commentator Peter Alliss said when Monty conceded the putt: "Well, that's going to affect a few bets". Moaning punters perhaps saw this accurate although innocent comment as a launchpad for complaint. But Alliss was merely demonstrating a commendable grasp of the Ryder Cup's importance to punters; he was not delivering a verdict.

Betting on golf, like football, is booming but that's no reason to expect the sport's top players to consider the needs of punters. Would we demand action against a football team that allowed, while leading 5-0, its keeper to take and miss a last-minute penalty just because we had a tenner resting on a 6-0 scoreline? Similarly, jockeys are entitled to ease up on a runaway winner without fearing the wrath of punters who have bought the winning distance on the spreads.

The only real surprise about those dramatic closing moments at Valderrama was that Montgomerie so readily obeyed the instructions of captain Ballesteros. Okay he'd already done enough to win the Ryder Cup for Europe, but his singles record before the 1999 contest read two wins and two halves from four outings when it could, maybe should, have read three wins and one half. To an athlete as competitive and proud as Monty, that will be a constant source of irritation.

One final point was missed in all of the Monty hullabaloo: who says Hoch would have missed that putt?

The Pebble Beach Pro-Am, the tournament referred to earlier, has caused more than its fair share of betting problems, but I will forever hold up the 1996 running as the perfect example of why sports betting in Britain is crying out for the appointment of an ombudsman.

Bookmakers were split over how to settle bets on the tournament, which was scrapped from the record books when only 36 of the scheduled 72 holes were completed. Previous rain-hit tournaments had been able to announce official results after 36 holes but the

Pebble Beach Pro-Am, for reasons explained earlier, is different.

Pebble Beach organisers ruled that the tournament should be treated as if it had never started. The 180 participants shared the prize-money equally ($3,000 each), but the cash was not added to that year's official money-list totals. Most bookmakers in Britain took that as their cue to void all bets, but Stan James and Surrey Racing settled on the 36-hole result, a particularly expensive option for the former firm who had offered top price (40-1) about the 36-hole leader Jeff Maggert.

Predictably, the decisions sparked an outcry from punters who for a week jammed the *Racing Post* switchboard to complain. Punters who'd backed Maggert or one of the placed finishers, but not with Stan James or Surrey, demanded their winnings, while clients of Stan James and Surrey not lucky enough to find one of the first four home insisted that their bets should be voided.

The unacceptable aspect of this Pebble Beach poser was that bookmakers, accountable only to their own shareholders, could have reached a decision that, for all we knew, was based upon the size of their liabilities. In the case of Stan James, whose crystal-clear rules demanded a pay-out on Maggert, that was clearly not the case. But how could we be convinced that other bookies had not merely taken the least expensive option?

A betting ombudsman would perhaps have seen things a little differently to the majority of bookies. He would have noted that bookmaker rules generally state that if 36 holes have been completed, bets will stand. The bookies, flying in the face of these rules, argued that as Pebble Beach was due to be played over three different courses of varying difficulty, three rounds (54 holes) needed to have been completed to give a fair result.

That was the view of the US PGA chiefs who scrapped the tournament from the record books. But why? Why did it need to be so fair and even-handed? Is it fair for instance that on the first day of the Open a player can tee off early in the morning in a howling gale, while for the golfer with an afternoon tee-off time there's not even a gentle breeze?

Some bookies argued that as there was no official winner, bets simply had to be made void. Yet only a couple of years earlier, one major firm was settling abandoned football matches on the score at the time of the abandonment, even though no official score would ever be recorded.

Whatever decision bookmakers reached on Pebble Beach, there was bound to be controversy; sure to be punters questioning their motives and their honesty. How much simpler it would have been if an independent arbiter had been consulted.

I've illustrated earlier in this book how gambling has been inextricably linked with certain sports throughout the course of history and no chapter on golf could be complete without an examination of how betting was the lifeblood of the sport from the 1930s to the late 1960s, by which time earnings were so vast that there was no longer the need for players to bet.

Writer Luke Friend in a memorable article recounted the story of the most notorious hustlers and I repeat it here, with the kind permission of Golf World magazine.

"In the 1930s gambling (in America) was as much a part of the times as illegal whisky and organised crime. The hustler then remained prominent right into the sixties, with the state of Texas gaining particular notoriety, with courses such as Memorial Park in Houston and Tenison Park near Dallas becoming the breeding ground for the golf gambler. The stories from these times and courses are rich and plentiful and have no doubt become more so with age. It was this environment which helped create some of golf's elite, such as Ray Floyd, Lee Trevino and Tommy Bolt, who were young guns looking for a game. Playing with money they didn't have, they emulated the pressure found in tournaments. 'Playing for your money is a great way to learn how to compete under the heat,' Floyd says. 'It's the best way I know.'

"These courses were also the offices of different professionals, full-time hustlers who could make more money from running their schemes than playing on the tour. In these days an oil man's wallet was much fatter than a professional tournament's purse. Jack Burke Jnr, who spent his early years around hustlers, believes they were instrumental in his development. As he says: 'I never learned much from guys who didn't have a little hustle in them.' The climate of the time was instrumental in creating the hustler. In early 1930s America, Herbert Hoover was the President, Prohibition was in force, Al Capone was on the rampage, and the hustler was in his element. The Depression was then to leave the economy decimated and crime and less-than-honest pursuits became commonplace, and the perpetrators part of folklore. Professional sports were no different, and they became the domain of the hustler. The golf tour was a gambler's paradise, both on the course and into the night.

"The best was born as one Alvin C Thomas in 1892 and grew up in Rogers, Arkansas. He also grew up to become the nation's most infamous hustler. His father was a gambler and his grandfather taught him as a young boy to play cards. It was in his blood. Titanic Thompson (as he became known) and gambling went together like Superman and phone-booths. The stories of his exploits were soon to become notorious. It is said he hustled Al Capone, winning $500 from throwing a lemon on to a high roof. This was one of his favourite tricks as his wonderful sleight of hand would enable him to switch the lemon for a weighted duplicate he had concealed.

"He didn't, however, start to play golf until he was into his thirties, but as soon as he began it became intertwined, like everything else in his life, with gambling. With his incredible hands the game came to him with ease. He soon found himself hanging around the professional tour, where everyone seemed to be looking for a game. 'It was all gambling,' Jack Burke Jnr, the 1956 Masters champion, said. 'They'd make more from gambling with each other than there was in the purse.'

"While there are endless stories of all-night poker games and tales of leaving Howard Hughes at the dice table $10,000 the poorer, there are two Titanic Thompson golf tales which will survive for ever. It was 1965. A young pro named Ray Floyd was in Dallas looking for a game. He was taken to Tenison Park, which at the time was to hustlers what Rome is to catholics, and introduced to a variety of players. They began to bargain – what Floyd calls 'proposition' games – on figuring out the scores they were going to shoot. Floyd was aware of an older man who seemed to be watching them with great interest. The man approached Floyd and introduced himself as Titanic Thompson. Floyd was acutely aware of who he was, and when he said that he liked what he saw in the youthful Floyd and suggested a match with another young pro from El Paso, Floyd was sold. The game was on.

"The young pro from El Paso had the backing of a very wealthy man from the area, while Thompson would back Floyd. They travelled down to the course by aircraft and introductions were made. Floyd's rival was called Lee Trevino. They played three rounds over three days at the Horizon course, with Trevino winning the first two with consecutive 63s to Floyd's 65-64. On the final day the betting doubled to $2,000, with Floyd, Titanic Thompson, and his friend, who Floyd says turned out to be a bookmaker, all putting in the required amount against the money of Trevino's backer. Floyd shoots a 63 and Trevino has a putt to tie him. As Floyd tells it, the ball entered the hole and then came out to perch on the lip. Floyd had won but realised it was a narrow escape. 'That's when I realised I didn't want to be playing this guy any more,' Floyd said. 'I then said the only thing I've ever said in Spanish – adios.'

"Titanic Thompson had brought together two of the game's greatest talents and no doubt came out the winner. Ray Floyd to this very day remembers the story in perfect detail and tells it with a passion. Floyd had grown up playing the game he loves for money, from nickels and dimes as a young boy learning the game to $1,000 a hole in Las Vegas. It was instrumental in the way he has played over the many decades, with a competitive fire that is rarely matched, and it is this trait which helped make him the great success he went on to be.

"The other great tale is of Titanic's meeting with Byron Nelson in 1934. While Ben Hogan, Tommy Bolt, Sam Snead, Lloyd Mangrum and others loved to gamble, Nelson was known for his abstinence. But Texas was full of rich oil men who were more than willing to back Nelson in a game of this magnitude – the consummate, mild-mannered professional against the most assured hustler of the time. Two oil men from Nelson's club in Dallas were his eventual backers, while Titanic Thompson was putting up his own money. The story differs, depending upon your source. Nelson stated that he shot a 69 to Thompson's 71, but Titanic loved to tell how he shot a back nine of 29 to win himself $3,000.

"However, the most remarkable thing is the impression that Titanic Thompson left on both of these great champions, and many others who were witness to his many exploits. Tommy Bolt, the 1958 US Open champion, states unequivocally that Thompson 'could have been the greatest'. It was Raymond Floyd, however, who made the most interesting observation, one that highlighted a reason for Thompson's genius. 'He had the hands of a 25-year-old,' Floyd said. 'He had long, elegant, linear fingers – just perfect, like they'd been drawn.'

"Tommy Bolt gained the reputation of being one of the best money players around. He learned to hustle in his native Shreveport, where he says 'there was always a doctor or dentist around with extra money I could use.' Bolt spent a lot of his time at Memorial Park in Houston, where he learned to refine his game and his gambling prowess. 'You had to shoot a 65 every time just to stay alive,' he said. These times helped produce some of the game's truly great players, who honed their skills and learned to play hard under the heat of a hustler's intimidatory tactics. The professional tour was all the richer for the quality of these players, who had gambled money they didn't have and in the process learned the game they would take with them on the tournament road."

# appendix

## for the notebook

### internet sites

### useful guides

### bookshop